The Grammar Network

Cognitive linguists and psychologists have often argued that language is best understood as an association network; however, while the network view of language has had a significant impact on the study of morphology and lexical semantics, it is only recently that researchers have taken an explicit network approach to the study of syntax. This innovative study presents a dynamic network model of grammar in which all aspects of linguistic structure, including core concepts of syntax (e.g., phrase structure, word classes, grammatical relations), are analyzed in terms of associative connections between different types of linguistic elements. These associations are shaped by domain-general learning processes that are operative in language use and sensitive to frequency of occurrence. Drawing on research from usage-based linguistics and cognitive psychology, the book provides an overview of frequency effects in grammar and analyzes these effects within the framework of a dynamic network model.

HOLGER DIESSEL is Professor of English Linguistics at the Friedrich-Schiller-Universität Jena. His publications include two monographs, *Demonstratives: Form, Function and Grammaticalization* (1999) and *The Acquisition of Complex Sentences* (Cambridge, 2004), and more than 50 articles in journals and edited volumes.

The Grammar Network

How Linguistic Structure is Shaped by Language Use

Holger Diessel

Friedrich-Schiller-Universität Jena, Germany

CAMBRIDGE
UNIVERSITY PRESS

University Printing House, Cambridge CB2 8BS, United Kingdom

One Liberty Plaza, 20th Floor, New York, NY 10006, USA

477 Williamstown Road, Port Melbourne, VIC 3207, Australia

314-321, 3rd Floor, Plot 3, Splendor Forum, Jasola District Centre, New Delhi - 110025, India

103 Penang Road, #05-06/07, Visioncrest Commercial, Singapore 238467

Cambridge University Press is part of the University of Cambridge.

It furthers the University's mission by disseminating knowledge in the pursuit of education, learning and research at the highest international levels of excellence.

www.cambridge.org
Information on this title: www.cambridge.org/9781108712767
DOI: 10.1017/9781108671040

First published 2019
First paperback edition 2022

A catalogue record for this publication is available from the British Library

Library of Congress Cataloging in Publication data
Names: Diessel, Holger, author.
Title: The grammar network : how linguistic structure is shaped by language use / Holger Diessel.
Description: New York, NY: Cambridge University Press, 2019.
Identifiers: LCCN 2019005966 | ISBN 9781108498814 (hardback)
Subjects: LCSH: Grammar, Comparative and general – Syntax. | Grammar, Comparative and general – Syntax – Study and teaching. | Grammar, Comparative and general – Study and teaching. | BISAC: LANGUAGE ARTS & DISCIPLINES / General.
Classification: LCC P291 .D545 2019 | DDC 415–dc23
LC record available at https://lccn.loc.gov/2019005966

ISBN 978-1-108-49881-4 Hardback
ISBN 978-1-108-71276-7 Paperback

Contents

Figures

Tables

Preface

Cognitive linguists have often argued that language is best understood as an associative network, but while the network view of language has had a significant impact on the study of morphology and lexical semantics, few studies have taken an explicit network approach to the analysis of syntax. This book presents a dynamic network model of grammar in which all aspects of linguistic structure, including core concepts of syntax (e.g., word classes, grammatical relations, constituent structure), are analyzed in terms of associative connections between different aspects of linguistic knowledge. These associations are shaped by domain-general learning processes that are operative in language use and sensitive to frequency of occurrence. A wealth of recent results indicate that frequency affects the activation and processing of lexemes, categories and constructions, which can have long-lasting effects on the development of linguistic structure.

Drawing on research from various subfields of linguistics (e.g., construction grammar, cognitive semantics, historical linguistics, linguistic typology) and cognitive psychology (e.g., language acquisition, sentence processing, structural priming), the book provides an overview of frequency effects in grammar and analyzes these effects in the framework of a dynamic network model.

The book is written for a broad readership, including researchers and graduate students of linguistics, psycholinguistics and cognitive science. It does not presuppose expert knowledge in any research area and approaches the study of grammar from an interdisciplinary perspective. While written as a monograph, the book can also be used as an advanced textbook for a seminar on usage-based linguistics or functional-cognitive grammar.

The idea of writing this book was born during my senior fellowship at the Freiburg Institute for Advanced Studies in 2011, when I also taught a seminar on usage-based grammar at the Graduiertenkolleg (Frequency Effects in Language) of the University of Freiburg. I would like to express my gratitude to the Freiburg linguists for providing me with a very stimulating environment and for many fruitful discussions.

After my visit to the University of Freiburg, it took another four years of reading and preparation before I eventually began to write the first chapters of the manuscript during my fellowship at the Wissenschaftskolleg in Berlin (WIKO), where I joined an interdisciplinary research group on language evolution. During my stay at the WIKO (2015–2016), I had numerous discussions with language scientists from other disciplines who convinced me that my project would be of interest not only to linguists but also to researchers and students of psychology and cognitive science. As a consequence, I have written this book from an interdisciplinary perspective so that it is accessible to readers from different backgrounds. I am very grateful for the support I received from the Wissenschaftskolleg in Berlin and would like to thank the members of our research group, in particular, Luc Steels and Peter Gärdenfors.

A special word of thanks is due to Martin Haspelmath, who read drafts of several chapters of the manuscript and provided many valuable and insightful comments. I am also grateful to Michael Arbib, Heike Behrens, Barthe Bloom, Merlijn Breunesse, Daniel Jach and Eva-Maria Orth for stimulating discussions and to my colleagues from the University of Jena for providing feedback on several colloquium presentations on topics related to this book. Finally, I would like to thank the editor of Cambridge University Press, Helen Barton, for her support and encouragement.

Abbreviations

1	first person
2	second person
3	third person
A	transitive agent
ACC	accusative
ADJ	adjective
ADV	adverb
AdvP	adverb phrase
A(G)	agent
AGR	agreement
AP	adjective phrase
ART	article
ASP	aspect
ASSOC	associative
ATTR	attribute
AUX	auxiliary verb
CAUS	causative
CC	complement clause
CL	classifier
CLIT	clitic
COMPL	complement
CONJ	conjunction
COP	copular verb
CV	consonant-vowel
DAT	dative
DEM	demonstrative
DET	determiner
DITRANS	ditransitive
DEC	declarative
DOM	differential object marking
DU	dual
DUR	durative

EMPH	emphasis
ERG	ergative
F	feminine
FUT	future
G/GEN	genitive
GER	gerund
IC	immediate constituent
IMPF	imperfective
INCEP	inceptive
IND	indicative
INF	infinitive
INST	instrument
INTER	interjection
INTR	intransitive
IRR	irrealis
L1	first (native) language
L2	second language
LOC	locative
M	masculine
MAIN	main clause
MOD	modal verb
N	noun
NC	noun class
NEG	negation
NML	nominalization
NOM	nominative
NP	noun phrase
NUM	numeral
O/OBJ	object
P	preposition
P(A)	patient
PL	plural
POSS	possessive
PP	prepositional phrase
P.PRO	personal pronoun
PRO	pronoun
PRS	present tense
PST	past tense
PTC	participle
PUNC	punctual
QP	question particle
RC	relative clause

REL	relative pronoun/relative marker
S	clause/sentence
SAI	subject–auxiliary inversion
SBJV	subjunctive
SFP	sentence-final particle
SG/S	singular
S/SUBJ	subject
SUB	subordinate (clause)
TAM	tense–aspect–mood
TH	theme
TOP	topic
TR	transitive
V	verb
VP	verb phrase
WH	question word

1 Introduction

1.1 Preliminary Remarks

There has been a long tradition in linguistics and related disciplines to separate the study of the linguistic system (i.e., langue, competence) from the study of language use (i.e., parole, performance). In formal linguistic theory, grammar is a self-contained, deductive system consisting of discrete categories and algorithmic rules that are usually analyzed without any consideration of how language is used and processed (e.g., Chomsky 1965, 1986).

This view of grammar has been challenged, however, by usage-based linguists and psychologists who have argued that linguistic knowledge, including knowledge of grammar, emerges from language use (e.g., Tomasello 2003; Goldberg 2006; Bybee 2006). In the usage-based approach, grammar is seen as a dynamic system consisting of fluid structures and flexible constraints that are shaped by general mechanisms of communication, memory and processing. Specifically, these researchers claim that grammar constitutes a network that is constantly restructured and reorganized under the influence of domain-general processes of language use (see Diessel 2017 for a review).

In order to understand the dynamics of the grammar network, usage-based researchers study the development of linguistic structure, both in history and language acquisition. One factor that has a great impact on language development is frequency of occurrence. As frequency strengthens the representation of linguistic elements in memory, it facilitates the activation and processing of words, categories and constructions, which in turn can have long-lasting effects on the development of linguistic structure. There is a large body of research indicating that frequency is an important determinant of language use, language acquisition and language change and that the cognitive organization of grammar is crucially influenced by language users' experience with particular lexemes and constructions (e.g., Bybee and Hopper 2001; Ellis 2002; Diessel and Hilpert 2016).

This book provides a comprehensive overview and discussion of usage-based research on grammar and grammatical development. The usage-based approach draws on research in functional and cognitive linguistics (e.g., Croft

2001; Hay 2003; Stefanowitsch and Gries 2003; Bybee 2010; Traugott and Trousdale 2013; Perek and Goldberg 2015) and related research in cognitive psychology and cognitive science (e.g., Elman et al. 1996; Seidenberg and MacDonald 1999; Christiansen and Chater 2008; Fedzechkina et al. 2013; Steels 2015; Ellis et al. 2016). These fields of research complement each other, but as it stands they are only loosely connected. It is the purpose of this book to integrate the various strands of research into a more unified framework and to elaborate some central principles of the usage-based approach. In particular, the book sets out to elaborate the network view of grammar.

It is a basic assumption of the usage-based approach that linguistic knowledge is organized in an associative network (e.g., Beckner et al. 2009), but although the network view of language is frequently invoked in the usage-based literature, it has not yet been developed into an explicit theory or model. To be sure, there are network accounts of morphology and lexical semantics, but syntactic phenomena are only rarely analyzed in the framework of a network model (see Diessel 2015 for discussion).

In this book, we will consider a structured network model of grammar in which all aspects of linguistic structure, including core concepts of syntax (e.g., noun, case, subject), are analyzed in terms of associative connections between lexemes, categories and constructions. The model is inspired by computational research with neural networks (e.g., Rumelhart and McClelland 1986a; Elman et al. 1996) and is intended to provide a unified framework for the analysis of language use and linguistic structure (e.g., Bates and MacWhinney 1989; Bybee 2006). Before we consider the details of the model, let us briefly consider three basic principles of the usage-based approach as a background for the subsequent discussion (see Diessel 2011a).

1.2   Three General Principles of Usage-Based Linguistics

The usage-based approach challenges basic principles of linguistic research that have long been taken for granted. In particular, it challenges the conception of three general divisions that have provided the foundation of syntactic theory since the advance of generative linguistics in the 1950s and 1960s, namely, (i) the division between linguistic knowledge and language use, or competence and performance, (ii) the dichotomy of synchronic states and diachronic development and (iii) the distinction between words and rules.

1.2.1   Linguistic Knowledge and Language Use

All (contemporary) linguists conceive of language, notably grammar, as a cognitive system that involves linguistic knowledge, but generative and usage-based researchers make very different assumptions about the nature and origin of linguistic knowledge and its relationship to language use (Newmeyer 2003; Bybee 2006).

In the classic version of the generative approach, knowledge of grammar is grounded in a particular faculty of the mind including categories and rules, or constraints, that are part of our genetic endowment and that can generate an infinite number of sentences (Chomsky 1986; Pinker and Jackendoff 2005). Language use, or performance, involves grammatical knowledge, commonly referred to as competence, but is also influenced by general psychological processes such as sensory perception and attention that do not immediately concern the representation of grammatical knowledge. Building on this view, generative linguists separate the study of grammar, or competence, from the study of language use, as the latter involves "performance phenomena," caused by general psychological processes, that are not part of the language faculty (and therefore commonly excluded from syntactic theory).

Usage-based researchers reject the innateness hypothesis of generative linguistics and with it the related distinction between competence and performance. In the usage-based approach, language is seen as a "complex adaptive system" that has evolved for the purpose of communication and processing (e.g., Steels 2000; Beckner et al. 2009). Rather than claiming that grammatical concepts are grounded in a particular faculty of the mind, usage-based linguists argue that all aspects of linguistic knowledge, including the core concepts of grammar, emerge from general cognitive mechanisms that are not only involved in the use of language but also in other cognitive phenomena such as vision, memory and decision-making. In accordance with this view, these researchers seek to explain how linguistic structure is shaped by (nonlinguistic) factors of performance, or as Bybee (2010: 1) puts it, it is the general goal of usage-based linguistics "to derive linguistic structure from the application of domain-general processes."

1.2.2 Synchronic States and Language Development

In order to study the (long-term) effects of language use on linguistic knowledge, one has to consider the way in which linguistic structures evolve over time. Ever since Saussure ([1916] 1994), the field of linguistics has been divided into two major research areas: synchronic linguistics, which is concerned with the analysis of linguistic states at a particular point in time, and diachronic linguistics, which is concerned with the analysis of language change. Prior to Saussure, linguistic structure was generally analyzed in light of its development – synchrony and diachrony were studied together in a unified framework (Paul [1880] 1920). But since the advance of linguistic structuralism, the study of synchronic states and language change has been split into separate fields of research with distinct goals and different methods. The division of labor has been reinforced by the innateness hypotheses of generative grammar. If grammar is grounded in a particular faculty of the mind, language change concerns only the periphery of grammar and the innate core can be studied from a purely synchronic perspective.

Usage-based linguists have questioned the usefulness of the structuralist division between synchronic and diachronic linguistics. If we conceive of grammar as an emergent system, all aspects of linguistic structure, including the core concepts of syntax, are subject to change, and in order to understand the nature of this system, one has to study language development, both in history and acquisition. This explains why usage-based linguists have emphasized the importance of grammaticalization for syntactic theory (Boye and Harder 2012) and why some usage-based scholars have turned to the study of language acquisition (Goldberg 2006). In the structuralist paradigm, grammatical research is primarily concerned with the analysis of linguistic states, but in the usage-based model, the focus of analysis is on the dynamics of the linguistic system (Hopper 1987).

1.2.3   Words and Rules

Finally, usage-based linguists have challenged the traditional distinction between words and rules, which is perhaps the most fundamental dichotomy of (traditional) linguistic theory (Pinker 1999). Words are signs or symbols that combine a particular phonetic form with a particular concept or meaning, whereas rules are commonly defined as (cognitive) algorithms that serve to combine abstract categories into larger structures. Phrase structure rules, for instance, combine word class categories (and phrases) into syntactic constituents (PP → P NP).

On this view, linguistic rules are completely different entities from words or lexemes, which are stored and processed in different modules of the mind. In the classic version of generative grammar, language consists of two general components: the mental lexicon, which includes words and idiomatic expressions, and grammar, which includes syntactic categories and rules or constraints (Chomsky 1965, 1986).

The distinction between lexicon and grammar has been a cornerstone of linguistic theory, but this distinction has lost some of its importance over the past 25 years as an increasing number of theoreticians has argued that linguistic structure is licensed by constructions rather than by algorithmic rules (Fillmore et al. 1988; Goldberg 1995). A construction is a holistic pattern in which a particular configuration of structural elements is associated with a particular function or meaning. A noun phrase such as *John's car*, for instance, can be seen

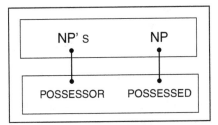

Figure 1.1 The English genitive construction

as a construction (with two slots for nominal expressions) that typically designates a particular semantic relationship of possessor and possessed (Figure 1.1).

The notion of construction is of central significance to the usage-based analysis of grammar. In fact, usage-based linguists have drawn so frequently on theoretical concepts of construction grammar that the two approaches are often presented as a unified framework (Tomasello 2003; Goldberg 2006). Note, however, that the notion of construction grammar subsumes a whole family of related theories that are not all usage-based (see Hoffmann and Trousdale 2013 for an overview). Indeed, one of the earliest and most influential construction-based theories, that is, the sign-based theory of construction grammar developed by Fillmore and Kay (1999), explicitly maintained the generative conception of competence and performance and paid little attention to usage and development. However, other varieties of construction grammar take a dynamic perspective and have made important contributions to the usage-based approach (e.g., Croft 2001; Goldberg 2006; Steels 2013; Hilpert 2014).

1.3   Goal and Scope of the Book

To summarize the previous discussion, usage-based linguists conceive of language as a dynamic system of emergent structures and flexible constraints that are in principle always changing under the pressure of domain-general processes, that is, processes that do not only concern the use of language but also nonlinguistic cognitive phenomena such as visual perception, memory retrieval and automatization. The focus of analysis is on the development of linguistic structure rather than on particular linguistic states.

The emergentist view of linguistic structure has far-reaching consequences for the study of grammar. Traditionally, grammatical analysis presupposes a "toolkit" of primitive categories that are defined prior to the analysis of any particular structure (Jackendoff 2002: 75). The "toolkit approach" has dominated syntactic theory for many decades (see Croft 2001 for discussion); but if we think of language as a dynamic system of emergent structures and fluid constraints, we cannot approach the study of grammar with a predefined set of primitive categories. On the contrary, what we need to explain is how linguistic categories evolve, stabilize and change. The underlying hypothesis is that all aspects of linguistic structure, including the most basic categories, such as noun, word and phrase, are emergent and fluid.

That does not mean, however, that linguistic structure is completely unconstrained in the usage-based model of grammar. Like any other grammatical theory, the usage-based theory of grammar rests on particular assumptions about the nature of linguistic structure and the overall organization of the linguistic system. As I see it, there are two general aspects of cognition that constrain grammar in the usage-based approach: (i) the domain-general processes that shape linguistic structure in the process of language use, and (ii) the network architecture of the grammatical system. It is the general goal of this book to elaborate on these two aspects of the usage-based model and to combine them into a coherent account.

The two following chapters introduce the basic assumptions of the current approach. We begin with the architecture of the grammar network (Chapter 2) and then turn to domain-general processes of language use (Chapter 3). In the remainder of the book, we will consider the various aspects of the model in more detail. Each chapter is concerned with particular cognitive processes and a specific aspect of the network model.

Part I

Foundations

2   Grammar as a Network

2.1   Introduction

It is a standard assumption of usage-based linguistics that grammatical structure consists of signs, that is, constructions, that are associated with each other in various ways so that the entire inventory of linguistic signs is commonly characterized as some kind of network. The network view of grammar has been expressed in a large number of studies (e.g., Bybee 1985; Langacker 1988; Bates and MacWhinney 1989; MacDonald et al. 1994; Goldberg 1995; Elman et al. 1996; Pickering and Branigan 1998; Croft 2001; Fried and Östman 2005; Hoey 2005; Hudson 2007; Steels 2011; Brown and Hippisley 2012; Traugott and Trousdale 2013; Hilpert 2014; Schmid 2016; van Trijp 2016; Ellis et al. 2016), but it has not yet been developed into an explicit theory or model (see Diessel 2015 for discussion).

Some researchers have argued that constructions are interconnected by particular types of links. Inheritance links, for instance, define connections between constructions at different levels of abstraction, and polysemy links specify relations between different senses of constructions (Goldberg 1995: 67–100; Hilpert 2014: 50–73). However, while the proposed links are certainly important, they are not sufficient to account for all aspects of linguistic structure. As we will see, in order to explain the full range of phenomena that constitute a speaker's linguistic knowledge, we need to consider additional types of links or relations.

This book delineates a theoretical network model of grammar in which all concepts of grammar (e.g., constituent structure, argument structure, word classes, grammatical relations, morphological paradigms and constructions) are defined by various types of links, or relations, that indicate associations between different linguistic elements. The present chapter introduces the general architecture of the network model, which will then be elaborated in the remainder of the book.

2.2   Some General Properties of Networks

Let us begin with some general remarks on the use of networks in science. Network models are used in many scientific disciplines to analyze a wide range of phenomena, e.g., ecosystems, social relations, the brain, economic circuits, traffic systems, cognitive processes and language (Buchanan 2002). On the face of it, these phenomena seem to be completely unrelated, but the network models that are used to analyze them have some interesting properties in common, which has led some scholars to argue that science needs a general "theory of networks" (Buchanan 2002; see also Baronchelli et al. 2013).

Formally, a network consists of two basic entities: (i) a set of nodes, sometimes referred to as vertices, and (ii) connections, also called arcs, links, relations or edges (Buchanan 2002). One reason why network models are so frequently used across disciplines is that they provide a useful framework for the analysis of dynamic processes. There are many different types of network models – some theoretical, some computational – that vary with regard to a wide range of parameters, but most network models are used to explain some kind of development.

The grammar network I propose is inspired, to some extent, by a family of network models known as neural networks, or connectionist models (Rumelhart and McClelland 1986a; Elman et al. 1996). Neural networks are computational models that are widely used by cognitive scientists for modeling cognitive processes, including language use and language acquisition (e.g., Rumelhart and McClelland 1986b; Elman 1990; Chang et al. 2006; Christiansen and MacDonald 2009). One feature that makes neural networks interesting for the usage-based analysis of language is that the links between nodes have "weights," or activation values, that are shaped by processing. In general terms, the more often a particular link, or a particular pattern of links, is processed, the stronger are the weight(s) of the connections and the higher is the probability that these connections (or links) will be reused in the future. This is one way in which many network models can change. In addition, network models may change by means of particular mechanisms that create, or delete, novel nodes and novel connections or that serve to reconfigure an existing constellation of nodes and connections (Buchanan 2002).

Network models provide a very flexible tool to explain development but will only be useful if they are theoretically motivated and constrained so as to generate particular hypotheses that can be tested. In the current case, the network architecture of grammar is motivated by the cognitive organization of grammatical categories and constructions and the network analyses presented in this book will allow us to make specific predictions that can be tested in experiments. With these general comments in mind, let us now turn to the particular architecture of the grammar network I propose.

2.3   A Nested Network Model of Grammar

Building on research in construction grammar (e.g., Goldberg 1995; Croft 2001; Bybee 2010; Hoffmann and Trousdale 2013; Hilpert 2014), usage-based morphology (e.g., Bybee 1985; Hay 2001; Hay and Baayen 2005) and cognitive psychology (e.g., Bates and MacWhinney 1989; Elman et al. 1996; Tomasello 2003; Steels 2011; Ellis et al. 2016), the current study outlines a network model of grammar in which all grammatical concepts are defined by particular types of links, or relations, that indicate associative connections between different aspects of a speaker's linguistic knowledge. Specifically, I propose a "nested network model" in which the nodes at one level of analysis are networks at another level of analysis.

The model crucially relies on the notion of construction. As pointed out in Chapter 1, constructions serve functions similar to those of traditional grammatical rules; but while grammatical rules are commonly defined as algorithms that operate over primitive concepts, constructions are meaningful templates that include slots for other linguistic expressions (Langacker 1987; Goldberg 1995; Croft 2001).

Two basic types of constructions can be distinguished: morphological constructions, which are multimorphemic words such as *teacher*, consisting of a slot for a verb stem and the nominalizing suffix *-er*, and syntactic constructions consisting of two or more slots for (free) lexemes. The genitive construction (e.g., *John's car*), for instance, is an example of a syntactic construction (§1.2.3). Other examples of syntactic constructions include questions (*Where is she?*), relative clauses (*The man I met*), prepositional phrases (*on the table*) and resultative clauses (*John painted the door red*).

Since all of these structures combine a particular structural pattern with meaning, constructions are commonly characterized as signs, parallel to lexemes. In fact, in some of the construction-based literature, the notion of construction has been extended from its traditional use for particular grammatical patterns to simple lexemes and bound morphemes (Goldberg 1995: §1; Croft and Cruse 2004: §9; Hilpert 2014: §1). In this (extended) use, all linguistic signs are subsumed under the notion of construction, which is then commonly characterized as a continuum ranging from simple morphemes to complex syntactic patterns (Goldberg 2006: 5). However, in keeping with the traditional notion of construction, we will restrict the use of this term to grammatical patterns that involve at least two meaningful elements, e.g., two morphemes, words or phrases, and will use the term lexeme for monomorphemic words and single morphemes (see Langacker 1987: 83–87). As we will see, since lexemes and constructions are learned and processed in very different ways, it is reasonable to keep them separate. Still, while there are important differences between lexemes and constructions, they can both be seen as signs, or symbols, as they both combine a particular form with meaning (see 1).

(1)

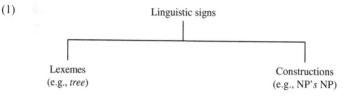

The sign-based view of linguistic structure has far-reaching implications for grammatical analysis. If linguistic structure consists of signs (i.e., constructions), it is a plausible hypothesis that the cognitive organization of grammar is similar to that of the mental lexicon, which is commonly characterized as a network of related signs or symbols. In accordance with this view, we may assume that a language user's knowledge of linguistic signs includes associative connections to other linguistic signs so that every linguistic sign – lexeme or construction – can be seen as a node of a symbolic network. However, while nodes are commonly defined as basic entities of network models, I suggest that the nodes of the grammar network can also be analyzed as networks. Specifically, I propose that a speaker's knowledge of linguistic signs, notably his/her knowledge of constructions, involves three basic types of links, or relations, that define associations between different aspects of linguistic signs (see Schmid 2016):

• SYMBOLIC RELATIONS connecting form and meaning,
• SEQUENTIAL RELATIONS connecting linguistic elements in sequences, and
• TAXONOMIC RELATIONS connecting linguistic patterns at different levels of abstraction.

Note that the three relations are related to well-known concepts of linguistic analysis. Symbolic relations are implicit in the traditional definition of linguistic signs as form-function pairings, and sequential and taxonomic relations specify associations that are closely related to the structuralist distinction between the syntagmatic and paradigmatic dimensions of language (Saussure [1994] 2016: 65–69, 121–125). The parallels are immediately obvious, but the structuralist view of these concepts is different from the dynamic network view of linguistic signs that will be outlined in this monograph.

Note also that while the three above-mentioned relations are of particular importance to the analysis of constructions, they can also be applied to lexemes. Like constructions, lexical expressions are symbolic, sequential and taxonomic: they combine a particular form with meaning, they consist of sequentially related speech sounds, or articulatory gestures, and they are taxonomic in the sense that lexical representations generalize over lexical tokens with similar semantic and phonetic properties.

Together the three relations define the basic units of speech – e.g., morphemes, words, phrases and constructions – which in turn are interconnected in various ways at a higher level of cognitive organization. In order to account for this higher-level network, I propose three further types of links, or relations, that concern the relationships between lexemes and constructions:

- LEXICAL RELATIONS connecting lexemes with similar or contrastive forms and meanings,
- CONSTRUCTIONAL RELATIONS connecting constructions at the same level of abstraction, and
- FILLER–SLOT RELATIONS connecting particular lexemes (or phrases) with particular slots of constructional schemas.

Lexical relations are well known from the study of the mental lexicon, but the two other types of relations are only rarely considered by linguistic scholars (or are analyzed in ways that are fundamentally distinct from their analysis in the current approach). However, as we will see, constructional and filler–slot relations are of central significance to the analysis of argument structure, word classes, grammatical relations, morphological paradigms and other grammatical phenomena that are traditionally analyzed by discrete categories and algorithmic rules. In the remainder of this chapter, I briefly introduce the six types of relations as a starting point for the analysis of the grammar network in later chapters of the book.

2.4   Signs as Networks

The general hypothesis that linguistic signs, notably constructions, constitute some kind of network has been proposed in previous studies (Langacker 2000: 13; Fried 2015; Schmid 2016); but to the best of my knowledge this hypothesis has never been elaborated.

2.4.1   Symbolic Relations

Symbolic relations constitute the heart of the traditional definition of linguistic signs. Focusing on words, Saussure ([1916] 1994: 66) defined the linguistic sign as a "two-sided psychological entity" that combines a particular sound pattern with a particular meaning. Traditionally, the notion of sign is restricted to lexemes, but, as pointed out above, constructions can also be seen as signs that combine a particular structure with meaning.

Cognitive linguists have analyzed the conceptual foundations of linguistic signs in great detail, but they usually look at the semantic pole of lexemes and constructions from a (purely) synchronic perspective. In the current approach, we are particularly interested in the development of symbolic associations. If we look at linguistic signs from a developmental perspective, we see that symbolic relations are emergent and gradient (like all other associative connections of the network). It is one of the central claims of this book that symbolic relations evolve from recurrent paths of interpretation that have become entrenched (and conventionalized) as a consequence of automatization (and social cognition).

The proposed analysis challenges the traditional distinction between encoding and inference and provides the basis for a dynamic theory of meaning in which linguistic elements are seen as cues or stimuli that activate a specific concept, that is, the figure node, of a semantic network (Figure 2.1) (Langacker 2008: 39). The word 'arm', for instance, activates the concept of a body part as figure node and entails the concept of 'body' as its base, but in addition to the base, 'arm' can also activate a wide range of other concepts such as 'muscle', 'strong' and 'raise'. Since the activation status of the network varies with the context (or a language user's mental state in a particular situation), the same linguistic cue can give rise to different interpretations in different speech situations. On this account, linguistic signs do not "have" meaning but serve to "create" meaning in communicative interactions (Elman 2009; see also Deppermann 2006).

Both lexemes and constructions can be seen as cues or stimuli that evoke meaning, but the cognitive processes that are involved in the semantic interpretation of constructions are different from those of lexemes. As we will see (Chapter 6), lexemes tap directly into world knowledge, whereas constructions serve to guide listeners' interpretation of lexical expressions. Specifically, it is

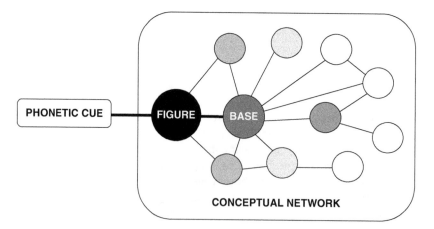

Figure 2.1 Symbolic associations

argued that constructions provide instructions to integrate the meanings that are evoked by multiple lexical expressions into a coherent semantic representation.

2.4.2 Sequential Relations

Sequential relations specify associations between linguistic elements in sequence. All linguistic entities (e.g., phonemes, lexemes, clauses) occur one after another in linear or sequential order. The linear arrangement of these entities is influenced by a wide range of cognitive factors including general principles of phonetic articulation, focal attention and common ground, but the strength of sequential relations is primarily determined by automatization. Since linguistic items that are frequently used together become associated with each other, they often develop into automated processing units, also known as "chunks" (Bybee 2010: 33–45). The expression *in any case*, for instance, consists of three lexemes that are so frequently combined with each other that they are stored and processed as one chunk.

Since language unfolds in time, sequential relations have an inherent forward orientation (but see §5.6 and §9.5), which is reflected in the fact that listeners are able to "predict" the occurrence of upcoming elements in the unfolding speech stream (Figure 2.2) (Altmann and Kamide 1999; Altmann and Mirković 2009).

Sequential processing influences all aspects of linguistic knowledge, but the effect is perhaps most obvious in the case of prefabricated lexical units such as *thank you, how are you,* and *I don't know* (Bybee and Scheibman 1999). Natural language abounds with "lexical prefabs" (or collocations), but sequential associations also play an important role in syntax. As we will see (Chapter 5), syntactic constituents are derived from recurrent strings of similar expressions that have developed into automated processing units with strong sequential links between their parts.

2.4.3 Taxonomic Relations

Finally, taxonomic relations concern the hierarchical organization of grammar. It is a standard assumption of the usage-based approach that linguistic

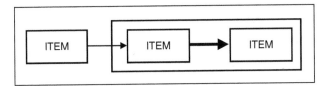

Figure 2.2 Sequential associations

knowledge varies on a scale of abstraction (Langacker 1987: 74–75; Croft 2001: 25–26; Goldberg 2006: 45–65). The scale is based on a language user's experience with particular lexical sequences. Every string of lexical expressions has particular phonetic and semantic properties that vary with the context, but there is overlap between individual sequences, which can give rise to the development of abstract representations of linguistic structure known as "constructional schemas" (Langacker 1991: 17–20, 25–26).

Constructional schemas can be more or less abstract, ranging from low-level generalizations over lexical sequences to highly abstract patterns of syntactic structure. The English possessive construction (§1.2.3), for instance, can be seen as a subtype of a constructional schema that does not only license constructions with two nominals combined by the possessive marker 's but may also subsume pronominal constructions including a possessive pronoun such as *my, your* and *his* (Figure 2.3).

Taxonomic relations are created by abstraction, which crucially relies on the recognition of similarity; but taxonomic relations are also shaped by frequency. Two different types of frequency must be distinguished in this context: token frequency, which refers to the frequency of the same or similar experiences, and type frequency, which refers to the number of distinct lexical types that are associated with a schema (Bybee 2001: 11–13). Both types of frequency affect the representation of linguistic concepts in memory. Token frequency has a well-known strengthening effect on lexical information and type frequency is of central significance to schema extraction (Chapter 4) and morphosyntactic productivity (§7.4–§7.5).

If and to what extent a language user extracts constructional schemas from lexical sequences is an empirical question. Traditionally, grammatical research has been mainly concerned with broad generalizations, but recent research has shown that language abounds with lexical prefabs, item-specific constructions and low-level schemas, suggesting that theoretical linguists may have

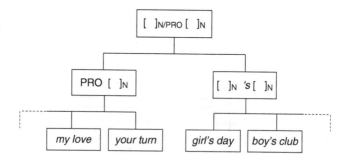

Figure 2.3 Taxonomic network of possessive/genitive constructions in English

overestimated the degree of abstraction in both language use and grammar (e.g., Frank et al. 2012; Frank and Christiansen 2018).

Moreover, a number of recent studies have shown that some of the high-level schemas that have been studied in formal syntax are not mastered (to the same extent) by all speakers. Challenging the widespread view that native speakers share the same basic knowledge of grammar, usage-based researchers have found substantial differences in the way individual speakers use and understand grammatical patterns (for reviews, see Dąbrowska 2012; Kidd et al. 2018). One reason for this is that linguistic experience varies across speakers and speech communities. Since some speakers do not have much experience with certain syntactic patterns (e.g., "tough movement," "parasitic gaps"; see Dąbrowska 1997), it does not come as a surprise that these patterns are not readily available to all native speakers (see also Dąbrowska 2012, 2018).

To summarize the discussion thus far, I have argued that a language user's knowledge of linguistic signs involves three basic types of associations: (i) symbolic relations connecting a particular form with a particular concept or meaning, (ii) sequential relations connecting linguistic elements in sequence, and (iii) taxonomic relations connecting linguistic representations at different levels of abstraction.

2.5   Networks of Signs

Linguistic signs are the basic units of the language system. They constitute the foundation of a speaker's linguistic knowledge at a higher level of cognitive organization, where every linguistic sign is connected to other linguistic signs, creating a symbolic network of interrelated lexemes and constructions that is of central significance to the analysis of linguistic structure. In order to analyze this higher-level network, we need three additional types of links, or relations, that specify associations between different types of linguistic signs (or symbols).

2.5.1   Lexical Relations

Lexical relations indicate associations between individual lexical items. They have been at the center of linguistic and psycholinguistic research on the mental lexicon. There is abundant evidence that a speaker's knowledge of lexical items includes associations to other semantically and/or phonetically related items. The lexeme *sky*, for instance, is semantically related to *cloud* and *sun* and phonetically associated with *skin* and *ski* (Figure 2.4).

Lexical relations are created by categorization and reinforced by automatization and priming. As we will see (Chapter 6), lexical expressions that are

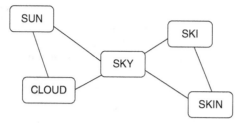

Figure 2.4 Lexical associations between the lexeme *sky* and four other
semantically and/or phonetically related items

frequently used together within the same frame or domain become associated
with each other.

   Although lexical associations are primarily concerned with words, they also
play an important role in the organization and development of grammar. As we
will see, lexical relations are of central significance to the network analysis of
complex words (Chapter 5), argument structure (Chapter 7) and grammatical
word classes (Chapter 8).

2.5.2   Constructional Relations

Like lexemes, constructions are interconnected. The underlying hypothesis is
that every construction has a particular "ecological location" in the grammar
network that is defined by its relationship to other constructions in the system
(Lakoff 1987: 492–494; see also Diessel 1997). This is perhaps most obvious in
the case of morphological constructions of inflectional paradigms. For
instance, in many languages, nouns are inflected for number and case and
verbs are inflected for person, tense, aspect and mood. Traditionally, inflectional paradigms are analyzed as the product of concatenating rules that
combine lexical stems with a set of (inflectional) affixes, but in construction
grammar, inflected word forms are licensed by constructional schemas
(Chapter 4). Although every schema constitutes a linguistic pattern in its own
right, the schemas of inflected word forms are closely related. They constitute a
system of interconnected schematic patterns that can be seen as a network in
which each schema is defined by its relationship to other schemas in the system,
as illustrated by the following example of conjugated verb forms in Latin
(Figure 2.5).

   On the face of it, the network in Figure 2.5 does not seem to be much
different from the structuralist view of a morphological paradigm, but there
is a significant difference. In the structuralist approach, linguistic paradigms are
considered closed and stable systems, but in the network approach, paradigms

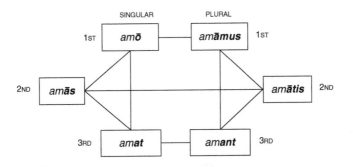

Figure 2.5 Constructional relations between six morphological schemas of an inflectional paradigm in Latin

emerge and are shaped by language use. As we will see in Chapter 11, there are cross-linguistic asymmetries in the encoding of complex words, often referred to as "structural markedness" (Croft 2003: 91–95), that reflect the influence of usage and cognition on the processing and development of related word forms (Greenberg 1966; Bybee 1985; Croft 2003).

Similar encoding asymmetries occur in the domain of syntax (i.e., phrase and clause structure) (Haspelmath 2008a, 2008b). Active and passive sentences, for instance, are licensed by syntactic schemas that complement each other in specific ways. Linguists have proposed many different analyses for the active-passive alternation in different frameworks. In the classic version of generative grammar, for instance, passive sentences were derived from active sentences by syntactic transformations (Chomsky 1965: 103–106). In construction grammar, there are no transformations (or other types of syntactic operations such as "move" and "merge"). Every surface pattern constitutes a construction in its own right (Goldberg 2002); but like all other grammatical theories, construction grammar must account for the active–passive alternation.

In Chapter 11, we will characterize active and passive sentences as "para-digmatic alternatives" that are associated with each other in a similar way as morphological schemas in an inflectional paradigm. One piece of evidence for this hypothesis comes from the fact that active and passive sentences (as well as many other syntactic constructions) exhibit the same encoding asym-metries as morphological constructions. As we will see, structural marked-ness is not a particular trait of morphology. The same marking asymmetries occur in the domain of syntax, suggesting that syntactic constructions enter into relations similar to those of morphologically complex words in inflec-tional paradigms.

2.5.3   Filler–Slot Relations

Finally, there are associative connections between individual lexemes and specific slots of constructional schemas to which we refer as filler–slot relations. In the structuralist and generative approach, individual lexemes are irrelevant for grammatical analysis, but in the usage-based approach, linguistic structure is lexically particular in the sense that grammatical categories and constructions are generally associated with specific lexical items (Diessel 2016).

Above, it was said that constructional schemas emerge from strings of lexical expressions with overlapping properties and that schemas and lexical sequences are connected by taxonomic links or relations. Filler–slot relations are based on the taxonomic organization of grammar, but they concern associations between individual lexemes and particular slots of constructional schemas rather than associations between entire grammatical patterns (§2.4.3). Consider, for instance, the filler–slot relations of English adjectives.

English has an open class of lexical items that are commonly used as adjectives in two major grammatical constructions: in noun phrases (e.g., *the big tree*) and in copular clauses (e.g., *the tree is big*). Most English adjectives can occur in both constructions, but there are item-specific differences: *utter*, for instance, is exclusively used as an attributive adjective in the noun phrase construction (**this is utter*), and *afraid* is only used as a predicative adjective in the copular construction (**an afraid child*). Moreover, many adjectives that appear in both constructions are statistically biased to occur in one or the other: *complete*, for instance, is primarily used in the noun phrase construction, whereas *impossible* is more frequently used in the copular construction.

The distributional biases and constraints are semantically motivated. There are some well-known preferences for using certain semantic types of adjectives in certain structural positions (Taylor 2012: 47, 107–109); but, as we will see in Chapters 7 and 8, semantic factors alone are not sufficient to explain how lexemes and constructions are related. Specifically, these chapters show that in addition to semantic considerations, it is a language user's experience with an established pattern that determines the combination of lexemes and constructions. To put it another way, speakers "know" from their experience with particular co-occurrence patterns that certain lexemes tend to appear in particular slots of constructional schemas and this has a significant impact on their choice of linguistic elements in language use. On this account, lexemes and constructions are associated with each other by probabilistic links that reflect the combined effect of semantic factors and frequency of occurrence (or entrenchment) (Figure 2.6) (Diessel 2015, 2016).

Elaborating on this account, I argue that filler–slot associations are of central significance to the analysis of certain types of grammatical categories.

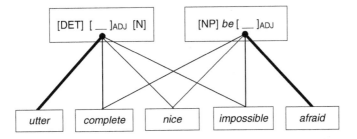

Figure 2.6 Filler–slot relations of property terms and two adjective schemas (in English)

Specifically, I show that argument structure, word classes and certain aspects of phrase structure are best analyzed in terms of associative connections between lexemes and constructions (which will resolve many of the problems that surround the analysis of these categories in other frameworks).

2.6   Summary

To summarize, this chapter has introduced a nested network model of grammar in which the various aspects of a speaker's grammatical knowledge are defined by a set of associative connections at two different levels of analysis. First, linguistic signs are defined by three basic types of relations, or associations: (i) symbolic relations connecting form and meaning, (ii) sequential relations connecting linguistic elements in sequence, and (iii) taxonomic relations connecting linguistic patterns on a scale of abstraction. And second, the various linguistic signs are combined to a higher-level network that involves another set of three associative connections: (iv) lexical relations connecting lexemes with similar (or contrastive) forms and meanings, (v) constructional relations connecting constructions at the same level of abstraction, and (vi) filler–slot relations connecting individual lexemes and particular slots of constructional schemas. Table 2.1 summarizes the previous discussion.

Crucially, each relation is shaped by particular cognitive processes. Symbolic relations, for instance, are determined by conceptualization and pragmatic inference (Chapter 6), whereas taxonomic relations are primarily created by abstraction (Chapter 4). As a consequence, the links in Table 2.1 can have very different properties. One aspect that needs to be considered in this context is the direction of associations (see Kapatsinski 2018 for a recent discussion). Specifically, we may distinguish between symmetrical and asymmetrical associations.

Table 2.1 *Overview of the various types of relations of the grammar network*

Signs as networks	
Symbolic relations	Associations between form and meaning
Sequential relations	Associations between linguistic elements in sequence
Taxonomic relations	Associations between representations at different levels of specificity
Networks of signs	
Lexical relations	Associations between lexemes
Constructional relations	Associations between constructions
Filler–slot relations	Associations between particular items and slots of constructions

Symmetrical associations involve a bidirectional link between two entities: when A occurs, B is also activated, and when B occurs, A is also active. In contrast, asymmetrical associations are unidirectional (or biased in one direction): A leads to the activation of B, but B does not necessarily activate A, or at least not to the same extent.

For instance, in Saussure's analysis of linguistic signs, symbolic associations are symmetrical. Given a particular phonetic form, listeners activate a particular concept (or more precisely, they construct a particular meaning), and given a particular concept (e.g., evoked by visual perception), speakers activate or select a particular linguistic form. In Chapter 6 we will see that symbolic associations are more complex than this, but for the time being we may say that symbolic links are symmetrical (in Saussure's analysis of the linguistic sign). Not all linguistic associations are symmetrical, however. For instance, above we said that sequential links have a forward orientation so that they can be seen as asymmetrical associations (Chapter 5).

We will consider the particular properties of the various types of links in detail throughout the book. Each chapter is concerned with a particular type of link that accounts for a particular grammatical phenomenon; but before we turn to the analysis of individual links, Chapter 3 will provide an overview of the cognitive processes that influence the various associations in usage and development.

3   Cognitive Processes and Language Use

3.1   Introduction

There is consensus among usage-based researchers that linguistic structure is shaped by domain-general processes. But what exactly are these processes? Different researchers have emphasized the importance of very different aspects of usage and cognition in order to explain how grammar is shaped by performance. Some linguists have emphasized the role of discourse (Givón 1979) and interaction (Auer 2005), others have focused on conceptual factors (Langacker 1987) or iconicity (Haiman 1985), and yet other researchers have claimed that grammar is shaped by cognitive constraints on sentence processing (Hawkins 2004), language acquisition (Chater and Christiansen 2008) and/or language production (MacDonald 2013). One factor that has been especially prominent in recent years is frequency of occurrence (Bybee and Hopper 2001; Ellis 2002; Behrens and Pfänder 2016). There is ample evidence that frequency is an important determinant of usage, acquisition and change (for reviews, see Diessel 2007; Diessel and Hilpert 2016).

The various proposals are not mutually exclusive, but there are so many different suggestions in the usage-based literature as to how grammar is shaped by performance that the whole approach has been rightfully criticized for being arbitrary and ad hoc (Newmeyer 2003). Obviously, what is needed is a more structured framework that attempts to predict the interaction of the various cognitive processes.

This chapter provides an overview of the various cognitive processes that are involved in language use and explains, in general terms, how grammar, usage and cognition are related. It is argued that language use involves a decision-making process that is determined by cognitive factors from three general domains: social cognition, conceptualization and memory. It is the purpose of the chapter to provide a background and orientation for the analysis of the emergence of linguistic structure in the grammar network in later chapters of the book.[1]

---

[1] Parts of the following discussion are based on Diessel (2017).

3.2   Linguistic Decisions

Let us begin with some general thoughts on language use or performance. Language use is a cooperative activity that is driven by interlocutors' communicative intentions. The German psychologist Karl Bühler (1934) characterized language as an "instrument," Greek "organon," which speakers use to provide information, to direct other people's actions, to ask questions or to express emotions (Austin 1962). Crucially, there are always multiple ways of expressing a particular communicative intention – of saying more or less the same thing, e.g., alternative constructions to describe the same scene (1a–b), alternative words to designate the same entity (2a–b) and alternative pronunciations (3a–b).

(1)   a. I sent Tom a letter.
          b. I sent a letter to Tom.

(2)   a. I didn't see the man.
          b. I didn't see him.

(3)   a. They are going to leave.
          b. They're gonna leave.

Of course, alternative does not mean equal. The examples in (a) and (b) are not equivalent. They differ with regard to style, information structure and conceptualization, but they are close enough that speakers can (often) choose between them. What is more, speakers cannot only choose between alternative means that are stored in (linguistic) memory, they can also produce novel forms and meanings. Language is productive in the sense that speakers are able to extend the use of previously established linguistic patterns within certain limits (Chapter 7). The productive use of language increases the range of linguistic means that are potentially available to express a particular communicative intention.

Given that there are always alternative ways of saying more or less the same thing, speakers have to make choices, that is, they have to "decide" how to express a particular intention or meaning. That does not mean, however, that they consciously consider the various alternatives and then make a deliberate decision. While there are situations in which language use proceeds in this way, notably in writing, the decisions speakers make in spontaneous conversation are often routinized and unconscious. Still, given that there are always alternative ways of expressing a particular communicative intention, we will say that language production involves an (unconscious) decision-making process that concerns the choice of linguistic means in a particular situation.

A parallel analysis applies to comprehension. Like speakers, listeners have to make decisions. Every word and every structure has multiple interpretations that are contingent on the context and listeners' knowledge. Psycholinguists have characterized sentence comprehension as a "constraint satisfaction process" (MacDonald et al. 1994) whereby listeners seek to derive a plausible and coherent interpretation from (i) the expressions they encounter, (ii) their understanding of the current interaction and (iii) general world knowledge (Trueswell et al. 1994; MacDonald and Seidenberg 2006). If we think of language comprehension in this way, it involves an (unconscious) decision-making process, just like language production.

The linguistic decision-making process is key to understanding how grammar, usage and cognition are related. In what follows, I argue that a language user's linguistic choices are motivated by competing cognitive processes from three general domains, namely, the domains of social cognition (§3.3), conceptualization (§3.4) and memory and processing (§3.5). The competing processes affect the linguistic decision-making process online, but since recurrent decisions tend to become automatized, they have long-term effects on language development in both history and acquisition. If we want to understand how grammar is shaped by performance, we have to study both the cognitive processes of language use and their effects on language development.

Note, however, that language use and language development are not only influenced by cognitive processes but also by social factors. Cognitive linguists and psychologists tend to focus on the analysis of cognitive processes, but there is ample evidence that linguistic decisions are also influenced by social factors such as prestige and group identity (e.g., Labov 1972). Many linguistic features are associated with particular social groups and social contexts. *I gotta go*, for instance, has a different social connotation from *I have to leave*. Historical linguists have shown that the sociolinguistic values of linguistic features have a significant impact on speakers' choice of linguistic means and their development in language history (Weinrich et al. 1968; Labov 1972; Trudgill 1974). Moreover, social factors are important to understand linguistic conventions. Since individual speakers seek to speak like their peers, speech communities develop group-specific patterns of language use that can be seen as linguistic conventions. There is no doubt that social factors influence language use and language change, but in this book the focus of analysis is on cognitive processes, including cognitive processes of social cognition.

3.3   Social Cognition

Language use is a particular form of social interaction, which crucially relies on the ability to take another person's knowledge, intentions and beliefs into account (Clark 1996). This ability is of fundamental significance in the use of linguistic symbols and has been characterized as a particular capacity of the human mind that distinguishes human communication from that of other species (Tomasello 1999). While other species are able to communicate in one way or another, their ability to understand mental states and linguistic symbols is limited compared to that of human beings (see Crockford et al. 2012 for a recent discussion).

A basic form of social cognition is "joint attention" (Carpenter et al. 1998; Tomasello 1999). In order to communicate, speaker and listener must focus their attention on the same experience, which may involve an object or event in the surrounding situation or a concept that is evoked by the preceding discourse. In face-to-face conversation, joint attention is commonly established by nonverbal means of communication such as eye gaze, head movement and gesture. Of particular importance is deictic pointing – a communicative device that is universally available to establish joint attention and that is commonly accompanied by demonstratives or spatial deictics (Diessel 2006; Stukenbrock 2015).

Interestingly, the ability to engage in joint attention emerges only gradually during early childhood (Carpenter et al. 1998; Tomasello 1999). While infants respond to adults' communicative behaviors from early on, it takes around nine months until they begin to follow the eye gaze and head movements of other people and it usually takes another three months until they begin to produce their first pointing gestures. Tomasello interprets the emergence of these behaviors as the first steps of a long-lasting process whereby children gradually acquire a "theory of mind" (Tomasello 2003: 3).

Joint attention is a basic aspect of social interaction, but in order to communicate, it is not only important that the speech participants are focused on the same object or scene, they also have to align their knowledge and beliefs; that is, communication presupposes that the interlocutors share a "common ground" (Clark and Brennan 1991). Clark (1996) defines common ground as language users' awareness of their shared knowledge, which does not only concern information about the physical speech situation surrounding the interlocutors, but also background information about the communicative partner and general world knowledge.

Common ground is a domain-general cognitive phenomenon that is not only relevant for the use of language but also for other, nonverbal forms of social interaction. Of particular importance to language are those aspects of common ground that emanate from discourse. As discourse unfolds, the communicative partners build up a body of shared representations providing a background and orientation for the interpretation of elements in the ensuing discourse. Functional linguists have emphasized the importance of discourse-based information for the analysis of various aspects of linguistic structure including nominal reference (e.g., Chafe 1994), word order (e.g., Givón 1979) and subordination (e.g., Verhagen 2005).

Common ground provides the basis for what some psychologists (and sociolinguists) call "audience design" (Clark and Marshall 1981), which is the process whereby speakers seek to construct a sentence according to what they think a hearer "needs" in order to understand their communicative intention in a particular situation (see also Horton and Keysar 1996; Arnold 2008). Audience design is of central significance to speakers' choice of linguistic means. Consider, for instance, the use of referring (nominal) expressions (see 4). In English, speakers can choose between definite and indefinite NPs, proper names, proximal and distal demonstratives, third-person pronouns and zero anaphors (in certain constructions):

(4)
The man	Definite noun phrase
A man	Indefinite noun phrase
Peter	Proper name
This	Proximal demonstrative
That	Distal demonstrative
HE	Stressed pronoun
He	Unstressed pronoun
ø	Zero anaphor

The inventory of referring terms is language-particular. Different languages have different sets of (pro)nominal expressions (Givón 1983; Ariel 1990), but all languages have multiple types of referring terms so that speakers are forced to choose between them. Functional linguists have shown that the various types of referring expressions serve particular pragmatic functions that correlate with aspects of the linguistic and nonlinguistic context (e.g., givenness, visibility) (Givón 1983; Chafe 1994). However, from a cognitive perspective we may say that speakers (often) choose a particular term based on what they think listeners know and see, and listeners interpret the chosen expressions based on the assumption that speakers construct sentences according to this strategy. In other words, the choice and interpretation of linguistic expressions is crucially influenced by interlocutors' "assessment of common ground" and the attempt to "tailor" an utterance according to "hearers' needs" (Clark and Marshall 1981; but see §3.6).

What is more, common ground and audience design do not only affect speakers' choice of linguistic expressions, they also influence grammatical development and grammar evolution. For instance, many languages have information-structure constructions such as left-dislocation (e.g., *That guy over there, he ...*) and cleft-sentences (e.g., *It is John who ...*), which can arguably be seen as grammatical strategies that have evolved from discourse patterns that were used to establish a thematic foundation (or common ground) for the interpretation of subsequent information in the unfolding speech stream (Clark and Brennan 1991: 228).

3.4   Conceptualization

Conceptualization is concerned with the construction of meaning. In (formal) semantics, linguistic meaning is commonly defined as some kind of correspondence relation between language and world, or language and thought, but in the usage-based approach, meaning is shaped by conceptualization, which is the cognitive structuring of experience or semantic content (Langacker 1987, 1991; Talmy 2000; Croft and Cruise 2004: §3).

Like all other cognitive processes of language use, conceptualization is not specific to language. In fact, the conceptual approach to semantics is inspired by general psychological research on vision (see Evans and Green 2006: §3 for a succinct summary). Pioneering research on conceptualization comes from gestalt psychology (Koffka 1935), which had a strong impact on cognitive semantics (Langacker 1991; Talmy 2000; Verhagen 2007). The gestalt psychologists showed that vision involves more than the passive recording of sensory cues – that visual perception is guided by general cognitive principles such as the figure–ground distinction and reification (which is the enrichment of perceptual information through inference).

Inspired by this research, cognitive and usage-based linguists have developed a conceptual theory of semantics in which the meaning of linguistic expressions is structured by general processes of conceptualization including metaphor, metonymy, fictive motion, force dynamics, reification and the figure–ground segregation (Lakoff and Johnson 1980; Lakoff 1987; Langacker 1991; Talmy 2000; Coventry and Garrod 2004).

Interestingly, Langacker (1991: 117) argued that there are always multiple ways of viewing the same experience so that speakers are (often) forced to decide how to describe and conceptualize a particular object or scene (see also Croft and Cruse 2004: §3 and Langacker 2008: 43). Consider, for instance, the use of *come* and *go* in the following examples.

(5)   She came to school.

(6)   She went to school.

Come and *go* are deictic verbs that can often be used with reference to the same scene, but they describe the scene from different perspectives, that is, they evoke different conceptualizations. In the case of *come*, the conceptual figure is moving toward the observer, but in the case of *go*, the figure is moving away from the observer (Figure 3.1).

Both verbs are interpreted relative to a particular point of reference, the deictic center, also called the "origo" (Bühler 1934: 107). The deictic center is the origin of a coordinate system that is usually grounded by the speaker's body or location at the time of the utterance, but the deictic center can be shifted from the speaker to another person or fictive observer. In narrative discourse, for instance, the deictic center is often located in one of the characters of the narration who uses deictic expressions in the same way as speakers use them for spatial orientation in the surrounding situation (see Diessel 2014 for discussion).

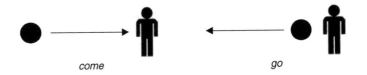

Figure 3.1 Conceptualization of *come* and *go*

Like words, constructions involve conceptualization. Consider, for instance, the active–passive alternation in examples (7) and (8).

(7)   The man kicked the ball.

(8)   The ball was kicked (by the man).

An active sentence construes a scene from the perspective of the agent. In sentence (7), the agent is the focus of attention and the patient is backgrounded relative to the agent, but in the passive sentence in (8) it is the other way around. In this case, the patient serves as figure and the agent is a secondary focal point (Langacker 1991: 101–148), which can be omitted, but, of course, conceptually, the passive construction entails an agent or agentive force. Analyzing grammatical relations in this way creates an explicit link between argument structure and general conceptual processes (Chapter 7).

To give one more example, in languages with perfective and imperfective aspect, action verbs can be construed in two different ways: as ongoing or imperfective actions (e.g., *I am writing a book*) and as completed or perfective actions (e.g., *I have written a book*). One feature that distinguishes ongoing from completed events is "conceptual boundedness" (Langacker 1987: 86–87; 1991: 93–95). Ongoing events are temporally unbounded, whereas completed events are temporally bounded. Of course, every event has a beginning and an ending, but perfective verb forms construe an event as temporally bounded, whereas imperfective verb forms present the same event as ongoing and expansible (Talmy 2000: 50–62).

In general, in the usage-based approach, semantic conventions emerge from recurrent conceptualizations of the same or similar experiences that become associated with particular lexemes and constructions. We will consider the conceptual approach to semantics in detail in Chapter 6. Here we note that conceptualization is not only the driving force behind the construction of meaning, it also plays a decisive role in the diachronic development of grammar. For instance, the early stages of grammaticalization are (often) motivated by general conceptual processes such as metaphor, metonymy and deictic projection, which lead to the development of grammatical function words from nouns, verbs and spatial deictics (Heine et al. 1991; Diessel 2012a).

Similar conceptual processes occur in first language acquisition (Diessel 2011b, 2012b). We will consider the conceptual processes of language change and L1 acquisition in later chapters (Chapters 5, 6 and 7) and now turn to memory-related processes.

3.5   Memory-Related Processes

Functional and cognitive linguistics have always emphasized that linguistic structure is motivated by semantic and pragmatic aspects of communication and discourse, but in the recent literature, the focus of analysis has shifted from communication and meaning to frequency and processing. Frequency and processing concern the storage, representation and activation of linguistic information in memory. In the older psychological literature, memory is often described as some kind of place where information is stored, but in current cognitive psychology, the term memory subsumes a set of cognitive processes that concern the processing and organization of knowledge (Cowan 2005; Jonides et al. 2008). In what follows, I briefly consider some of the memory-related processes that influence speakers' choice of linguistic means. All of these processes will be described in more detail in later chapters.

3.5.1   Attention and the Flow of Consciousness

Traditionally, the human memory system is divided into two basic "stores": long-term memory, which includes a person's entire knowledge, and working memory, which holds the information that is currently activated and processed (Baddeley 1986). A number of recent studies have argued, however, that information in working memory cannot really be delineated from information in the long-term store (MacDonald and Christiansen 2002; Cowan 2005). Challenging the traditional division between long-term memory and working memory, these studies argue that memory constitutes a "unitary system" in which working memory serves as an "attention mechanism" that activates specific information at a particular point in time. In particular, Cowan (2005) argued that one should think of memory as an encompassing network with an inherent focus of attention (see also Oberauer 2002).

Above, we have seen that the creation of joint attention is an important aspect of communication (§3.3); but the attention mechanism of the memory system is not only influenced by social interaction but also by memory and sensory perception, which can interfere with interlocutors' attempt to coordinate their attention.

Crucially, at any given moment in time, the focus of attention centers on only one item, but this item is connected to semiactivated items, which in turn are linked to other memory traces that are currently not activated but easily

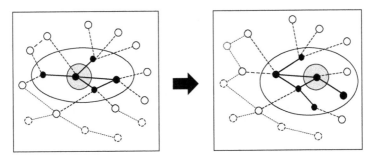

Figure 3.2 Long-term memory with moving focus of attention (see Oberauer 2002: 412)

accessible through the activated item (Oberauer 2002; Cowen 2005). On this view, the traditional notion of working memory corresponds to a cluster of conceptually related elements with graded activation values in the overall network of a person's knowledge.

In accordance with this view, linguistic researchers have argued that the focus of attention in speaking and listening constitutes an open-ended set of activated and semiactivated items (Chafe 1994). Crucially, since language unfolds in time, the focus of attention is moving and the whole cluster of activated elements is constantly in flux (see Figure 3.2). Chafe refers to this as the "flow of consciousness" and argues that the moving focus of attention is an important determinant for language users' choice of linguistic means. Word order, for instance, is crucially influenced by the flow of attention, or flow of consciousness (Chafe 1994: 162–165).

3.5.2   Categorization, Abstraction and Analogy

Categorization is the process whereby a new experience is classified as an instance of an existing category or schema. Traditionally, categories are defined by necessary and sufficient features, but in current cognitive psychology, categories are commonly defined in terms of prototypes and exemplars (see Murphy 2002: Chapters 3 and 4 for a review).[2]

Like attention and the flow of consciousness, categorization is a domain-general process that concerns both linguistic and nonlinguistic concepts (Lakoff 1987). Crucially, there are always multiple concepts (or categories) that are potentially available to license (or categorize) a new (linguistic) token. Consider, for instance, the categorization of speech sounds.

---

[2] Note that while categorization is here subsumed under memory-related processes, it also involves cognitive processes of conceptualization (Lakoff 1987; Langacker 1991).

There is an enormous amount of variation in the phonetic realization of speech sounds, especially in the domain of vowels. Very often, a vowel token falls somewhere in between two or more speech-sound categories, but listeners are forced to categorize (unconsciously) any given phonetic token as a particular phoneme in order to arrive at a coherent interpretation. A listener's choice of category is determined by a number of factors including the context, frequency and, perhaps most importantly, the similarity between the new token and the phonetic properties of the competing speech-sound categories. Similarity is a key concept of categorization and does not only concern the classification of speech sounds, but all linguistic elements including morphemes, words, phrases and constructions (Chapters 4, 7, 8 and 9).

Closely related to categorization are two other cognitive processes: abstraction and analogy. By abstraction I mean the process whereby language users generalize across multiple experiences with overlapping properties and thereby create a new concept or schema (Anderson 2005: 165–167; see also Langacker 2008: 17, who refers to abstraction as "schematization"). Abstraction plays a central role in language acquisition, notably in grammar learning (Chapter 4).

The notion of analogy is used in many different ways by different scholars. In historical linguistics, it is often used as a descriptive term for a certain type of structural change, notably morphological change (Trask 1996: 105–115), but in usage-based linguistics, analogy is a domain-general phenomenon that accounts for an important aspect of linguistic productivity (Bybee and Moder 1983; Barðdal 2008; Behrens 2017). In the usage-based approach, linguistic productivity is commonly defined as the extension of an existing schema to a new item (Langacker 2000: 26; Bybee 2010: 94). Two general factors influence the analogical extension of a constructional schema to novel expressions: (i) the strength of a particular schema in memory, and (ii) the similarity between lexical expressions that are licensed by a schema.

We will consider these factors in detail in later chapters (Chapters 4, 7, 8 and 9). Here we note that there are two different types of similarity that influence analogy (and also categorization and abstraction): (i) "object similarity," which refers to overlapping attributes, and (ii) "structural similarity," which involves overlapping structures or relations (Gentner 1983; Holyoak and Thagard 1995). Consider, for instance, the three sets of circles and squares in Figure 3.3.

As can be seen, set A and set B are structurally similar – they involve similar arrangements of geometric figures, but C is different. There is no structural overlap between C and the two other sets, but C includes circles that are similar in shape, color and size to those in B, that is, C and B exhibit object similarity. Both types of similarity affect analogy (and categorization and abstraction), but, as we will see (Chapters 4 and 7), structural similarity is of particular importance to grammar learning as grammar is concerned with relations.

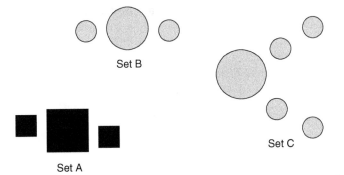

Set B

Set C

Set A

Figure 3.3 Object similarity and structural similarity

3.5.3   Priming

Priming is a well-known recency effect of activation in memory that is related to analogy. Like analogy, priming is driven by similarity, both object similarity and structural similarity, which has led some researchers to argue that priming can be seen as a (particular) form of analogy (Leech et al. 2008; Goldwater et al. 2011). Yet, in contrast to the term analogy, the notion of priming is specifically used to characterize the role of recency on activation spreading. Elements that have been recently activated increase the likelihood that the same or related elements will be (re-)used in the unfolding situation. Two basic types of (language) priming are commonly distinguished: lexical priming and structural priming.

Lexical priming refers to the facilitatory (or inhibitory) effect of a lexical item, the prime, on the activation of a related item, the target. For instance, people are faster and more accurate in identifying a word such as *dog* if the word is preceded by a semantically related item such as *cat* than if it is preceded by an unrelated word such as *city*. There is also evidence that the phonetic features of a word affect the activation of phonetically related expressions that rhyme or alliterate with the prime and that repetition speeds up lexical access and word recognition (Harley 2001: 145–150).

Like lexical priming, structural priming is an implicit memory effect that concerns the activation of knowledge, but structural priming involves relations or structures rather than lexemes. If speakers can choose between alternative constructions, and if one of them has been previously used, speakers are likely to reuse the construction in the ensuing discourse. For instance, as Bock (1986) demonstrated in a pioneering study, English speakers are more likely to describe an act of transfer by the *to*-dative construction (*She gave the book to John*) than the double-object construction (*She gave John the book*), if they have used a *to*-dative construction prior to the experimental task (*He sent a picture to his friend*). Bock's study launched a whole new line of research in psycholinguistics (see Pickering and Ferreira 2008 for a review). There is now a plethora of results indicating that both lexical priming and structural priming have a significant impact on language users' choice of linguistic means and the development of linguistic knowledge in acquisition (e.g., Chang et al. 2006; Goldwater et al. 2011; Rowland et al. 2012) and change (e.g., Jäger and Rosenbach 2008, Pickering and Garrod 2017).

3.5.4   *Exemplar Learning and Automatization*

Repeated decisions strengthen the representation of linguistic elements in memory. There is general consensus among usage-based linguists that repetition or frequency is an important determinant of linguistic knowledge, but the strengthening effect of frequency can be analyzed from different perspectives (Diessel 2016).

Some usage-based linguists have argued that exemplar learning provides a cognitive mechanism that explains the role of frequency in language (Bybee 2006; Goldberg 2006). On this account, every piece of information, that is, every token, encountered in experience leaves a trace in memory. Over time, tokens with similar or identical features reinforce each other creating clusters of overlapping memory traces known as "exemplars." The whole token cluster can be interpreted as an emergent category that functions as an "attractor" or "cognitive reference point" for the classification of novel experiences (Nosofsky 1988).

Exemplar theory has been especially influential in research on phonetics and phonology, where speech-sound categories (e.g., vowel phonemes such as /ɛ/ and /ɔ/) emerge from many slightly different phonetic tokens that a language user encounters in experience (Johnson 1997; Bybee 2001; Pierrehumbert 2001), but parallel analyses have also been proposed for the emergence of linguistic elements in morphology and syntax (Bybee 1985; Goldberg 1995; Bod 2009). Specifically, it has been argued that speakers' knowledge of constructional schemas is based on their experience with particular lexical instances of constructions.

Exemplar theory provides a plausible explanation for certain aspects of categorization, category learning and the storage of linguistic information (Chapter 4), but in the current approach, most frequency effects are explained by automatization, which is immediately related to the network view of language (Diessel 2016).

Automatization is a well-known concept of cognitive psychology (Anderson 2005: 99–103) that is closely related to the distinction between "automatic" and "controlled processes" (Logan 1988; Schneider and Chein 2003). Automatic processes occur without conscious control and effort – they are fast and can be performed in parallel to other tasks. Using a computer keyboard, for instance, is an automatic process that most people can perform parallel to other tasks (e.g., watching the computer screen). Controlled processes, by contrast, require attention and monitoring and cannot be so easily combined with other tasks. Entering new values into an electronic database, for instance, is a controlled activity that requires attention and monitoring.

Automatization transforms controlled processes into automatic processes through repetition or practice. This is a very common cognitive phenomenon that concerns both motor actions and cognitive processes. Automatization enables people to perform complex activities with little effort (Logan 1988) but is also a common source for certain types of mistakes, e.g., slips, that occur for lack of attention or lack of conscious control (Schneider and Chein 2003).

Language use is a highly automated process, which involves the rapid production of articulatory gestures, the choice of lexemes and constructions and the monitoring of the addressee. All of this occurs in milliseconds and would not be possible without automatization (or routinization). In particular, the motor movements of speech production are highly automated, but automatization also affects the choice of lexical and grammatical means.

If we think of grammar as an encompassing network in which the various aspects of a speaker's linguistic knowledge are interconnected by associative relations, we can define automatization as the process that strengthens the associations between linguistic elements in memory through repetition. For instance, if two or more lexemes are frequently used together, they become associated with each other and develop into a holistic lexical unit (§2.4.2 and §5.2).

Let me emphasize, however, that automatization is not the only factor that affects the strength of associative connections. As we will see, the various types of links that constitute the grammar network are subject to different cognitive processes. While all of them are strengthened by automatization, some are also influenced by semantic and pragmatic factors. Symbolic links, for instance, are crucially influenced by relevance. As we will see in Chapter 6, there is evidence that speakers are able to memorize the meaning of a new form with no or little repetition if the new expression is relevant to the speaker, suggesting that relevance (or salience) has a particular impact on symbolic associations.

Automatization has far-reaching consequences for the linguistic decision-making process and the storage of linguistic information. Linguistic elements (or linguistic features) that are frequently processed together develop into cognitive routines that are executed without any further decision once the routine has started; that is, automatization reduces the number of linguistic decisions that are involved in the production and comprehension of an utterance (§5.2).

3.6   Competing Motivations

Table 3.1 provides an overview of the cognitive processes that have been considered in this chapter. The various processes concern different aspects of language use and complement each other but can also be in competition. The notion of "competing motivations" plays a key role in the usage-based analysis of language (DuBois 1985; Bates and MacWhinney 1989; MacDonald et al. 1994; see also Diessel 2005). Of particular importance is the competition between social cognition and memory-related processes.

There is general agreement that communication involves audience design, but several recent studies have argued that speakers and listeners do not constantly assess the other person's mental state (Horton and Keysar 1996; Pickering and Garrod 2004). More specifically, these studies argue that inter-locutors often act in a self-oriented way without taking the other person's knowledge, beliefs and attention into account (see Arnold 2008 for a review).

For instance, in a series of studies Horton, Keysar and colleagues have shown that speakers often disregard their listeners' needs when choosing a particular referring expression (Horton and Keysar 1996; Keysar et al. 2000; Horton and Gerrig 2005). In one of their studies, they examined the way speakers describe a spatial scene that was not visible to the listener under two different conditions. In condition 1, speakers performed the task at their own pace, but in condition 2, they were put under time pressure. In accordance with their hypothesis, Horton and Keysar (1996) found that in condition 1 speakers carefully considered what listeners could potentially know about the hidden scene when describing it; but when speakers were put under time pressure, they often acted in a self-oriented fashion and disregarded their hearers' needs, as evidenced by the fact that the chosen expressions were not always informative

Table 3.1 *Some domain-general processes of language use*

Social cognition	• Joint attention
	• Common ground
	• Audience design
Conceptualization	• Figure–ground segregation
	• Metaphor and metonymy
	• Deixis and perspective
	• Force dynamics
Memory-related processes	• Attention and flow of consciousness
	• Categorization, abstraction, analogy
	• Lexical and structural priming
	• Exemplar learning and automatization

to the addressee (as they were when speakers performed the task at their own pace). Parallel results have been found in several other studies on speakers' choice of linguistic means (Arnold 2008).

In accordance with this research on production, Hanna et al. (2003) observed that comprehension can proceed in an automatic fashion. Specifically, these researchers showed that the semantic interpretations listeners assign to linguistic expressions are not always consistent with what they know about speakers' current mental states, suggesting that comprehension, like production, does not generally involve a careful assessment of common ground.

Similar results have been reported in linguistic and psycholinguistic research on phonetic reduction. If listeners are likely to be able to predict the occurrence of a particular word or utterance from the context, speakers tend to reduce articulatory effort, but if there are no contextual cues that would allow listeners to anticipate upcoming expressions, speakers tend to produce them carefully. There is plentiful evidence that the degree of phonetic reduction correlates with the predictability of linguistic expressions in a particular context (e.g., Jurafsky et al. 2001; Bell et al. 2003, 2009; Gahl and Garnsey 2004; Kuperman and Bresnan 2012; Arnon and Priva 2013). There is, however, also evidence that phonetic reduction is influenced by production-internal processes, notably by automatization (Bybee 2001) and priming (Fowler and Housom 1987), and that reduction processes are not always adjusted to the hearers' needs (Bard et al. 2000).

In general, there is now a large amount of research indicating that the linguistic decision-making process is the result of an intricate interplay between other-oriented and self-oriented processes. In production, we can distinguish between "hearer-oriented processes" of common ground and audience design, and "speaker-oriented processes" of memory retrieval, priming and automatization (Arnold 2008). A similar contrast occurs in comprehension: very often, listeners' interpretations of linguistic stimuli are based on their assessment of common ground, but under time pressure, they may solely rely on their experience with particular words and constructions without considering the speaker's current mental state. More generally, as we will see throughout this book, while communication needs some audience design, there is evidence that both speakers and listeners often act in a self-oriented or mechanistic way (Pickering and Garrod 2004; Horton and Gerrig 2005; Arnold 2008).

3.7   Acquisition and Change

The linguistic decision-making process has long-term effects on language development, which can be studied in two different time frames: (i) in ontogenetic time (i.e., L1 acquisition) and (ii) in diachronic time (i.e., language change). There are many parallels between L1 acquisition and language change that have intrigued linguists for a very long time. At the end of the nineteenth century, many scholars were convinced that the diachronic development of language is crucially influenced by language acquisition. Henry Sweet, for instance, argued that sound change can be the result of children's defective imitation of adult speakers' pronunciations, and Max Müller claimed that the regularization of irregular morphology is caused by children's errors (see Diessel 2012b for discussion).

Child-based explanations of language change have been very prominent in historical linguistics until today (e.g., Lightfoot 1999; Culbertson and Newport 2015); but a number of recent studies have questioned the validity of child-based theories of language change (Croft 2001: 45; Bybee 2010: 114–119). Specifically, these studies argue that diachronic innovations do not arise from errors and misanalyses in child language but from small changes in adult language use (see also Sankoff and Blondeau 2007). One piece of evidence for this view comes from the fact that children's errors do not seem to survive through adolescence into adulthood. If language acquisition was the source of language change, one would expect children's errors to persist through adolescence into adulthood, but this is not the case (see Diessel 2011b, 2012b for reviews of relevant research).

That does not mean, however, that language acquisition is irrelevant to the study of language change. That speakers of Present-Day English do not understand the Old English sentence *Ne com se here* 'The army did not come' is, of course, a consequence of the fact that they have no direct experience with the words and structural patterns in this sentence, indicating that the transmission of language from one generation to the next plays an important role in the diachronic development of language (e.g., Hare and Elman 1995; Kirby 1999).

Moreover, while children's errors are usually eliminated in the development from childhood into adolescence, there are striking parallels between L1 acquisition and language change that are interesting from a usage-based perspective, as the comparative analysis of language acquisition and language change can help to better understand the dynamics of the language system. As I have argued in Diessel (2011b, 2012b), while diachronic innovations are unlikely to originate from errors in L1 acquisition, the two developments involve the same (or very similar) cognitive processes, which account for the many parallels between them. However, since L1 acquisition and language change occur under very different circumstances, they also differ in important ways. There are two points to note here.

First, an important aspect of grammar learning is the extraction of structural patterns from the analysis of lexical sequences with overlapping properties (Chapter 4). Schema abstraction plays a key role in L1 acquisition. Once the first constructions are in place, they are often modified and extended under the influence of new experiences; but the first steps of grammar learning crucially involve the extraction of novel schemas from the analysis of lexical sequences, which is a relatively rare phenomenon in language change. As we will see (throughout the book), language change typically involves the modification and extension of existing schemas rather than the extraction of entirely new ones.

Second, child and adult language are subject to different sociolinguistic constraints. Young children seek to imitate the speech of adult speakers. The ambient language provides a model for children's speech during the preschool years; but when children get older and reach adolescence, they begin to pay attention to the speech of their peers. There is copious evidence indicating that the language of adolescents and adults is influenced by social prestige and group identity (Labov 1972; Trudgill 1974). In other words, while young children strive to imitate the language of a few adult speakers, notably the language of their parents, adults seek to speak in accordance with the linguistic conventions of particular speech communities.

3.8   Summary

To summarize the discussion in this chapter, I have argued that language use involves an unconscious decision-making process that is influenced by a wide range of cognitive processes, which may be divided into three basic types: (i) processes of social cognition, which concern the interaction between the speech participants, (ii) processes of conceptualization, which concern the cognitive structuring of experience, and (iii) memory-related processes, which concern the storage, retrieval and processing of linguistic information.

The various cognitive processes affect the linguistic decision-making process online and have long-term effects on language development. These effects can be studied in two different time frames: in ontogenetic time (or language acquisition) and in diachronic time (or language change). Since child and adult speakers are influenced by the same cognitive processes, there are conspicuous parallels between acquisition and change, but there are also important differences between them that reflect the different conditions under which linguistic structures evolve in L1 acquisition and language change (Diessel 2011b, 2012b). In what follows, we will consider usage-based research on both acquisition and change in order to better understand how grammar (or linguistic knowledge in general) is shaped by language use.

Part II

Signs as Networks

4   The Taxonomic Network

4.1   Introduction

Having introduced the general framework of the current approach, we will now consider the grammar network in more detail. We begin with the analysis of linguistic signs, that is, lexemes and constructions (Part II), and then turn to the analysis of grammatical categories (Part III) and the global organization of the grammar network (Part IV).

Recall that linguistic signs, notably constructions, are here defined by three basic types of links or associations: symbolic links connecting form and meaning, sequential links connecting linguistic elements in sequences and taxonomic links connecting linguistic representations at different levels of abstraction.

In what follows, we will consider the three types of links in turn, beginning with the taxonomic organization of grammar in the current chapter, followed by sequential and symbolic links in Chapters 5 and 6. As the book unfolds, we will consider a wide range of grammatical phenomena that have never been analyzed in the framework of a network model (especially in Parts III and IV), but since the taxonomic organization of grammar has been at center stage of usage-based research on L1 acquisition, the current chapter provides primarily a review of the previous literature. Readers who are familiar with the usage-based literature on L1 acquisition may thus immediately turn to Chapter 5.

4.2   The Taxonomic Organization of Constructions

All aspects of linguistic knowledge are ultimately based on our experience with lexical expressions. Usage-based linguists have emphasized the importance of lexical tokens for the development of linguistic knowledge (Bybee 2006), but of course, knowledge of language, notably grammar, exceeds speakers' memory of particular tokens. Grammar is abstract in the sense that it includes schematic representations of form and meaning to which we refer as constructional schemas (§2.4.3).

Constructional schemas represent generalizations over lexical sequences with similar forms and meanings. They enable language users to produce and categorize linguistic elements they have never heard or used before. Schema extraction is influenced by many factors but of particular importance is language users' experience with particular lexemes and constructions (§3.5.4). Since linguistic experience varies across the members of a speech community, individual speakers can have different representations of constructional schemas (Dąbrowska 2012; Kidd et al. 2018). Moreover, since constructional schemas are derived from lexical units, they are usually associated with particular words (or morphemes). In formal grammar, syntactic representations are disassociated from individual lexical expressions, but in the usage-based approach, schemas are generally linked to particular lexemes. Questioning the widespread view that the linguistic system is maximally economical and nonredundant, usage-based linguists have argued that the same information of linguistic structure is often stored redundantly at different levels of abstraction (Langacker 1987: 132–137; Croft 2001: 56).

It is one of the most basic principles of usage-based linguistics that the emergence of linguistic generalizations, notably the emergence of constructional schemas, does not automatically efface a language user's memory of particular lexical units (or even lexical tokens) from which all schemas are eventually derived (Abbot-Smith and Tomasello 2006; Goldberg 2006; Bybee 2010). On the contrary, there is good evidence that linguistic generalizations are never fully independent of lexical expressions. Building on this view, it has become a basic principle of usage-based linguistics that schemas and lexical units are associated with each other in a "taxonomic network" (Goldberg 1995: 5; Croft 2001: 25; Hilpert 2014: 57). Let us consider English relative clauses as an example (1–5).

(1)	The man who met John.	Subject RC
(2)	The man (who[m]) John met.	Object RC
(3)	The man (who) John talked to.	Oblique RC
(4)	The place (where) we met.	Oblique RC
(5)	The man whose friend John met.	Genitive RC

As can be seen, English has a family of relative-clause constructions that are formally and semantically distinguished, but the common properties of these constructions can be represented in a general relative-clause schema. All relative clauses are subordinate clauses that modify a noun in the main clause which serves a particular semanto-syntactic role in the relative clause. Subject and nonsubject relatives are distinguished by word order and the optional omission of the relative marker in nonsubject relative clauses (6–7).

(6)   Subject RCs: NP [*who/that/which* VERB . . .]$_{RC}$

(7)   Nonsubject RCs: NP [*(who/that/which)* NP VERB . . .]$_{RC}$

The latter (i.e., nonsubject RCs) comprise object, oblique and genitive relative clauses, which are differentiated by the use of different pronouns (*whom* vs. *who* vs. *whose*), adpositions (*which* vs. *of which*), verb valency (transitive vs. intransitive) and the omission of the relativized noun (which is the semantic referent that is coreferential with the noun being modified by the relative clause). The various types of relative clauses constitute a taxonomic network of constructions ranging from highly frequent lexical units, which (some) speakers may memorize as prefabricated chunks, to highly abstract schemas (Figure 4.1).

The taxonomic relationships between schemas and lexical units can be analyzed from two different perspectives. On the one hand, we can study the way constructional schemas arise from language users' analysis of lexical sequences through abstraction, or "schematization" (Langacker 2008: 17), and on the other hand, we can study how existing schemas are used to categorize novel linguistic experiences or novel tokens (Figure 4.2).

In this chapter, we will look at the taxonomic organization of grammar from both perspectives, but the focus of analysis is on abstraction, or schematization, rather than on categorization (which will concern us in later chapters). The presentation is divided into two main parts. The first part reviews empirical research on schema extraction in L1 acquisition (§4.3, §4.4 and §4.5), and the second, much shorter part considers two case studies on the emergence of constructional schemas in language change (§4.6).

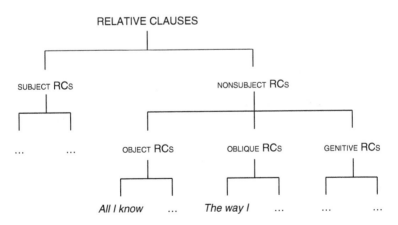

Figure 4.1 Hierarchical network of English relative-clause constructions

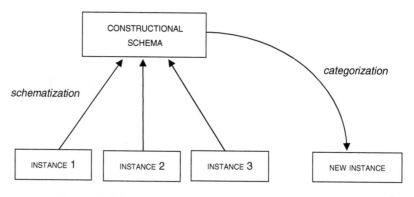

Figure 4.2 Schematization and categorization

4.3   Schema Extraction in Infancy

Constructional schemas emerge as generalizations over similar lexical sequences. While this may happen at any time, the basic inventory of constructional schemas is learned during the preschool years. Schema learning has been a central topic of research on first language acquisition and has played an important role in the development of the usage-based model of grammar (for reviews, see Behrens 2009; Diessel 2013).

One of the tasks children face in infancy is the segmentation of the speech stream. Utterances consist of phrases including words and words consist of morphemes. How do children identify the various units of speech? According to Jusczyk (1997), there are two important types of cues that help the child to segment phonetic sequences: (i) phonetic cues such as intonation, stress and pauses that correlate with utterance, phrase and word boundaries, and (ii) distributional cues that reflect the order of linguistic elements in phrases and sentences.

In a highly influential study, Saffran et al. (1996) observed that infants are very sensitive to distributional regularities in phonetic sequences. Specifically, these researchers found that 8-month-old infants are able to recognize phonetic chunks (which Saffran et al. call "words") in continuous speech based on their distribution. Inspired by this finding, infant researchers began to explore the role of statistical learning mechanisms in the acquisition of grammar. There is now abundant evidence that infants can easily extract structural templates, or schemas, from phonetic sequences based on very little data (see Aslin and Newport 2012 for a review).

4.3.1   Schema Extraction in Seven-Month-Old Infants

For instance, Marcus et al. (1999) exposed seven-month-old infants to 16 artificial three-word sentences consisting of CV "words" that were combined by two simple "word order rules." One group of children heard sentences that followed an AAB pattern, whereas the other group of children listened to sentences that followed an ABA pattern. The sentences were produced by a speech synthesizer and did not include any prosodic cues (8).

(8)   AAB: leledijijijededeli ...
         ABA: ledilejijejidelide ...

In the test phase, children listened to sentences that consisted entirely of new "words." Half of the test sentences were formed according to the same "word order rule" as the sentences infants had heard during training (e.g., AAB); the other half was constructed according to the second "word order rule," which they had not encountered in the training phase (e.g., ABA). Using the listening preference procedure (Jusczyk 1997), Marcus et al. found a significant difference between infants' responses to the two stimuli. They conducted three related versions of the same experiment and in all three versions infants looked significantly longer at a flashing light above the loudspeakers producing the acoustic stimuli when listening to the unfamiliar pattern than when listening to the pattern they had heard during the training phase (Table 4.1).

   Since the only difference between the two stimuli was infants' experience with one of the two patterns, Marcus et al. suggested that infants had extracted a schema or "rule" (in a broad sense of the word rule) from the sentences they had heard during the training phase, which now influenced their perception (or categorization) of novel sentences, as shown in Figure 4.3.

   Gómez and Gerken (1999) conducted a parallel experiment in which 12-month-old infants were exposed to sentences with different length and different word orders. Although the stimuli of this experiment were more complex and diverse than those in the Marcus et al. study, the results were very similar: Unfamiliar ordering patterns caused longer looking responses than familiar ones, supporting the hypothesis that children are able to extract fully abstract

Table 4.1 *Mean looking times to matching/nonmatching word order stimuli*

Experiment	Mean looking time(s) (SE)		
	Matching word order patterns	Nonmatching word order patterns	
1	6.3 (0.65)	9.0 (0.54)	$p < 0.0001$
2	5.6 (0.47)	7.36 (0.68)	$p < 0.0005$
3	6.4 (0.38)	8.5 (0.5)	$p < 0.0001$

Source: Marcus et al. (1999)

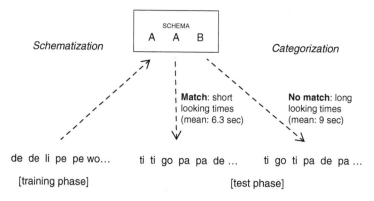

Figure 4.3 Pattern matching (data from Marcus et al. 1999)

schemas from phonetic sequences even before they begin to produce mean-ingful words and sentences (see Gómez and Gerken 2000 for a review).

4.3.2   Schematization and Item-Specific Knowledge

In a related study, Gerken (2006) made another important observation. When children can "choose" between schemas at different levels of abstraction, they "select" the more specific one. In this study, Gerken reconsidered and modified the experimental design of the study by Marcus and colleagues. As can be seen in Table 4.2, the 16 AAB strings Marcus et al. had used in the learning phase of their experiment do not only support a fully schematic AAB pattern, they also support an item-specific pattern in which the final word of a sentence (i.e., the B-slot) is expressed by a particular CV-word (e.g., the word *di* in the first column).

What Gerken wanted to find out is whether infants generalize to an abstract AAB schema if the final word does not vary across sentences. In order to examine this question, she exposed 9-month-old infants to two different sequences of CVCVCV strings consisting of two identical syllables at the beginning of each string and a different syllable at the end. One group of children was familiarized with strings that all ended in the same syllable (e.g., *di*, as in the first column of Table 4.2); the other group of children was familiarized with strings that ended in different syllables (as the strings in the diagonal of Table 4.2). Although both sets of stimuli instantiate an AAB pattern, children performed differently under the two conditions. In condition 2 (diagonal strings), they generalized to an (abstract) AAB schema, as in the Marcus et al. study, but in condition 1 (column strings), they did not acquire a

Table 4.2 *AAB stimuli used by Marcus et al. (1999)*

Syllable A	Syllable B			
	di	je	li	we
le	lele**di**	leleje	leleli	lelewe
wi	wiwi**di**	**wiwije**	wiwili	wiwiwe
ji	jiji**di**	jijije	**jijili**	jijiwe
de	dede**di**	dedeje	dedeli	**dedewe**

fully schematic AAB pattern and restricted the generalization to an item-specific schema including a particular syllable at the end (e.g., *AAdi*).

Considering this result, Gerken hypothesized that in situations in which infants can "choose" between schemas at different levels, they prefer the more specific one because item-specific schemas are more similar to the lexical sequences from which they are derived than fully schematic patterns. Altogether, these findings suggest that children are excellent "pattern finders" (Tomasello 2003: 28) and able to extract fully schematic representations of linguistic structure from phonetic sequences, though they seem to prefer item-specific ones.

4.4   Statistical Patterns in the Ambient Language

Note that it is not immediately clear from these experiments if and to what extent children's ability to recognize distributional regularities in phonetic sequences helps them to learn grammatical categories outside of the laboratory. After all, it is a long-standing hypothesis of generative grammar that the "input" children receive during the preschool years is not sufficient to learn grammar from experience alone. According to Chomsky (1972: 78), the ambient language is so "meager and degenerated" that distributional analysis is unlikely to play an important role in grammar learning. The so-called argument from the poverty of the stimulus has been at center stage in the psycholinguistic literature on linguistic nativism (Chomsky 1980; Pinker 1994), but a number of recent studies have shown that this argument is unfounded as the ambient language is much richer and more regular than previously assumed (Redington et al. 1998; Mintz et al. 2002; Scholz and Pullum 2002; Monaghan et al. 2005; Behrens 2005).

For instance, Redington et al. (1998) examined the distributional properties of English word classes in child-directed speech from the CHILDES database. Concentrating on the 1000 most frequent words in their data, they collected bigram statistics to analyze the distributional behavior of these words. That is,

Table 4.3 *Bigram frequencies of 1000 target words in the ambient language*

	Context 1 [the old __]	Context 2 [the __ of]	Context 3 [I am __]	Context 4 [is __ to]	Context vectors
Target word 1	210	176	2	5	210–176–2–5
Target word 2	367	56	1	0	367–56–1–0
Target word 3	0	1	987	298	0–1–987–298
Target word 4 ...	1	1	354	421	1–1–354–421

Note: see Redington et al. (1998)

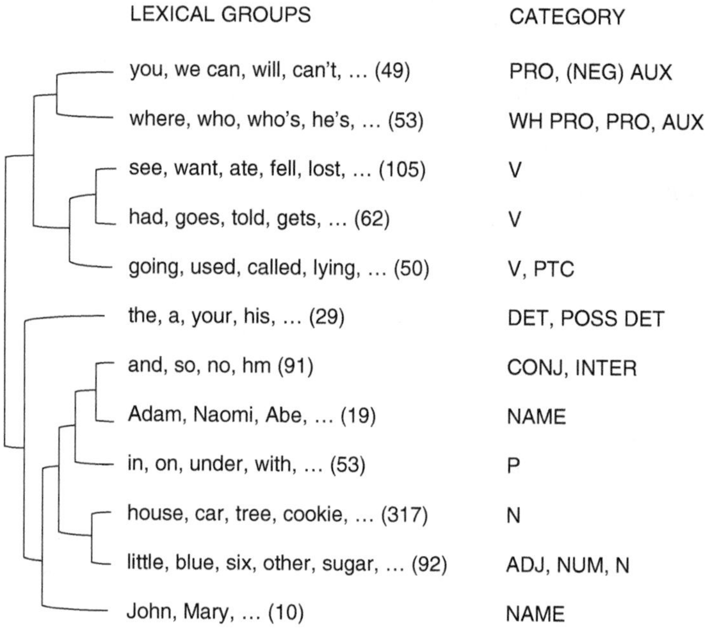

LEXICAL GROUPS   CATEGORY

you, we can, will, can't, ... (49)   PRO, (NEG) AUX

where, who, who's, he's, ... (53)   WH PRO, PRO, AUX

see, want, ate, fell, lost, ... (105)   V

had, goes, told, gets, ... (62)   V

going, used, called, lying, ... (50)   V, PTC

the, a, your, his, ... (29)   DET, POSS DET

and, so, no, hm (91)   CONJ, INTER

Adam, Naomi, Abe, ... (19)   NAME

in, on, under, with, ... (53)   P

house, car, tree, cookie, ... (317)   N

little, blue, six, other, sugar, ... (92)   ADJ, NUM, N

John, Mary, ... (10)   NAME

Figure 4.4 Cluster analysis of lexical items based on their distribution in the ambient language (Redington et al. 1998: 443)

for each target word, they considered the frequency of the two preceding and the two following context words. In order to keep it simple, they concentrated on the 150 most frequent context words. If we indicate the frequency of the various bigrams in a contingency table as in Table 4.3 and combine the numbers in the rows to one long string, we obtain "context vectors" that provide a distributional profile of the target words.

Using hierarchical cluster analysis, Redington et al. examined the distributional profiles (or context vectors) of the 1000 target words in their corpus. The cluster analysis yielded a hierarchical structure (a "dendrogram") in which target words with similar numerical profiles are grouped together in clusters. Comparing the items in these clusters to the categories that are commonly assigned to particular words in dictionaries and grammars, Redington et al. found a highly significant correlation between the groups created by the cluster analysis and the traditional classification of words in English grammar (Figure 4.4), suggesting that the linguistic context provides a rich source of information for the acquisition of word class schemas.

Subsequent research confirmed this finding and improved the results of the Redington et al. study by including phonetic features in the analysis (Mintz et al. 2002; Monaghan et al. 2005). What all of these studies have shown is that the ambient language includes more information than commonly assumed and that this information is readily available to young children as distributional and phonetic cues are especially informative in local contexts that involve a relatively small number of high-frequency words (Mintz 2003). Considering these results together with the research on statistical grammar learning in infancy (§4.3), we can conclude that distributional analysis plays a highly important role in the acquisition of grammatical categories and constructional schemas.

4.5   The Acquisition of Constructional Schemas

While the first schemas infants extract from adult speech may be purely structural patterns (or phonetic templates), constructions combine a particular structure with meaning. Since constructions are meaningful, statistical learning mechanisms alone are not sufficient to explain the acquisition of grammar. In order to understand how children learn constructions, we have to consider both distributional and semantic/communicative aspects of language use (Tomasello 2003: 169–173).

The earliest utterances children produce are holophrases consisting of isolated words or unanalyzed chunks of multiword sequences that function as speech acts. Since children's early holophrases are embedded in daily routines, their interpretation is tied to the specifics of particular contexts (Tomasello 2003: 88).

As children grow older, holophrases are replaced by multiword utterances that become increasingly more independent of contextual support from the child's daily routines. Children create these early multiword utterances by two strategies. In some cases, they use intonation to combine two or more words in a communicative unit (Clark 2003: 162–165). This is the classic scenario whereby syntactic structures are derived from smaller, primitive units, but there is a second scenario whereby children decompose some of their early frozen chunks into separate lexical units (e.g., *What-s-this* → *What is this)* (Dąbrowska 2000). One aspect that has been stressed by many usage-based scholars is that children's early two- and three-word utterances are commonly organized around particular lexical items (e.g., Braine 1976; Lieven et al. 1997; Tomasello 2000; Lieven et al. 2003; Dąbrowska and Lieven 2005).

4.5.1   Pivot Schemas

In a classic study, Martin Braine (1976) referred to children's early item-based constructions as "pivot schemas." They typically include a relational expression, a "pivot word," that provides a "slot" for a class of nonrelational expressions that are semantically compatible with the pivot word. The prototype of a pivot word is the verb, which is generally associated with one or more structural positions for its participants (e.g., [[HITTER] *hit* [HITTEE]]), but pivot schemas can also be organized around other types of expressions. For instance, as Braine (1976) observed, children combine quantifiers, demonstratives and adjectives with certain types of referring terms in structures that are strikingly similar to their early argument-structure constructions (see 9 from Braine 1976: 7, 34, 38).

(9)   [MORE ___]   [THERE ___]   [BIG ___]

More care.	There book.	Big plane.
More cereal.	There rhino.	Big book.
More cookie.	There hammer.	Big car.
More fish.	There ball.	Big sock.
More juice.	There boat.	Big ball.
More hot.	There milk.	Big rock.

Not all child utterances include a lexical frame as in these examples, but the "pivot look" is characteristic of early child language and not a particular trait of English. As Braine showed in his pioneering study, children learning Swedish, Hebrew, Finnish and Samoan produce lexically specific constructions that are reminiscent of those produced by English-speaking children (see also Behrens 2005 on German). Consider, for instance, the utterances in (10) from a 2-year-old Hebrew-speaking child, which are very similar to children's pivot schemas in English (Braine 1976: 40).

(10)   Tire kos.   'see glass'   Ten li.   'give me'
         Tiri rakevet.   'see train'   Ten li kova.   'give me hat'
         Tire kise.   'see chair'   Ten li mayim.   'give me water'
         Tire susim.   'see horses'   Ten li oto.   'give me car'

Hine migdal.	'here tower'	Efo buba?	'where doll'
Hine sus.	'here horse'	Efo uga?	'where cake'
Hine kova.	'here hat'	Efo Aba?	'where daddy'
Hine buba.	'here doll'	Efo sus?	'where horse'

Braine (1976: 4) characterized pivot schemas as "limited scope formulas" that typically occur with a narrow range of semantically defined expressions. Every slot is initially limited to particular semantic types of expressions denoting, for example, objects, persons, animals, animate beings, locations, physical processes or mental processes, but as children get older they extend the range of expressions that can occur in particular positions. Consider, for instance, the development of children's constructions including the verb *want* in (11a–d) (data from Diessel 2004: 68–72).

(11)	a. I wan(na) bag.	I want THING
	b. I wan(na) ride.	I want PROCESS
	c. I wan(na) my book here.	I want THING LOCATION
	d. I wan(na) Daddy to help me.	I want PERSON ACTION

Want is initially always combined with the first person pronoun *I* and variably pronounced as *wan* or *wanna*. In the earliest uses, *want* is followed by nominal expressions denoting a thing (11a). Shortly thereafter children begin to use *want* with verbs denoting processes (11b), but then it takes several months until they also use *want* with complex arguments denoting the location of a thing (11c) or the action of another person (11d). Interestingly, when children reach this stage, they sometimes overextend the use of *want* to structures that seem to include finite complement clauses, as the examples in (12a–c) (from Diessel 2004: 71).

(12)	a. I want [dat came out].
	b. I want [my doll's waking up].
	c. You want [I do a cartwheel]?

What these examples illustrate is that the slots of children's early pivot schemas increase in scope as they get older (Lieven et al. 1997; Dąbrowska 2000; Lieven et al. 2003; Dąbrowska and Lieven 2005), but while the positions for nonrelational expressions are readily expanded to a wider range of terms, children tend to cling to the lexical parts of their early pivot schemas. Fully schematic constructions in which relational expressions are represented by a slot or category, rather than a pivot word, emerge only later.

4.5.2   Fully Schematic Constructions

The appearance of fully schematic constructions has been a central topic of research on the acquisition of argument-structure constructions (Brooks and

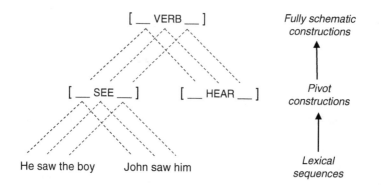

Figure 4.5 Development of fully schematic constructions from lexical sequences via pivot constructions

Tomasello 1999; Tomasello 2000, 2003; Goldberg et al. 2004; Goldberg 2006; Ambridge et al. 2008). According to Tomasello (1992), every argument-structure construction is initially a "constructional island" that is organized around a particular (pivot) verb providing a lexical frame for the construction. It takes months and years before children begin to generalize across verb-island constructions with overlapping semantic and syntactic properties and to form constructional schemas that include a slot for the verb (Figure 4.5).

The development involves the same cognitive processes as the formation of purely structural schemas in infancy (§4.3), except that argument-structure constructions are not just structural templates. They also capture semantic generalizations over recurrent semantic roles and event schemas. One piece of evidence that indicates the emergence of fully schematic argument-structure constructions is the appearance of overextension errors at a particular age. Consider, for instance, the following examples from Bowerman (1988) and Pinker et al. (1987).

(13)   Kendall fall that toy. (2;3) [= 2 years and 3 months]
        Who deaded my kitty cat. (2;6)
        Don't giggle me. (3;0)

(14)   I'll brush him his hair. (2;3)
        I said her no. (3;1)
        Button me the rest. (3;4)

As can be seen, the examples in (13) include intransitive verbs in a transitive clause, and the examples in (14) include transitive verbs in a ditransitive clause. We will consider the occurrence of these mistakes in more detail in Chapter 7. Here we note that children's overextension errors presuppose the existence of constructional schemas that include a slot for the insertion of verbs that (usually) do not occur in these positions. Since overextension errors of this type are absent from children's early pivot schemas, Tomasello and colleagues have argued that children only generalize across verbs at a later age.

This hypothesis is supported by evidence from a series of experiments in which children of different age groups were taught novel verbs in particular constructions and were then asked to extend them to other syntactic contexts, that is, constructions in which the novel verbs had not yet been used. For instance, in one study children were taught new causative verbs in active transitive constructions and were then encouraged to use these verbs in passive sentences (Brooks and Tomasello 1999). As expected, the researchers found that older children had no difficulties in extending the novel causative verbs from active transitive to passive constructions, but the younger children were reluctant to do so; that is, they restricted the use of the novel verbs to the active construction, supporting the hypothesis that fully schematic constructions including a verb slot arise only gradually from pivot schemas (see Tomasello and Brooks 1998 for parallel experiments with other constructions).

Interestingly, Goldberg et al. (2004) observed that the acquisition of verb-argument schemas is crucially influenced by the relative frequency of individual verbs (for a summary, see also Goldberg 2006: 79–90). There are two important points to note.

First, the argument-structure constructions children encounter in the ambient language typically include one verb that is much more frequent than all others (see also Ellis et al. 2016). The intransitive motion construction, for instance, is very frequent with *go* (e.g., AGENT *goes* PATH/LOCATION) and the caused-motion construction is very frequent with *put* (e.g., AGENT *puts* OBJECT PATH/LOCATION). In the data Goldberg et al. (2004) analyzed, 39 percent of the intransitive motion constructions (in child-directed speech) included the verb *go* and 38 percent of the caused-motion constructions included the verb *put*. All other verbs were much less frequent (in both constructions).

Second, there is evidence that the occurrence of frequent verbs facilitates the acquisition of verb-argument constructions. As Goldberg et al. (2004) showed in a learning experiment, children (aged 5 to 7) find argument-structure constructions much easier to learn when they occur with a skewed distribution of verb types. Specifically, they found that children have fewer difficulties with constructions that include one frequent verb and several infrequent ones than with constructions in which all verb types are about equally frequent. Building on this finding, the authors claim that the acquisition of verb-argument constructions is driven by "pathbreaking verbs" that constitute the prototype of a new schema (see also Ninio 1999; Madlener 2016; Ellis et al. 2016).

Taken together, these studies provide strong evidence for the view that children acquire a taxonomic network of constructions from the analysis of lexical sequences. The development is driven by domain-general processes, notably by categorization and abstraction. In §4.6, we will consider the emergence of constructional schemas and the taxonomic organization of grammar from a diachronic point of view.

4.6   The Emergence of Constructional Schemas in Language History

The constructional schemas children learn are implicit in the ambient language. But where do these schemas come from? What are their origins in language change and language evolution? For most constructions, this question is difficult to answer. If we look at diachronic corpora, we find that even the oldest languages (of which there are historical records) have a rich inventory of complex constructions similar to those of modern languages. Old Akkadian, for instance, has a wide range of highly complex structures including argument-structure constructions, content and polar questions, genitive constructions, relative clauses, adverbial clauses and quotative constructions (Deutscher 2000), making it very difficult to study the ultimate origins of these constructions in language evolution with empirical (i.e., corpus linguistic or comparative) methods.

In §4.5, we have seen how children derive constructional schemas from lexical sequences. When children are born, they have no grammatical knowledge and everything they learn about grammar is ultimately based on their analysis of the ambient language. Language change is different. Since language change occurs in adult language use (§3.7), it typically involves the extension or modification of existing schemas rather than the creation of entirely new ones. What we observe in diachronic corpora is how constructions change through structural reanalysis, lexical diffusion and grammaticalization (Harris and Campbell 1995; Bergs and Diewald 2008; Hilpert 2013; Traugott and Trousdale 2013), but there is relatively little evidence for the emergence of new schemas that are not based on, or influenced by, existing schemas.

In what follows, however, we will consider the development of two grammatical categories in the recent history of English (i.e., secondary modals and determiners) which arguably involved the emergence of new schemas. As we will see, in both cases the development originated from a number of lexical patterns with similar semantic and syntactic features that converged upon a new schema.

4.6.1   The Emergence of a Secondary Modal Verb Schema

English has a large number of modal verbs that are often described as a continuum ranging from central modals such as *can* and *may* to verb-infinitive constructions such as *hope to* and *want to* (15) (based on Quirk et al. 1985: 137):

(15)

↑	CENTRAL MODALS	can, may, will
│	MARGINAL MODALS	dare, need, used to
│	MODAL IDIOMS	had better, would rather, have got to
│	SEMI-AUXILIARIES	have to, be going to, be supposed to
↓	VERB PLUS INFINITIVE	hope to, want to, wish to

All of the verbs in (15) have modal meanings but different structural properties. The central modals differ from main verbs with respect to the following features: they occur with bare infinitives (*She can leave*), do not take the third-person agreement suffix *-s* (*He may go*), are negated without "*do*-support" (*I cannot sleep*) and occur in clause-initial position in questions (*Can we leave?*). Some of these features are also found in marginal modals and modal idioms, but the noncentral modals do not form a structurally coherent class: some of them consist of a single verb, others are phrases (*need* vs. *have got to*); some can occur with bare infinitives, others are exclusively found with *to*-infinitives (*I don't dare ask* vs. *I have to ask*); and some can be negated with *not*, whereas others need *do*-support (*I need not say more* vs. *I don't want to say more*).

Obviously, the expressions in (15) are structurally diverse. They do not form a coherent syntactic category, but, interestingly, some of these expressions have become more similar to each other in the recent history of English. As Krug (2000) showed (based on extensive data from diachronic corpora), English has acquired a new class of "secondary modals" that are organized around three central category members: *be going to, have (got) to*, and *want to*.

The development of *be going to* is the paradigm case of grammaticalization (Hopper and Traugott 2003: 1–3). Since this development has been described in many other places, I will just briefly summarize the main points. *Go* is a motion verb that is commonly combined with an agentive subject and an allative prepositional phrase (*I am going to the store*), but in Present-Day English, *be going to* is (also) often used as a future tense auxiliary that has lost its original meaning as motion verb (*There is going to be a meeting*). The development of the future tense marker originated from a bi-clausal structure in which the clause including *be going to* was followed by an infinitive construction denoting a metaphorical goal or purpose of the motion event described in the *be-going-to* clause (see example 16).

(16)   I am going to the store to buy something to drink.

This construction has undergone a series of related changes whereby the motion verb *go* developed into a future tense auxiliary and the infinitive into the main verb of a periphrastic verb phrase construction. First, the motion sense of *go* was backgrounded under the influence of the purpose clause and then extended to the meaning of intention and later to future (17a). Second, as the meaning of *go* shifted from motion to future, the main clause event was no longer perceived as an independent state of affairs and the whole structure was reanalyzed as a simple sentence (17b). Third, parallel to these developments the semantic profile of the subject slot was extended from nouns denoting animate beings to things and abstract entities and finally to dummy pronouns (e.g., *It is going to rain*) (17c). And fourth, *going to* was reduced to *gonna* and the auxiliary *be* is now often omitted in colloquial speech (*I gonna miss you*) (17d).

(17)   a. motion > intention > future
        b. complex sentence > simple sentence
        c. animate subject > inanimate subject > dummy subject
        d. be going to > gonna

Like *be going to,* the modal uses of *have got to* and *want to* developed from main verbs that were accompanied by an infinitive construction. As main verbs, *have* denotes possession (*I have a bike*) and *want* desire (*I want ice cream*). There are many parallels in the development of *be going to, have got to* and *want to* into modal verbs, but note that these developments originated from different source constructions. *Go* is an intransitive verb and the future tense marker is based on a progressive verb form including the auxiliary *be*, whereas *have* and *want* are transitive verbs that do not occur in the progressive tense when used as modal verbs. The three verbs have undergone different reduction processes of assimilation, cliticization and deletion, but, interestingly, these processes have given rise to phonetically similar verb forms. As Krug (2000) showed, *be going to, have got to* and *want to* converged on a phonetic template consisting of two CV syllables including the same vowels and similar consonants (see 18a–c).

(18)   a. going to   > gonna /gɒnə/
        b. want to   > wanna /wɒnə/
        c. have got to > gotta /gɒtə/

What is more, while the emerging modals are based on different source constructions, *wanna, gonna* and *gotta* are now used in the same constructional schema consisting of a nominal slot for the subject, a phonetically specified slot for the auxiliary and a subsequent slot for the infinitive or main verb (Figure 4.6).

Interestingly, the new schema has attracted new verbs in the recent history of English that have been (formally) accommodated to *wanna, gonna* and *gotta* in this context. According to Krug (2000: 230), these verbs are now the prototypes of a new category of secondary modals that includes a group of phonetically and structurally related verb forms including *have to* /hæftə/, *had better* /(hæd)

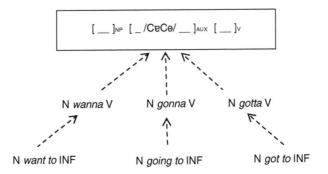

Figure 4.6 Emerging constructional schema of secondary modal verbs (in English)

betə/, *need to* /niːtə/, *try to* /traɪtə/, *dare to* /dæɾtə/, *ought to* /ɔtə/ and perhaps also *supposed to* /səpɔztə/. All of these verbs have modal meanings and are phonetically and structurally similar to the three prototypes but are based on different source constructions. *Dare (to)*, for instance, was a true modal verb in Early Modern English that was exclusively used with bare infinitives until the sixteenth century, but is now often used with *to*-infinitives and *do*-support like other secondary modals (Krug 2000: 200–202), and *supposed to* is based on a passive construction that has developed into an idiomatic modal verb with both deontic and epistemic meanings. Generalizing across all of these expressions, we may characterize the new category of secondary modals as an "attractor" in a self-organizing system of similar constructions that has given rise to the constructional schema in Figure 4.6 and that is organized around a center or prototype as shown in Figure 4.7 (Krug 2000: 239).[1]

4.6.2   The Emergence of a Determiner Schema

Another grammatical category that has emerged only recently in the history of English is the category of determiner. The prototype of the English determiner is the definite article *the*, which developed from a demonstrative pronoun (Diessel 1999: 62–70). Old English did not have articles, and definite nouns were sometimes used without a definite marker, as in example (19a). But very

---

[1] Interestingly, Warner (1993) proposed a similar analysis for the class of central English modals. They too emerged from a small class of verbs with fairly different properties that have become more similar over time and have attracted other category members. According to Warner (1993: 238), the development of the central modals started with only three verbs, namely, *mot* 'must', *sceal* 'shall' and *uton* 'lets' (which later disappeared). Today, the class of central modals includes more than 10 verbs that are related by family resemblance similar to the secondary modals in Figure 4.7.

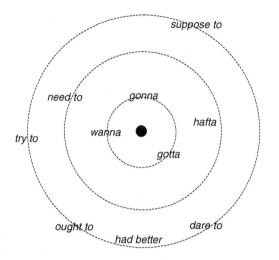

Figure 4.7 Radial category of secondary modal verbs

often definite nouns were accompanied by a demonstrative or possessive pronoun (Sommerer 2015). Crucially, while these markers indicate (semantic) definiteness, as in Present-Day English, their syntactic behavior was different from their behavior today. As can be seen in (19b), demonstratives and possessive pronouns could occur together before a noun and could follow a co-occurring adjective (19c).

(19)   a. He   is   swiðe   biter   on   muðe.
           It   is   very   bitter   in   mouth
           'He has a bitter taste in his/the mouth.' (Sommerer 2015: 110)
        b. his   þa   œfestan   tungan
           his   that   pious   tongue
           'that pious tongue of his' (Van de Velde 2010: 270)
        c. on   wlancan   þam   wicge
           on   proud   that   horse
           'on that proud horse' (Van de Velde 2010: 270)

Today, demonstratives and possessive pronouns are mutually exclusive in pre-nominal position and the elements that accompany a noun are arranged in a particular order such that adjectives generally follow demonstratives or possessive markers. If we look at the development of the English noun phrase since the time of Old English, we find that its structure has become increasingly more rigid and constrained. In Present-Day English, count nouns are generally accompanied by a determiner that precedes adjectives and other noun modifiers, but in Old English, nouns were only loosely combined with demonstratives, possessive

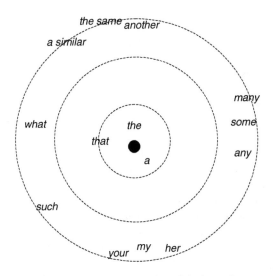

Figure 4.8 Radial category of English determiners

pronouns and nouns in some kind of appositional construction (Traugott 1992: 173). In contrast, the noun phrase of Present-Day English is licensed by a tightly organized constructional schema including a specific slot for the category determiner that precedes the slots for adjectives and the head noun (see also Van de Velde 2010 on a parallel development of determiners in Dutch).

Like the class of (secondary) modals, the class of English determiners is an emerging category that has evolved from a number of related constructions that have converged on a new schema (Sommerer 2015). In the course of this development, the unstressed demonstrative *se* developed into a definite article, which soon became the prototype of the new category or schema. Over time, the emerging category attracted additional category members including the indefinite article *a(n)*, which evolved from the numeral 'one,' possessive pronouns such as *my, your* and *her*, and quantifiers such as *many, all* and *some*, which developed from diverse sources (see Figure 4.8). All of these expressions are now commonly used as determiners at the beginning of a noun phrase, though some of them have idiosyncratic properties (Culicover 1999: 61–68) that reflect aspects of their earlier uses in Old and Middle English.[2]

---

[2] Interestingly, Breban and Davidse (2003) observed that in the recent history of English, the articles *the* and *a* are commonly combined with expressions of similarity and contrast resulting in a new set of "secondary determiners" such as *the same, a similar* and *another* at the margin of the new category (Figure 4.8) (see also Breban et al. 2011).

4.7   Conclusion

To briefly sum up, this chapter has been concerned with the taxonomic organization of grammar and the emergence of constructional schemas. Schemas represent generalizations over linguistic strings with similar semantic, phonological and distributional properties. They are related to particular lexical units in taxonomic networks in which linguistic information of the same kind is (often) represented at multiple levels of abstraction. Children acquire the taxonomic network in a piecemeal, bottom-up fashion that is driven by both distributional and communicative aspects of language use. The emergence of constructional schemas can also be studied from a diachronic perspective, but usually, language change involves the extension and modification of existing schemas rather than the rise of entirely new ones. The taxonomic organization of linguistic structure has been very prominent in usage-based research on grammar and L1 acquisition. In fact, many construction grammarians conceive of grammar primarily as a taxonomic network (Goldberg 1995; Croft 2001; Fried and Östman 2005; Hilpert 2014). In what follows, however, we will see that in addition to taxonomic links speakers' knowledge of constructions includes sequential and symbolic associations.

5 Sequential Relations

5.1 Introduction

Language is a linear medium in which all linguistic elements – speech sounds, morphemes, words, phrases, clauses and sentences – are arranged in sequential order. Functional and cognitive linguists have argued that the sequential organization of language is motivated by general semantic and pragmatic factors. There is, for instance, a well-known tendency to place conceptually related elements next to each other (Behaghel 1932) and to present given or old information before new information (Chafe 1994). Semantic and pragmatic factors can influence speakers' choice of a particular sequential order, but very often linguistic sequences are fixed (and conventionalized) as a result of automatization (and social cognition) (§3.5.4). If the same string of linguistic elements is repeatedly processed, automatization creates sequential links between them.[1]

Since language unfolds in time, sequential links are asymmetrical: they usually have an inherent forward orientation, which is reflected in the fact that language users are able to anticipate, or to "predict," the occurrence of upcoming elements in the unfolding speech stream (Altmann and Mirković 2009).

Since automatization is a gradual process driven by frequency of occurrence, sequential relations vary on a continuum. Other things being equal, the more often a string of linguistic elements is processed, the stronger are the sequential links between them (Bybee 2002; 2010: 33–37). The cognitive result of this development is the gradual emergence of a "unit" or "chunk." Langacker (1987) uses the notion of "unit" as a technical term for automated sequences that speakers activate and execute as integrated wholes (see also Langacker 2008: 60–73):

---

[1] Automatization is the driving force behind entrenchment, which must not be confused with conventionalization (Schmid 2015). The latter is influenced by both automatization and social cognition. In order to communicate, language users must adjust their speech to the linguistic norms, or conventions, of a particular speech community, which can reinforce the sequential associations that are created by automatization.

The term 'unit' is employed in a technical sense to indicate a thoroughly mastered structure, i.e., one that a speaker can activate as a preassembled whole without attending to the specifics of its internal composition. (Langacker 1987: 494)

Bybee (2010) refers to units as "chunks" and to the process of unit formation as "chunking": "Chunking is the process by which sequences of units that are used together cohere to form more complex units" (Bybee 2010: 7; see also Ellis 1996). Bybee adopts the notion of chunking from general psychological research on the organization of memory (Miller 1956; Newell 1990; Gobet et al. 2001). In a seminal study, the psychologist George Miller (1956) characterized chunking as a cognitive process whereby individual pieces of information are grouped together into one item or chunk that is stored and processed as a single cognitive unit.

There is a close connection between sequential processing and the taxonomic organization of linguistic knowledge. Linguistic sequences that are grouped together in one chunk (as a consequence of automatization) may be combined with other chunks in larger units at higher levels of linguistic structure. Sequences of speech sounds, for instance, are grouped together into syllables and word chunks, which in turn are grouped together into prefabs, multiword phrases and sentences (Miller 1956; Gobet et al. 2001; Green 2017). In this way, sequential processing creates a "chunk hierarchy" (Gobet 2017: 258) that increases the amount of information people can activate in a particular situation.

According to Miller, the maximal number of items that one can hold in working memory is seven, plus/minus two, but the actual amount of information that is available for processing at a particular point in time varies with the structure and size of the items, or chunks, that are currently in working memory (or focus of attention) (§3.5.1). Later research by Cowan (2005) and others argued that Miller's "magical number seven" should be reduced to four (Green 2017), but while Miller may have overestimated the number of items that can be held in working memory (see also Oberauer 2002), there is general consensus among cognitive psychologists that chunking is of utmost significance to the cognitive organization of memory and linguistic knowledge (see Cowen 2005: Chapter 3 for a review; see also Ellis 1996).

This chapter considers the sequential organization of grammar and the emergence of linguistic units or chunks. The chapter is divided into two main parts. The first part is concerned with lexical chunks and the usage-based analysis of morphology (§5.3, §5.4 and §5.5), and the second part is concerned with constructional schemas and sequential relations in syntax (§5.6 and §5.7). Like Chapter 4, the current chapter provides an overview of the usage-based literature, but it also includes some novel suggestions and combines the linguistic analysis of prefabricated chunks with recent psycholinguistic research on sequential processing and syntactic predictions.

5.2   Lexical Prefabs and Idiomaticity

Natural language abounds with lexical chunks, commonly referred to as "lexical prefabs" or "collocations." While the co-occurrence of lexical expressions is always semantically motivated, semantic factors alone are not sufficient to explain the existence of lexical prefabs (see Taylor 2012: Chapter 7 for a recent discussion). Consider, for instance, the following examples:

(1)   That's a powerful computer.

(2)   How long ago did she leave?

The sentences in (1) and (2) are consistent with general syntactic and semantic principles – their structures are regular and their meanings are compositional; and yet, both sentences include lexical prefabs that cannot be altered even if the alternation is consistent with general principles of semantics (or conceptualization). For instance, although *powerful* may be paraphrased by *strong*, it is not customary to say *strong computer* because *powerful computer* is an automated string that is stored and processed as one chunk. Likewise, *how long ago* constitutes a unit or chunk as evidenced by the fact that *long* cannot be replaced by *short* even if the time period in question is very limited (*how short ago).

Lexical prefabs are semantically (and pragmatically) motivated and shaped by automatization. If the same string of words is repeatedly used, it develops into a processing unit – a cognitive routine with strong sequential associations between its (lexical) parts (Figure 5.1).

Lexical prefabs of this type are very frequent in everyday language use (Erman and Warren 2000). They constitute an important aspect of speakers' linguistic knowledge and must not be ignored in grammatical analysis. For one thing, prefabs reduce the number of lexical choices in language use. In a classic study, Sinclair (1991) argued that language use is governed by two general principles: The "open choice principle," which refers to contexts in which speakers can freely choose between alternative expressions, and the "principle of idiom," which refers to contexts in which speakers' choice of lexemes is predetermined by the sequential context. As Sinclair (1991: 110) put it:

The principle of idiom is that a language user has available to him a large number of semi-preconstructed phrases that constitute single choices, even though they might appear to be analyzable into segments.

Figure 5.1 Sequential links of lexical prefabs

Table 5.1 *Examples of prefabricated lexical sequences*

Fully specified sentences	Phrasal collocations
How are you?	unmitigated disaster
Thank you, I am fine.	powerful computer
What time is it?	keep apart
I don't know.	take into account
Say that again.	to the right
Preconstructed sentence fragments	**Grammatical prefabs**
Do you mind if __	not at all
Why don't you __	be about to
I was wondering if __	some kind of
How do you know (that) __	must have been
I can't help Ving __	as if

In accordance with this view, corpus linguists have shown that both spoken and written discourse proliferate with prefabricated sequences that do not allow for lexical variation (Erman and Warren 2000; Wray 2002). Some of these prefabs are complete sentences or sentence fragments, others are phrasal collocations, and yet others are composed of multiple function words (Table 5.1).

Most research on lexical prefabs is based on corpus data, but there is also experimental evidence for the hypothesis that frequent word strings are stored and processed as units. Arnon and Snider (2010), for instance, conducted an experiment in which participants responded much faster to frequent word strings in lexical decision tasks than to infrequent strings, and Tremblay et al. (2011) report the results of a reading time experiment in which frequent word sequences were read significantly faster than infrequent or novel ones (see also Bannard and Matthews 2008 for a parallel study with children and McCauley and Christiansen 2014 for a computational model in which the acquisition of lexical chunks is foundational to (adult) sentence processing).

Crucially, lexical sequences that are highly routinized often develop idiosyncratic properties that are not predictable from their components. Lexical prefabs with idiosyncratic properties are known as idioms. Traditionally, idioms are thought to form a small class of irregular expressions that are stored alongside words in the mental lexicon, whereas the vast majority of phrases and sentences are derived by means of fully productive rules. This view of stored idioms and derived expressions is not consistent, however, with the widespread use of prefabricated lexical sequences. In fact, if we look at the semantic and formal properties of lexical prefabs, we find that many of them have some idiosyncratic properties that are not predictable from general rules, suggesting that idiomaticity is a continuum that concerns a much wider range of expressions than commonly assumed (Fillmore et al. 1988; Nunberg et al. 1994; see also Wulff 2008; Taylor 2012).

5.3   Words, Clitics and Morphemes

Since lexical prefabs are based on phrases, they have the structure of syntactic units, but they often behave more like words rather than phrases. In fact, morphologically complex words are frequently derived from lexical prefabs, which in turn may develop into simple words. In the literature, the unit of word is commonly treated as a primitive concept. There is, perhaps, no other linguistic category that is so closely associated with the toolkit approach than the notion of word. Words are of central significance to the analysis of linguistic structure and the traditional view of grammar. As Lyons (1968) notes:

> The word is the unit par excellence of traditional grammatical theory. It is the basis of the distinction which is frequently drawn between morphology and syntax and it is the principal unit of lexicography. (Lyons 1968: 194)

To be sure, the word is a key concept of grammatical analysis, but contrary to the way the notion of word is used in most linguistic studies, it is NOT a basic or primitive concept. Like all other aspects of linguistic structure, the unit word is emergent, fuzzy and language-particular.

5.3.1   The Word as an Emergent Unit

If we look at words from a cross-linguistic perspective, we find an enormous amount of variation. There are languages like Lao in which words typically consist of a single morpheme (3), and there are languages like Mohawk in which words can easily consist of half-a-dozen morphemes (4).

(3)   khon2   (thii1)   laaw2   lèèn1   siø   bòø   paj3
       person   (REL)   3SG   run   IRR   NEG   go
       'The person who ran will not be going.' (Enfield 2007: 115)

(4)   t-v-hshakoti-ya't-ayest-áhsi-'
       DU-will-they/them-body-mix-REVERSE-PUNC
       'They will pick them out.' (Mithun 1984: 868)

In the typological literature, words are usually defined by a combination of syntactic and phonological features. Syntactic features of wordhood concern the order and position of morphemes, the possibility of interrupting a lexical sequence by a (free) item and certain scope phenomena. Phonological features that are widely used to define words include stress and tone assignment, vowel harmony, assimilation and sandhi (Dixon and Aikhenvald 2002; Haspelmath 2011; Schiering et al. 2011).

Crucially, while some of these features tend to co-occur, there is a great deal of variation, making it difficult to define the unit word by a fixed set of features. Since the features linguists use to define words are often language-particular, Haspelmath (2011) argues that words can only be defined at the level of individual languages. There is no universal concept of "wordhood" according to Haspelmath, but even if we restrict the definition of word to particular languages, the notion of word is not without problems as the language-particular features of wordhood do not always coincide. In fact, there is a well-known mismatch between syntactic and phonological criteria for wordhood that is commonly characterized by the notion of clitic or cliticization.

5.3.2   Cliticization and Phonetic Reduction

Clitics are often defined as syntactically independent words that are phonetically attached to a host similar to an affix (Spencer and Luis 2012). In English, for instance, auxiliaries are free lexemes (or words) that can appear in various structural positions (e.g., before and after subjects: *You are . . ., Are you . . .?*), but in declarative sentences they are often phonetically reduced and attached to a preceding host (e.g., *I'm, you've, he's*). Interestingly, Krug (1998, 2003) observed that the occurrence of auxiliary clitics correlates with the frequency of the auxiliary and a preceding (pro)noun (see also Labov 1969). For instance, in one of his studies, Krug found that the proportion of the contracted use of the auxiliary *have* correlates with the joint frequency of *have* and the preceding pronoun: The more frequently *have* follows a particular pronoun, the higher the contraction rate (Figure 5.2). Later research confirmed this finding and showed that the same correlation occurs with other contracted auxiliaries and other types of subjects (see Bresnan and Spencer 2013; Barth and Kapatsinski 2017).[2]

The results of these studies are representative of a large body of research indicating that phonetic reduction (and contraction) correlates with frequency of occurrence (e.g., Bybee 2001; Jurafsky et al. 2001; Bell et al. 2003, 2009; Aylett and Turk 2004; Pluymaekers et al. 2005). There is clear evidence that speakers are overall more likely to produce frequent word strings with less articulatory effort than infrequent ones, but the cognitive processes that lead to phonetic reduction (and contraction) are not fully understood.

Some researchers have argued that phonetic reduction is primarily caused by the routinization of articulatory gestures (Bybee 2001) or the automatization of lexical access (Pluymaekers et al. 2005). On this view, frequent word strings are prone to be phonetically reduced because of self-oriented (or speaker-oriented) processes of articulation and activation that are facilitated by repetition and practice.

---

[2] In addition to the joint frequency of pronoun and auxiliary, there are several other factors that correlate with the occurrence of auxiliary contraction in English, e.g., the phonetic context and constituent type (see Bresnan and Spencer 2013 and Barth and Kapatsinski 2017).

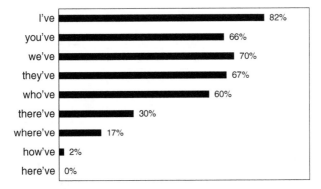

Figure 5.2 Proportion of contracted auxiliary *have* after certain pronouns (arranged in accordance with their frequency in a large corpus) (based on data from Krug 2003: 25)

Other researchers have claimed that phonetic reduction is primarily caused by other-oriented (or hearer-oriented) processes of common ground and audience design (Jurafsky et al. 2001; Haspelmath 2008a). On this view, linguistic elements are phonetically reduced if their components are predictable (for the hearer) from the context. One aspect that affects the predictability of words in continuous speech is language users' experience with linguistic sequences. In a classic study, Pollack and Pickett (1964) showed that about 50 percent of all words are not phonetically recognizable if they are spliced out of context; but since listeners are able to predict the occurrence of words from the linguistic (or nonlinguistic) context, they do not even recognize that many words are phonetically underdetermined.

The two factors, that is, the automatization of articulatory gestures (and lexical access) and the predictability of co-occurring words, are not mutually exclusive. In fact, there is good evidence that they complement each other (Lorenz and Tizón-Couto 2017; see also Bybee 2010: 38–43). If linguistic expressions are easily predictable from the context, speakers are inclined to reduce them, but if linguistic elements are not (or not so easily) predictable from the context, speakers may resist the tendency that is inherent in automatization to produce linguistic expressions with less articulatory effort in order to avoid misunderstandings.

For instance, although basic numerals such as *one, two* and *three* are very frequent, they are unpredictable in many contexts (e.g., exchange of money) and therefore unlikely to be reduced, as evidenced by the fact that numerals are fairly stable in language change (Pagel and Meade 2018). As can be seen in Table 5.2, the English numerals *one, two* and *three* are phonetically similar to

Table 5.2 *Number words in old and modern Indo-European languages*

English	Latin	Sanskrit	Gothic	Welsh	Spanish	Russian
one	ūnus	ekam	ains	un	uno	a'deen
two	duo	dve	twai	dau	dos	dva
three	trēs	treeni	þrija	tri	tres	tri

the corresponding numerals in other Indo-European languages (including old IE languages such as Latin and Sanskrit), suggesting that these items have changed very little over centuries, whereas other linguistic expressions are readily reduced if speakers have reason to assume that listeners are able to predict their occurrence from the context. Most function words, for instance, are easily predictable from the linguistic context and therefore frequently reduced, whereas the basic numerals exhibit slow rates of reduction and lexical change.

5.3.3   Bound Morphemes

Linguistic expressions that are frequently reduced and attached to a host can develop into bound morphemes. The development is driven by automatization and predictability but is also influenced by semantic factors. Clitics that are attached to semantically related hosts are prone to undergo affixation, whereas clitics that are attached to semantically unrelated hosts are unlikely to develop into affixes. Auxiliary clitics, for instance, often develop into verbal affixes (indicating tense, aspect and mood) if they are attached to a verb (Bybee et al. 1994), but they tend to remain clitics (that is, grammatically independent words) if they are attached to (pro)nouns (see English *I've, John's*).[3]

Two basic types of affixes are commonly distinguished: (i) derivational affixes, which serve to form complex nouns, verbs and adjectives (e.g., *govern-ment, fals(e)-ify, hand-ful*), and (ii) inflectional affixes, which provide information that typically concerns the syntactic or semantic organization of a clause or phrase (e.g., *animal-s, want-s*). Both types of affixes are derived from free items that have fused with co-occurring content words, but the source constructions of inflectional and derivational affixes are different.

Derivational affixes are commonly derived from content words that are routinely combined with other content words in lexical compounds or phrases. The derivational suffix *-ly*, for instance, evolved from the noun *lice* meaning

---

[3] Note, however, that there are languages in which pronouns appear with verbal affixes that seem to have developed from auxiliary clitics (e.g., in Quileute; see Andrade 1933).

'body', which was originally combined with a preceding noun or adjective where the meaning of *lice* 'body' had changed to mean 'like', as in *man-lic* 'manlike' (= manly) and *cwicu-lice* 'quicklike' (= quickly). Parallel examples from Romance and German are given in (5) and (6).

(5)   *-ment* as in Fr. *gouverne-ment* > from Latin *mente*, ablative SG of *mēns* 'mind'

(6)   *-sam* as in Germ. *streb-sam* 'ambitious' > from *samo* 'of the same kind'

Like derivational affixes, inflectional affixes are commonly derived from free items, but in this case, the source of the affix is usually a grammatical function word – that is, a pronoun, auxiliary or adposition – rather than a content word. The English past tense suffix *-ed*, for instance, seems to have evolved from the dummy auxiliary *do* (Hill 2010).

The development of inflectional morphemes from grammatical function words has been a central theme of research on grammaticalization. There is a very rich literature on this topic that cannot be reviewed in this chapter (e.g., Heine et al. 1991; Bybee et al. 1994; Lehmann [1995] 2015; Hopper and Traugott 2003), but here are some well-known examples. Person-number affixes of verbs are commonly derived from personal pronouns as illustrated by the following examples from Basque (adopted from Trask 1996: 117):

(7)   *n-oa*   'I am going'   *ni*   'I'
         h-oa   'you are going'   *hi*   'you'
         d-oa   's/he is going'   ∅   's/he'
         g-oaz   'we are going'   *gu*   'we'
         z-oaz   'you are going'   *zu*   'you'
         d-oaz   'they are going'   ∅   'they'

As can be seen, the verb *joan* 'to go' occurs with person-number prefixes that are phonetically similar to the corresponding pronouns. In particular, the verb forms of first and second person (both singular and plural) include the same initial consonants as the pronouns *ni* 'I', *hi* 'you', *gu* 'we' and *zu* 'you.PL', which, according to Trask (1996: 117), reflects the fact that the verbal prefixes are derived from subject pronouns that fused with the verb stem.

Parallel developments of verbal person-number affixes have been found in many other languages including languages from Proto-Indo-European, Bantu, Pama-Nyungan and Iroquoian (see Van Gelderen 2011 for a survey). If verbal person-number affixes are accompanied by co-referring nouns in the same clause, they are commonly described as agreement markers. Consider, for instance, the use of French *il* 'he' in example (8).

(8)   Jean,   il=parle.
         John   he=speak.
         'John speaks/is speaking.'

Traditionally, *il* is considered a subject pronoun that may be reduced to a clitic in preverbal position. A number of recent studies have argued, however, that French is currently in the process of acquiring a new agreement system. If the subject is expressed by a noun in colloquial French, as in (8), it is commonly resumed by a bound form that one could analyze as an emergent agreement affix of the verb (see Culbertson 2010 for empirical evidence and further references).

Other diachronic paths that are cross-linguistically very frequent (and well known from the grammaticalization literature) include the development of oblique case affixes from adpositions and serial verbs (Heine 2008), the development of tense, aspect and mood affixes from free auxiliaries (Bybee et al. 1994), and the development of definiteness markers and noun class markers from demonstratives (Greenberg 1978).

Considering the data presented in this section, we must rethink the status of words and morphemes in linguistic theory. Although words and morphemes are commonly treated as primitive categories in the linguistic literature, they are undoubtedly the (diachronic) products of domain-general processes. Like all other aspects of linguistic structure, words and morphemes are fluid categories derived from language use.

5.4   Morphological Gradience

In accordance with the emergentist view of words and morphemes, a number of recent studies have argued that morphological decomposition is a matter of degree (Hay 2001; Bybee 2010). Traditionally, complex words are formed from morphemes that are combined by concatenating rules, but in the usage-based approach, complex words are analyzed as holistic processing units that can be more or less cohesive.

5.4.1   Morphological Networks

Consider, for instance, the English verb *walked*. In the traditional approach, *walked* is analyzed as a composite structure formed from two separate morphemes, that is, *walk* and *-ed*; but in the network approach, *walked* is a lexical unit, a prefabricated chunk, in which *walk* and *-ed* are sequentially related. The diachronic origin of the English past tense suffix is unclear, but one common view is that the sequential link between verb and *-ed* evolved from the frequent co-occurrence (and fusion) of lexical verbs and the auxiliary *do* (Hill 2010). However, whatever the diachronic origin of V-*ed* may be, synchronically, sequential relations are determined by a language user's experience with particular linguistic strings; that is, synchronically *walk* and *-ed* are sequentially related because language users have encountered the string *walked* so frequently that it is stored and processed as an automated unit (for experimental evidence supporting this view, see Sereno and Jongman 1999; Alegre and Gordon 1999).

Since sequential links are crucially influenced by automatization, frequent complex words constitute stronger lexical units than infrequent ones. This is reflected in the structure and meaning of complex words and the way they are processed (in psycholinguistic experiments). Other things being equal, frequent complex words tend to be structurally and semantically less transparent than infrequent ones (Bybee 1985; Hay 2001) and they are accessed faster in lexical decision tasks (Sereno and Jongman 1999; Alegre and Gordon 1999). Considering the effect of frequency on morphological transparency and lexical access, some researchers have argued that there are two different routes of lexical access: while infrequent complex words are accessed via their morphological parts, frequent complex words are accessed directly as one chunk (Frauenfelder and Schreuder 1992; Hay 2003).

The "dual-route model" of lexical access is useful to explain the effect of frequency on the storage and processing of complex words, but since automatization and predictability have a continuous effect on unit formation or chunking, there is no sharp division between the two routes of lexical access. Both routes can be processed in parallel to access a complex word (Hay 2003: 95), but depending on a language user's experience with particular expressions, the two routes can have different activation values, or different "weights."

In the current approach, language users' experience with complex words is modeled by two different types of links. On the one hand, a word such as *walked* involves a sequential link between verb and affix that is shaped by automatization and predictability, and on the other hand, it involves lexical links to other items in the system that are established by categorization. As Bybee (2007: 207–209) explains, the internal structure of complex words is determined by their connections to other items with the same or similar parts in the network. *Walked*, for instance, is lexically related to other inflected verb forms and the simple form *walk* (Figure 5.3). On this account, the internal structure of complex words is determined by categorization rather than by concatenating rules.

Morphological network models of this type were pioneered by Bybee (1985, 1988, 1995, 2001) and are now widely used in usage-based morphology (e.g., Hay 2001; Hay and Baayen 2005). In this approach, every expression has a unique representation in the network that is determined by the interaction between sequential and lexical relations. The interaction reflects a language user's experience with particular words and morphemes. Sequential links are determined by automatization and the predictability of upcoming elements, and lexical links are created by categorization and analogy. Since categorization and analogy are based on similarity (§3.5), lexical links are gradient, just like

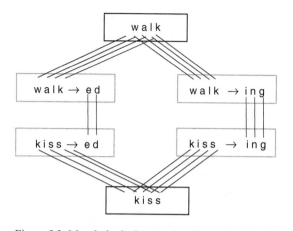

Figure 5.3 Morphological network with sequential and lexical associations

sequential links (§3.7), but for a different reason. As a consequence, morphological structure is inherently graded and compositionality is a matter of degree.

5.4.2   Empirical Evidence for Morphological Gradience

Building on this view, Hay (2001) showed that people's perception of morphological structure is crucially influenced by the relative frequencies of complex words and their lexical bases (Hay 2003). Consider, for instance, the words *refurbish* and *rekindle*. Both words consist of a verbal base and the prefix *re-*, but the composite form *refurbish* is much more frequent than the base *furbish*, whereas *rekindle* is less frequent than the base *kindle* (Table 5.3).

Earlier studies had shown that the total frequency of complex words strengthens their status as lexical units (Bybee 1985), but Hay argued that the representation and processing of lexical units is not only influenced by the overall frequency of a particular item, but also by the "relative frequency" of a complex word and its base. Specifically, she hypothesized that complex words that are more frequent than their base (such as *refurbish*) are not so easily decomposable as complex words that are less frequent than their base (such as *rekindle*). In order to test this hypothesis, Hay conducted two clever experiments.

In the first experiment, she prepared two separate lists of word pairs consisting of a complex word and a base. The word pairs on the first list (List A) included items such as *refurbish* and *furbish*, where the complex form is more frequent than the base, and the word pairs on the second list (List B) included items such as *rekindle* and *kindle*, where the base is more frequent than the complex form. Table 5.4 shows some of Hay's stimuli from both lists.

Table 5.3 *Token frequencies of* refurbish/furbish *and* rekindle/kindle

	Frequency of complex form	Frequency of base
refurbish–furbish	33	1
rekindle–kindle	22	41

Source: Hay (2001: 1047)

Table 5.4 *Frequency of complex forms and base forms*

List A	Complex freq.	Base freq.	List B	Complex freq.	Base freq.
Prefixed words			**Prefixed words**		
re-furbish	**33**	1	*re-kindle*	22	**41**
in-animate	**34**	4	*in-accurate*	53	**377**
un-canny	**89**	20	*un-common*	114	**3376**
...	...	...	...	...	...
Suffixed words			**Suffixed words**		
slim-y	**61**	35	*cream-y*	74	**540**
hap-less	**22**	13	*top-less*	27	**3089**
respir-ation	**39**	4	*ador-ation*	49	**218**
...	...	...	...	...	...

Source: Hay (2001: 1047–1048)

For each pair of words, participants were asked to indicate which member of the pair they consider more "complex" (in the sense that it includes more morphemes). As predicted, complex words that were more frequent than their bases (List A) were rated less complex than complex words that were less frequent than their bases (List B). Since the effect was independent of the overall frequency of a complex word form, it seems reasonable to assume that morphological decomposition is crucially influenced by the relative frequencies of the lexical base and the complex form. As Hay (2001: 1049–1050) explained: "When the base is more frequent than the whole [List B], the word is easily and readily decomposed. However, when the derived form is more frequent than the base it contains [List A], it is more difficult to decompose and appears to be less complex." This holds for both prefixed and suffixed forms and is not contingent on the absolute frequency of a complex word form (which may affect morphological decomposition as an additional factor; see Bybee 2010: 46–48 for discussion).

In the context of the current study, we may say that there is a negative correlation between the strength of sequential links and the strength of lexical

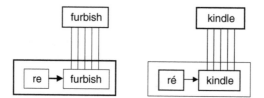

Figure 5.4 Lexical and sequential links of morphologically complex words

associations. Words such as *refurbish* include a strong sequential link between base and affix and weak lexical connections to other items in the network, whereas words such as *rekindle* exhibit a strong lexical link to the base *kindle* and a relatively weak sequential link between base and affix (Figure 5.4). The analysis is supported by the occurrence of pitch accent. As Hay (2003: 88–95) showed, words such as *rekindle* are more likely to carry pitch accent on the prefix than words such as *refurbish* indicating that in the former case the prefix *ré-* is perceived more strongly as an independent semantic component.

Elaborating on this analysis, Hay hypothesized that the relative frequency of complex words and their lexical bases has an effect on semantic transparency. Specifically, she proposed that morphologically complex words of the A List (i.e., complex words that are more frequent than their bases) are semantically less transparent than complex forms of the B List (i.e., complex words that are less frequent than their bases). In order to test this hypothesis, she examined the definitions of complex word forms in dictionary entries. If the definition of the complex word includes the base (as in "Dishorn: to deprive of horns"), this was taken as a sign of semantic transparency, but if the definition of the complex word did not mention the base, this was interpreted as a sign of semantic opaqueness. While this approach can only provide a rough estimate of semantic transparency, the data overwhelmingly confirmed Hay's hypothesis: "Words for which the derived form is more frequent than the base are significantly less likely to mention their base in their definition than words for which the derived form is less frequent than the base" (Hay 2001: 1057).

Taken together, Hay's research provides strong evidence for the hypothesis that morphological structure is gradient and shaped by language use. Specifically, we may say that morphological gradience results from the interaction between two different types of links: sequential links, which are strengthened by automatization and predictability, and lexical links, which are determined by categorization and analogy (i.e., the recognition of similarity). As automatization and predictability reinforce the association between base and affix, complex words become increasingly "autonomous" (Bybee 2010: 44–45).

5.4.3   Lexical Autonomy

Lexical autonomy is a key concept of Bybee's network model of morphology (e.g., Bybee 1995; 2001: 125–126). The basic idea is that while morphologically complex words are connected to other items in the system (as shown in Figure 5.4), these connections can vanish. Consider, for instance, the word *breakfast*. Historically, *breakfast* consists of two lexemes, the verb *break* and the noun *fast* (meaning: to end the nightly fast), but although these elements are still recognized in the written form of *breakfast*, the spoken form ['brekfəst] has lost its connections to *break* [breɪk] and *fast* [faːst], that is, *breakfast* has become autonomous in the sense that its parts are no longer associated with (diachronically) related items in the network (Figure 5.5). Needless to say that this does not only concern the form of *breakfast* but also its meaning.

The same process can be observed in many instances of grammaticalization. The phrase *(be) going to*, for instance, has evolved into a future tense auxiliary that is about to lose its lexical connections to *go, -ing* and *to*. As noted in Chapter 4, *(be) going to* is often phonetically reduced to *(be) gonna* if it is used with a subsequent infinitive to indicate future tense. While speakers of English are still aware of the fact that *gonna* is related to the progressive form of the motion verb *go, gonna* is on its way to becoming a fully autonomous item as evidenced by the fact that the main verb *(be) going to* cannot be reduced to *gonna* (9–10) (Lorenz 2013).

(9)   Peter's going to leave.   →   Peter's gonna leave.

(10)   Peter's going to school.   →   *Peter's gonna school.

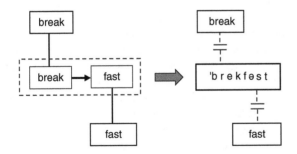

Figure 5.5 Lexical autonomy: the development of sequential and lexical relations (as a result of fusion)

Autonomy, also known as "emancipation" (Haiman 1994), is an important aspect of grammatical change that finds a natural explanation in the network model of morphology. As we have seen, when a morphologically complex word becomes autonomous, it loses its internal sequential links and its connections to other items in the system.

5.5   The Suffixing Preference

Having considered the cognitive processes behind fusion and morphological decomposition, the current section will take a closer look at a phenomenon to which typologists refer as the "suffixing preference" (Croft 2003: 67–69). Since grammatical affixes are commonly derived from independent function words, they typically appear in the same position relative to the associated content word as their diachronic sources. In other words, grammatical function words (short GRAMS) that precede their lexical hosts usually develop into prefixes, whereas grammatical function words that follow their hosts usually develop into suffixes (Givón 1971; Bybee et al. 1990) (11a–b).

(11)   a.

b.

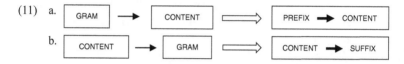

Interestingly, if we look at the positions of bound morphemes from a cross-linguistic perspective, we find that suffixes are much more frequent than prefixes. According to the World Atlas of Language Structures, 63.9 percent of the world's languages make more frequent use of suffixes than of prefixes, but only 18.4 percent have more prefixes than suffixes (in the remaining 17.8 percent, suffixes and prefixes are about equally frequent; see Dryer 2005). The suffixing preference varies with the function of the grammatical marker. Case markers, for instance, are predominantly suffixing, whereas agreement markers are also often expressed by prefixes (Siewierska and Bakker 1996). Notwithstanding these differences, there is a general suffixing preference for all types of grammatical affixes (Himmelmann 2014).

Why are inflectional suffixes so much more frequent than inflectional prefixes? One possibility is that the suffixing preference reflects a general tendency to postpose function words. There is, indeed, some evidence that grammatical function words are overall more frequent after than before their hosts (Bybee et al. 1990: 6), but in addition, postposed grammatical function words are more likely to undergo affixation than preposed grammatical function words. Consider Figure 5.6, which is based on data published in Bybee et al. (1990), who compiled a large cross-linguistic database on free and bound grammatical

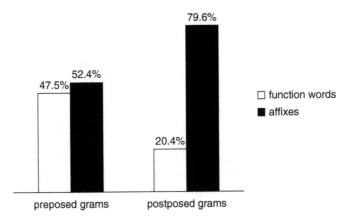

Figure 5.6 Frequency of (free) verbal grams and (bound) verbal affixes in pre- and postverbal position in a controlled sample of 50 languages (based on data from Bybee et al. 1990: 5)

markers of verbs, collectively referred to as "verbal grams," indicating tense, aspect, mood, person and valency.

As can be seen, the vast majority of verbal grams that follow their hosts are affixes: only 20.4 percent of all postposed grams are free function words in Bybee's data. In contrast, preposed verbal grams are only marginally more often expressed by affixes than by free function words. Assuming that verbal affixes are commonly derived from free function words in parallel positions (Bybee et al. 1990), the data in Figure 5.6 suggest that free postposed verbal grams are more likely to develop into affixes than free preposed verbal grams (Bybee et al. 1990; see also Himmelmann 2014).

There are various proposals in the literature to explain the suffixing preference of inflectional affixes (see Song 2012: 55–66 for a review). Some scholars have argued that languages tend to avoid prefixation because words are difficult to access if a bound morpheme precedes the stem (Hawkins and Cutler 1988: 305), but there is an alternative explanation that stresses the importance of sequential processing for the development of inflectional affixes.

As pointed out above, sequential processing has an inherent forward orientation. Both speakers and listeners are usually ahead of the speech stream and anticipate the occurrence of upcoming elements in an unfolding sentence (§5.6). Building on this observation, we may hypothesize that the asymmetry between pre- and postposed grams reflects the availability or predictability of an item in a particular context.

Grammatical function words constitute small classes of high-frequency expressions, whereas content words comprise large numbers of less frequent items. It is thus much more difficult to predict the occurrence of a particular content word from a given function word than to predict the occurrence of a particular function word from a given content word. For instance, disregarding semantic and contextual factors, a preposed article such as English *the* can be followed by the whole class of common nouns. As a consequence, speakers have the choice between a very large number of items that can go into the noun slot after the determiner. Yet, if the article follows the noun, as for instance in Lakhota (cf. *mathó ki* 'bear the'), there are only few items that can go into the determiner slot after the noun (as the class of determiners is fairly limited in Lakhota and other languages). In other words, given that there are many more nouns than determiners, it is much easier to access (and to predict) a determiner after a given noun than to access (and to predict) a noun after a given determiner (Figure 5.7).

Both type and token frequency affect the accessibility (and predictability) of a word given a previous word. Type frequency is important because it determines the number of lexical alternatives between which speakers can choose in order to fill a particular structural position (as illustrated in Figure 5.7), and token frequency is important because lexical decisions are crucially influenced by a language user's experience with particular word sequences. Consider for instance the effect of token frequency on the (forward) predictability of English nouns in definite NPs.

The definite article *the* occurs more than 3 million times in the British National Corpus. It is followed by a wide range of noun types that occur with

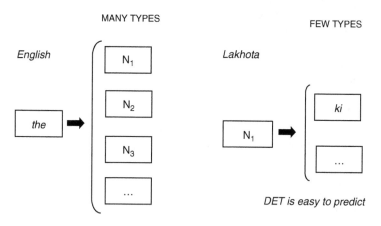

Figure 5.7 Sequential relations of NPs with pre- and postposed determiners

different frequencies. The noun *boy*, for instance, appears 5162 times after *the*, but it also appears in other contexts. Overall, *boy* has a token frequency of 19,915 in the BNC. In order to estimate the strength of the sequential link between *the* and *boy*, we can use "conditional probability" as a statistical measure.

Conditional probability, also known as transitional probability, is often used by corpus linguists to determine the likelihood that a word w_y will occur given a previous word w_x (Jurafsky et al. 2001). It is calculated by dividing the frequency with which the two words, w_x and w_y, occur together (in the same order) in a particular corpus by the total frequency with which the first word occurs in the same corpus. As can be seen in (12), the transitional probability that the article *the* is followed by *boy* is extremely low.

(12) $$P = \frac{\text{the boy}}{\text{the}} = \frac{5162}{3,004,338} = 0.0017$$

Now image a language in which *the, boy* and *the boy* occur with the same frequencies as in English, but in which *the* and *boy* are arranged in reverse order, that is, in the order *boy the* (as in Lakhota). As can be seen in (13), in this case the transitional probability of *boy* being followed by *the* is much higher than in a language like English, in which articles precede nouns, indicating that the occurrence of articles after nouns is predictable with a much higher degree of certainty than the occurrence of nouns after a previous article.

(13) $$P = \frac{\text{boy the}}{\text{boy}} = \frac{5162}{19,915} = 0.25709$$

If sequential processing involves an anticipatory component, as many psycholinguists have claimed, it seems reasonable to assume that the sequential associations between content words and postposed function words are significantly stronger than the sequential associations between preposed function words and their ensuing hosts (14).

(14)

In accordance with this analysis, Himmelmann (2014) observed that postposed function words are prosodically more tightly bound to their lexical hosts than preposed function words. Analyzing transcripts of spoken discourse from a number of unrelated languages, he showed that there are often disfluencies between free preposed grams and semantically related content words, whereas postposed function words typically follow their lexical hosts without any interruption. In English, for instance, it is not unusual that determiners, auxiliaries and prepositions are separated from the following content word by a pause or hesitation signal (e.g., *the ... ah ... argument*), whereas in languages like Japanese postposed function words are only rarely separated from their hosts (Himmelmann 2014: 935–945).

Especially interesting are languages in which the same types of function words occur in both positions (that is, before and after the associated content word). In German, for instance, auxiliaries can precede or follow the verb, but although both orders are frequent, Himmelmann found a striking asymmetry between them: while preposed auxiliaries are often separated from their ensuing hosts by a pause (15a), there were no disfluencies between the main verb and the auxiliary when the latter was postposed (15b) in Himmelmann's data.

(15)   a.   [das] wird . . . gezeigt
        b.   [das] gezeigt wird

Prosodic integration is one aspect that reflects the strength of the associative connections between words in sequential processing. A second aspect, which is closely related to prosodic integration, is fusion. Since postposed function words are easily predictable from previous content words, they are bound by intonation and prone to undergo affixation, whereas preposed function words are (quite) often separated from their hosts by pauses and disfluencies and therefore less likely to develop into bound morphemes. To put it another way, since the sequential links between content words and postposed function words are stronger than the sequential links between preposed function words and ensuing content words, postposed function words are more likely to fuse with their hosts than preposed function words, and as a consequence of this, inflectional suffixes are cross-linguistically more frequent than inflectional prefixes (see Himmelmann 2014 for a related explanation).

5.6   Syntactic Predictions

Like all other aspects of linguistic structure, sequential links are shaped by a language user's experience with (phonetically concrete) lexical items, but sequential relations do not only concern lexical prefabs and morphologically complex words, they also concern constructional schemas. Like words and lexical prefabs, constructional schemas are automated processing units that involve sequential associations.

One piece of evidence supporting this hypothesis comes from psycholinguistic research on syntactic predictions. Above, we have seen that words and affixes are often easily predictable from previous words, but predictions also occur at the level of schematic processing units, that is, the level of (abstract) syntax. In fact, recent research on sentence comprehension has argued that syntactic processing involves an anticipatory component as listeners anticipate or predict the structure of an unfolding sentence (e.g., Elman 1990; Altman and

Kamide 1999; Konieczny 2000; Hale 2001; Kamide et al. 2003; Levy 2008; Fine et al. 2013; Kuperberg and Jaeger 2016).

For instance, Altmann and Kamide (1999) showed that verbs generate particular expectations as to how a sentence will continue. Using the "visual world paradigm" (Tanenhaus et al. 1995), these researchers examined listeners' eye movements while they were exposed to different stimuli. In one of their experiments, participants looked at a scene containing a boy, a cake, a ball and a toy car while listening to sentences including the verbs *eat* and *move* (16–17).

(16)   The boy will eat the cake.

(17)   The boy will move the cake.

As expected, there was a highly significant difference in participants' eye movements when they were listening to these stimuli. Specifically, Altmann and Kamide observed that listeners were much more likely to look at the cake upon hearing the verb *eat* than upon hearing the verb *move*, indicating that they anticipated the occurrence of different types of nominal referents after the two verbs. Since verbs select particular semantic participants (Chapter 6), it does not come as a surprise that they generate specific expectations as to how a sentence will continue. However, interestingly, Kamide et al. (2003) showed that listeners' expectations are also influenced by their experience with structural aspects of constructions.

Of particular importance is a study they conducted with speakers of Japanese. Since Japanese is a head-final language in which arguments precede the verb, the argument frame of the verb does not immediately affect listeners' linguistic expectations, but like speakers of English, speakers of Japanese are often ahead of the speech stream and anticipate the occurrence of upcoming elements in an unfolding sentence (see also Konieczny 2000 for evidence from German). Using the same experimental paradigm as Altmann and Kamide (1999), Kamide et al. (2003) examined the "anticipatory looks" of Japanese speakers who looked at a restaurant scene including a waitress, a customer, a hamburger and some nonedible objects, while listening to transitive and ditransitive sentences. While the order of arguments is nonrigid in Japanese, there is a strong tendency to place the subject at the beginning of a sentence and to place the dative NP before the accusative NP in ditransitive sentences (as in 18).

(18)   weitoresu-ga   kyaku-ni   tanosigeni   hanbaagaa-o   ha-kobu
         waitress-NOM   customer-DAT   merrily   hamburger-ACC bring
         'The waitress will merrily bring the hamburger to the customer.'
         (Kamide et al. 2003: 147)

What Kamide and colleagues wanted to find out is if listeners anticipate the occurrence of the third argument of a ditransitive sentence after they had heard the two initial NPs. To this end, they exposed their participants to two different stimuli: (i) sentences beginning with a nominative NP followed by a dative object, and (ii) sentences beginning with a nominative NP followed by an accusative object (19).

(19)   Condition 1: NP_{NOM} NP_{DAT} $\cdots$
         Condition 2: NP_{NOM} NP_{ACC} $\cdots$

Both stimuli can be continued in more than one way (in Japanese), but there are statistical biases. Sentences beginning with a subject and a dative NP (condition 1) are almost always expanded to ditransitive sentences. A few transitive verbs occur with dative NPs in Japanese, but usually sentences including a dative object are ditransitive. In contrast, sentences including an accusative NP after the subject (condition 2) are usually transitive, so that in this case, the sentence is unlikely to include a third NP. Yet, while accusative NPs are usually followed by a transitive verb in Japanese, they may also be followed by a dative NP, though dative NPs typically precede accusative NPs in ditransitive sentences.

Given these tendencies, Kamide et al. (2003) hypothesized that the two strings in (19) would cause different responses. In accordance with their hypothesis, they found that listeners looked significantly more often to the hamburger as the potential theme of the transfer scene when the sentence included a dative object after the subject (condition 1) than when the subject was followed by an accusative NP (condition 2), indicating that the relative frequencies of the strings $[NP_{NOM}$ NP_{DAT} $\ldots]$ and $[NP_{NOM}$ NP_{ACC} $\ldots]$ in transitive and ditransitive constructions create different expectations as to how these sentences will evolve.

Taken together with similar results from parallel studies (see Altmann and Mirković 2009 for a review), this research provides strong evidence that constructional schemas include sequential associations. While listeners' predictions are influenced by general world knowledge, they are also influenced by linguistic knowledge from two sources: (i) the meaning of relational expressions, notably the meaning of verbs, and (ii) language users' experience with particular structural patterns or constructions. Specifically, the study by Kamide et al. (2003) showed that the string $[NP_{NOM}$ NP_{DAT} $\ldots]$ creates a strong sequential link to a third NP due to the frequency with which Japanese speakers experience an accusative object after a dative NP. Note that since the clause-final verb of a ditransitive sentence evokes an event frame with three participants (Chapter 6), we may hypothesize that the occurrence of a particular theme object after the dative NP is not only predictable from the two initial case roles, but also from the clause-final verb once the listener has reason to expect the occurrence of a particular ditransitive verb (Figure 5.8).

Interestingly, while automatization creates sequential links with an inherent forward orientation, relational expressions at the end of a phrase create

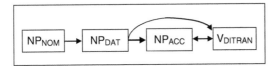

Figure 5.8 Sequential links of the (default) ditransitive construction in Japanese

(semantically motivated) sequential links with an inherent backward orientation. This constitutes a crucial difference between head-initial languages like English, in which relational expressions tend to occur at the beginning of a phrase, and head-final languages like Japanese, in which relational expressions typically occur at the end of a phrase or sentence (§9.5).

5.7   Syntactic Constituents

Sequential links between syntactic categories are of central significance to constituent structure, also known as phrase structure. Functional and cognitive linguists have often argued that syntactic constituents are semantically motivated (e.g., Langacker 1997), but in addition to the semantic factors that underlie syntactic constituency, phrase structure is crucially influenced by automatization and predictability. We will consider the semantic foundations of syntactic constituency in Chapter 9. Here we concentrate on some general sequential aspects of phrases (which will also be discussed in more detail in Chapter 9).

According to Bybee (2010: 136–164), chunking, or automatization, plays an important role in the shaping of syntactic structure (Bybee 2002; Bybee and Scheibman 1999). Since automatization is a continuous process, there are many "degrees of constituency" (Bybee and Scheibman 1999). Above, we have seen that the strength of sequential links between lexical items is contingent on frequency. Other things being equal, the more often a particular word is followed by another word, the tighter the sequential association between them. The same mechanism affects the sequential organization of constructional schemas. Consider, for instance, the structure of the English noun phrase.

Nouns are preceded by determiners and adjectives in English and followed by prepositional attributes and relative clauses (e.g., *an old friend of mine who moved to Berlin*). There is good evidence that the syntactic categories preceding nouns are more tightly connected to the nominal head than the syntactic categories that follow it. As Bybee (2002) demonstrated (based on data from the Switchboard corpus), there are many more pauses and disfluencies between nouns and postposed attributes (i.e., prepositional phrases and relative clauses) than between nouns and preposed determiners and adjectives. While this may

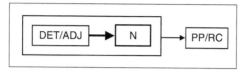

Figure 5.9 Sequential structure of the English noun phrase

reflect, at least in part, the strengths of conceptual associations between nouns and other categories, it also correlates with frequency. As Bybee showed, nouns are much more frequently accompanied by preceding determiners and adjectives than by postposed prepositional phrases and relative clauses.

In §5.6, we have seen that the probability of the definite article *the* to be followed by a particular noun is low, but note that the probability of the category DET to be followed by the category N is extremely high, almost absolute, as determiners are generally succeeded by nouns in English. Compared to the probability that a determiner is followed by a noun, the probability of a noun to be followed by a prepositional attribute or relative clause is low, suggesting that the associative connections between nouns and postposed noun modifiers are much weaker than the associative connections between nouns and (preceding) determiners and adjectives, irrespective of any conceptual differences that may distinguish pre- and postposed noun modifiers in English (Bybee 2002) (Figure 5.9).

Moreover, Bybee (2002, 2010) argues that the tightness of constituency varies with the size of syntactic units. Since smaller units are usually more frequent than larger ones, they tend to be more cohesive, as evidenced by the occurrence of more pauses and disfluencies in complex NPs than in simple ones. As a consequence of this, smaller and more tightly organized units appear to be embedded in larger and less automated units, creating a hierarchical organization of linguistic structure that is traditionally represented in phrase structure trees. Note, however, that traditional phrase structure representations of syntactic structure do not capture the gradience of constituency. On the contrary, in formal syntax, phrase structure is analyzed by a predefined set of discrete categories, which is not appropriate in accounting for syntactic constituency if we assume that phrase structure is gradient (Chapter 9).

What is more, while constituency is commonly defined in terms of general syntactic categories (e.g., N, PP, S), it must be emphasized that the high-level generalizations described by syntactic constituents constitute only one aspect of speakers' phrase structure knowledge. Traditionally, syntactic analysis abstracts away from individual lexical items, but in the usage-based approach, syntactic structure is derived from strings of concrete lexical expressions and therefore never fully independent of particular lexical items (Chapter 4). In accordance with this view, Bybee (2010: 136–150) argues that syntactic constituency involves a large amount of lexical-specific information that must not be ignored in the analysis of syntactic phrases (see also Bybee and Scheibman 1999; Bybee 2002; Christiansen and MacDonald 2009; Christiansen and Chater 2016; Diessel 2017; Jach 2018). Consider, for instance, the structure of an English verb phrase consisting of a verb and a prepositional phrase, as in the following examples (20–22).

(20)   They swam in the lake.

(21)   They waited for John.

(22)   They belong to me.

At one level of analysis, we may say that all of these sentences include a verb phrase with two immediate constituents, namely, V and PP, but note that in some of these examples the preposition is more strongly associated with the preceding verb than with the following noun. *Belong to*, for instance, is a lexical chunk that takes the following noun as complement, whereas *swim* is followed by a prepositional adjunct. Many linguists distinguish between phrasal verbs such as *belong to* and free combinations of verb and preposition such as *swim in*, but note that the sequential relations between verbs, prepositions and nouns vary on a continuum that is crucially influenced by a language user's experience with particular V-P-NP sequences and that cannot be neatly divided into phrasal verbs and free combinations of verb plus prepositional phrase (Figure 5.10).

Considering this variation, it is not immediately obvious how one should analyze the sequential associations between V, P and N(P) at the level of syntactic schemas. Given that the occurrence of prepositional phrases is not restricted to the position after verbs and that verbs are not generally followed by a PP, we may assume (in accordance with the traditional phrase structure analysis) that the sequential link between P and N(P) is stronger than that between V and P (Figure 5.11), but that does not mean that all linguistic

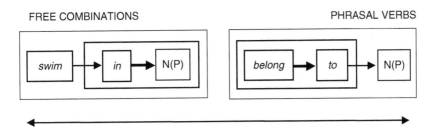

Figure 5.10 Continuum of V-P-N(P) sequences (in English)

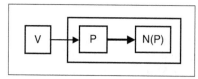

Figure 5.11 Sequential links of English V-PP construction

sequences of V-P-N(P) have the same structure. Phrasal verbs such as *belong to* deviate from the canonical pattern in Figure 5.11.

In general, the traditional phrase structure categories do not always match the structure of lexical units. Although prepositions are commonly grouped together with nouns in syntactic phrase structure trees, they are often more strongly associated with verbs than with nouns. Similar "violations" of syntactic constituency occur with other grammatical phrases (see §9.6 for additional examples). Since the canonical constituents of syntactic structure are derived from many lexical sequences with similar properties, they usually match the groupings of lexical expressions, but there are some well-known discrepancies between lexical and syntactic units that can be explained by competing motivations. As we will see in Chapter 9, syntactic phrase structure is semantically motivated by general principles of conceptualization. These principles underlie the canonical constituents of syntactic phrase structure (e.g., NP, VP, PP), but constituent structure is not only motivated by conceptual factors, it is also influenced by automatization (and predictability). Usually, automatization reinforces the sequential associations that are created by conceptualization, but, as we have seen, if the two forces pull in opposite directions, they create structures in which the lexical and syntactic units of a sentence (or phrase) do not match each other, as in the case of (English) phrasal verbs.

5.8   Conclusion

To summarize, this chapter has argued that linguistic knowledge includes a vast array of prefabricated processing units of different length and different strength at different levels of abstraction. Since these units are activated by single choices, they facilitate utterance planning and sequential processing. Once a unit (or chunk) has been selected, a language user can execute the unfolding sequence with little attention and control, which then often leads to phonetic reduction and fusion. Chunking increases the amount of linguistic information that can be held in working memory and is of central significance to the analysis of linguistic structure.

Traditionally, the units of speech are seen as primitive concepts, or building blocks, of grammatical structure, but the current chapter has argued that even the most basic units, that is, the units of word, morpheme and phrase, emerge from domain-general processes. The rise of these units is motivated by general principles of conceptualization, but is also influenced by automatization and predictability. One can think of automatization and predictability as general processing mechanisms of online language use, but these mechanisms have long-term effects on the development of linguistic structure. If the same string of linguistic elements is repeatedly processed, automatization and predictability create sequential links between them and the whole string evolves into a single unit.

Since the units of speech are shaped by automatization and predictability (in conjunction with several other factors; see Chapter 9), they can be more or less cohesive. The most cohesive meaningful unit is the morpheme, which usually does not allow for any variation. Larger units, such as complex words and phrases, are more variable and therefore less cohesive, but there is a great deal of cross-linguistic variation.

Since the various units of speech are diachronically related, there are no clear-cut boundaries between them. As we have seen, phrases, words and affixes constitute a continuum of fluid processing units leading from multiword sequences to simple morphemes.

6   Symbolic Relations

6.1   Introduction

Linguistic communication is symbolic in nature. Symbols combine a particular form – a sound pattern or grammatical structure – with a particular meaning or function. The ability to communicate with symbols is a uniquely human capacity and a design feature of (human) language (Tomasello 1999). Symbols enable speakers to talk about objects and events that are not present in the speech situation and provide a particular format for the representation and processing of knowledge (Deacon 1997). But what exactly are the cognitive processes that underlie the use of linguistic symbols? And where do symbols come from? How do they emerge in L1 acquisition and language change?

In the current framework, symbols are defined by particular types of associations referred to as symbolic links or relations. Symbolic links connect representations of linguistic form with conventionalized paths of semantic interpretation. Like sequential and taxonomic links, symbolic links are created by domain-general processes, notably by conceptualization and social cognition (or pragmatic inference). In addition, automatization can reinforce the strength of symbolic associations.

Cognitive linguists have analyzed the conceptual processes of symbolic communication in great detail (Langacker 1987; Lakoff 1987; Talmy 2000; Bergen 2012), but they usually look at linguistic symbols from a synchronic perspective. In the current approach, we are also interested in the development of linguistic symbols. If we look at symbols from a diachronic or ontogenetic perspective, we see that symbolic associations are emergent and gradient, just like all other associative connections of the network. It is one of the central claims of this chapter that symbolic links evolve from recurrent paths of semantic interpretation that have become automatized through repetition.

Note that symbolic links are not only a property of words but also of constructions. It is a standard assumption of the usage-based model that constructions are linguistic signs, or symbols, that combine a particular form with meaning, similar to lexemes (§1.2.3). Nevertheless, while both lexemes and constructions are commonly characterized as signs or symbols, it is important to recognize that the meanings of constructions reside in different cognitive processes than the meanings of lexemes.

Following Langacker (1987), the current chapter argues that lexemes induce listeners to derive a particular semantic interpretation from a network of encyclopedic knowledge (see also Fillmore 1985; Barsalou 1999), but constructions are different: they do not immediately evoke world knowledge, but serve to process lexical information. Specifically, the chapter argues that constructions provide processing instructions that guide listeners' semantic interpretation of lexical expressions.

6.2   The Creation of Symbolic Associations in L1 Acquisition

Let us begin with some general findings on word learning in L1 acquisition. The first linguistic signs children learn are simple words or lexemes – constructions appear only later. How do children learn that (phonetic) words express meaning? In the literature, it is commonly assumed that word learning presupposes the co-presence of a phonetic signal and a referent in a particular situation (e.g., Trueswell et al. 2013). For instance, in order to learn the meaning of the word *dog*, the child must experience the phonetic string [dɔg] while being focused on a dog in the surrounding situation. Of course, in adult language the meaning of the word *dog* is not restricted to one specific animal but applies to a whole class of animate beings; but irrespective of the fact that common nouns designate concepts or categories (rather than individual beings or entities), the co-presence of a particular phonetic form and a particular referent seems to provide a natural starting point for the acquisition of word meanings (Quine 1960).

However, as it turns out, word learning is more complex than in this scenario, which is somewhat reminiscent of the behaviorist view of association learning. What children have to learn are indeed associative links between form and meaning, but the co-presence of a phonetic string and a referent, or a whole group of similar referents, is not sufficient to explain how children acquire the meaning of new words.

Words are learned in social interactions. In order to understand that words express meaning, children must be able to understand basic concepts of communication. In particular, they must be able to recognize that other people have mental states and intentions – a capacity that develops only gradually during the first years of life (see Tomasello 2003: 43–93 for a summary).

The earliest words children produce are one-word utterances or holophrases that express the child's intention in recurrent situations involving frequent actions such as giving, showing, eating, playing or diaper changing (Tomasello 2003: 88). Food items, for instance, such as *milk, apple* or *juice* are commonly used to indicate that the child would like to obtain something to eat, and spatial particles such as *up, down* and *back* are used to instruct the adult to perform a particular action. Moreover, expressions such as *bye bye, night night* and *hi* are used with reference to daily routines in the child's life.

Building on these observations, Tomasello and colleagues conducted a series of experiments in which they examined the role of communicative intentions and social routines in word learning (see Tomasello 2003: 69–72 for a summary). For instance, in one of these experiments Akthar and Tomasello (1996) introduced two-year-old children to several new objects without giving them a name. Then these objects were hidden behind the doors of five toy barns and the experimenter said to each child "Now let's find the toma," went to the toy barns, opened the doors one after another, looked at the objects and expressed disappointment; but one of the doors could not be opened and the experimenter said: "It's locked. I can't open it." Then, he turned to the next toy barn, while the child was watching him, opened the door, looked at the object and expressed again disappointment. When all five barns had been visited, the child was shown the objects to which s/he was introduced at the beginning of the experiment and was asked to pick up the "toma." Although the word "toma" was never used with direct reference to any object, most children identified the object behind the closed door as the "toma."

Considering these results, together with parallel results from several other experiments (Tomasello 2003: 65–72), Tomasello makes two important points. First, he argues that the co-presence of a linguistic form and a referent is not sufficient to explain how children acquire the meaning of a new word. Although the novel words did not appear in the presence of any object in these experiments, children were able to link new phonetic strings to novel referents. And second, Tomasello contends that the acquisition of early words crucially relies on the ability to apprehend social interactions. If the situation is meaningful to the child, s/he is able to infer the referent of a new word from his/her emerging understanding of social interactions and world knowledge, suggesting that symbolic links are established by pragmatic inference, or as Tomasello puts it "children acquire linguistic symbols as a kind of by-product of social interactions with adults" (Tomasello 2003: 90).

A third lesson that one might draw from these experiments is that children are very quick to grasp the meaning of a new word. This has also been observed in many other studies. As Carey and Bartlett (1978) demonstrated in a classic paper, children are often able to infer the meaning of a new word from a single exposure in a particular situation – a phenomenon that has become known as "fast mapping." Fast mapping is a particular aspect of symbol learning. While association learning is usually influenced by frequency, symbolic associations can be learned very quickly, and if the new word is relevant to the learner, symbolic associations persist in memory even if they are not reinforced by repetition. Of course, like all other associative connections, symbolic associations are strengthened by frequency, but in addition to frequency (or repetition), relevance has a significant impact on the strength of symbolic associations (see Bower 2000 for some discussion).

Fast mapping has been studied intensively in child language research (see Vlach and Sandhofer 2012 for a review). Note, however, that word learning involves more than the mapping of a new phonetic form onto a particular referent. As we will see shortly, words are interpreted against the background of an entire network of related concepts that vary with the context. Learning how to use a new word in the context of such a network is a complex and long-lasting task whereby new items must be accommodated to concepts that are already in the system (Clark 2003: 131–158). The experiments Tomasello and colleagues conducted concern thus only the very beginning of word learning. In order to fully understand the nature of symbolic associations, we will now look at the way lexemes are used in adult language.

6.3   The Network Approach to Lexical Semantics

Young children infer the referent of a new lexeme from its use in a particular communicative situation. There is a very close connection between the pragmatic context and the meaning of a word in early child language, but this connection becomes more variable as children grow older. In adult language, every word is used across a wide range of contexts that reflect a language user's experience with particular items in many different situations. The totality of a person's experience with words constitutes a vast network of symbols that is ultimately grounded in a language user's experience with objects and events in the world (Langacker 1987: 154–166; see also Barsalou 1999).

Traditionally, most linguists make a sharp distinction between linguistic knowledge and world knowledge, but in cognitive semantics, word meanings are based on encyclopedic knowledge. Let us consider the meaning of the word *car* to characterize this view of semantics.

Our encyclopedic knowledge of cars is based on many experiences with cars in different situations. Some of these experiences are likely to be shared by all members of the speech community. We all know, for instance, that a car is a vehicle, that it has wheels, an engine, a gear shift and a bumper, that cars are used for transportation, that they are produced in factories and that they cause air pollution and traffic jams. In addition, a person's knowledge about cars may include particular experiences that are not shared by (all) other speakers.

Crucially, when the word *car* is used in a particular situation, speakers typically focus on certain aspects of their knowledge about cars. For instance, the sentence *The car crashed into a truck* invokes knowledge about car accidents, but is unlikely to activate knowledge about the car industry or air pollution. Since the activation of knowledge varies with the context in which a word is used, it has become a basic principle of lexical semantics to restrict the analysis of word meaning to those aspects of speakers' knowledge that do not vary with the speech situation. On this view, the interpretation of a word is generally influenced by certain aspects of the context, but these aspects are excluded from semantic analysis and relegated to the domain of pragmatics.

The division between semantic encoding and pragmatic inference is a cornerstone of (traditional) linguistic theory, but in practice, the two aspects of meaning are difficult to distinguish. In fact, cognitive linguists have argued that there are no objective criteria for establishing a precise boundary between (stable) semantic representations and context-dependent aspects of pragmatically inferred meanings (Fillmore 1985: 233; Langacker 2008: 38). Questioning the rigid division between encoding and inference, these scholars contend that the traditional view of word meaning is fundamentally flawed.

Specifically, they claim that the encoding theory of semantics should be replaced by a general inference model of understanding in which words are seen as "prompts" or "cues" that do not "encode" particular semantic features, but "evoke," or "create," semantic interpretations in particular contexts (Fillmore 1982, 1985; Langacker 1987, 2008; Barsalou 1999; Evans and Green 2006: 206–244; Elman 2009; Bergen 2012).

Every lexeme designates a particular concept in language users' encyclopedic knowledge, but since concepts are interconnected, word meanings are usually derived from a whole system of related concepts. Following Langacker (1987), we will say that words provide a "point of access" to a network of conceptually related nodes that are activated together with the "access node" (see also Fillmore 1982: 381). As Langacker puts it:

The entity designated by a symbolic unit can therefore be thought of as a point of access to a network. The semantic value of a symbolic unit is given by the open-ended set of relations . . . in which this access node participates. (Langacker 1987: 163)

Cognitive psychologists have characterized this phenomenon as "activation spreading" (Collins and Loftus 1975; Anderson 1983; Dell 1986; see also Hudson 2007: 36–41). When one node is activated by a lexeme (or some other type of cue), activation spreads to conceptually related nodes in the network (Figure 6.1).

One piece of evidence for activation spreading comes from lexical priming. When people are given a lexeme in a word recognition task, their responses to semantically related items are much faster than their responses to semantically unrelated items (§3.5.3). The direction and amount of activation spreading is determined by two factors: (i) the structure of the network and (ii) the context. In what follows, we will consider the two factors respectively.

Conceptual network

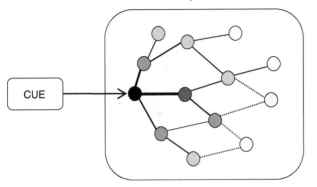

Figure 6.1 Point of access and spreading activation

6.4   The Structure of the Knowledge Network

Every lexeme is interpreted against the background of a whole network of concepts in a particular domain. For instance, the items *car, street, drive, highway* and *stop light* pertain to a conceptual network that is based on a language user's experience with the domain of traffic. The strength of the associative connections between concepts is determined by two general factors: (i) the frequency with which individual concepts are jointly activated in usage and cognition, and (ii) the nature of the connections between individual concepts.

Some concepts evoke particular conceptual relations that entail other concepts. The part-whole relationship, for instance, involves a connection between two concepts that are inextricably related (e.g., head → body). Likewise, action concepts presuppose particular conceptual relations between an action and its participants that cannot be separated (e.g., write → writer, text). If the network accessed by a lexeme involves conceptual relations of this type, the access node specifies a "figure concept" of a "conceptual gestalt" that presupposes one or more "base concepts" (Fillmore 1985; Lakoff 1987).

Crucially, not all lexemes evoke conceptual relations of this type. A noun such as *stone*, for instance, designates a nonrelational entity that does not presuppose a specific base concept. But while nonrelational concepts such as *stone* do not entail particular conceptual relations, they are also associated with other concepts in the network (e.g., *hard, heavy, throw*) that can influence their interpretation in a particular situation (see §6.5).

The figure-base relationship is of particular importance to the semantic analysis of lexical expressions (Fillmore 1982, 1985; Langacker 1987, 2008; Talmy 2000). Building on frame semantics, we will use Fillmore's notion of

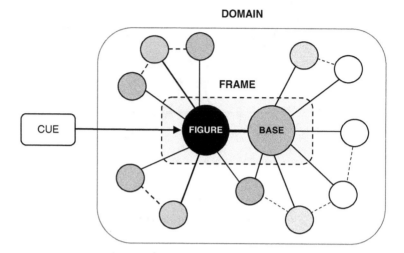

Figure 6.2 Frames and domains

"frame" for conceptual gestalts that involve a particular figure concept and one or more base concepts; and we will use the notion of "domain" for larger knowledge structures that may surround a frame (Figure 6.2).[1]

6.4.1   Frames

Although Fillmore did not specifically propose a network model to explain semantic frames, his notion of frame is immediately compatible with the current network approach. Here is how Fillmore defined the notion of frame in a seminal paper:

By the term frame I have in mind any system of concepts related in such a way that to understand any one of them you have to understand the whole structure in which it fits; when one of the things in such a structure is introduced into a text, or into a conversation, all of the others are automatically made available. (Fillmore 1982: 373)

Of particular importance for the study of grammar is Fillmore's analysis of "event frames." Event frames are conceptual gestalts that involve a relationship between an action and its participants. An example is the "transfer frame," which involves an act of transfer and three general participant roles: a sender, a

---

[1] Note that Langacker (1987, 2008) uses the notion of "domain" in a way that overlaps with Fillmore's notion of frame (Croft and Cruse 2004: 7–32; Cienki 2007), but here we distinguish between frames and domains as shown in Figure 6.2.

theme and a recipient (Fillmore et al. 2003: 238–239). English has a large
number of transfer verbs that presuppose these three roles: *give, send, receive,
obtain, consign, keep, sell, buy* and *retain* to mention just a few. Some of these
verbs have a general meaning, others are more specific. The verbs *sell* and *buy*,
for instance, are interpreted based on what Fillmore calls the "commercial
transaction frame," which can be seen as a subtype of the general transfer frame
(Fillmore 1982; Fillmore et al. 2003: 238–239).

The transfer frame provides a uniform conceptual foundation for all verbs of
transfer, but individual verbs present the transfer event from different perspectives and assign different degrees of prominence to particular participant roles
(Fillmore et al. 2003: 238–239). Consider, for instance, the following
examples:

(1)   John sent Jane twenty emails.

(2)   Jane received twenty emails.

Both *sent* and *receive* evoke the transfer frame, but they conceptualize the scene
in different ways. In the case of *send*, the sender is highlighted as an agent of the
described action, but in the case of *receive*, the recipient is the primary focus of
the scene. Note that the sender is not explicitly mentioned in example (2), but,
of course, it is implicit in the event described by the verb as the transfer frame
generally entails the role of a sender (Figure 6.3).

Event frames are foundational for the analysis of argument structure
(Fillmore et al. 2003). As we will see in Chapter 7, while argument structure
is not directly predictable from a verb's meaning, event frames constrain the
verbalization of participant roles and their degree of prominence in argument-
structure constructions.

Like verbs, adjectives evoke a frame. Since adjectives entail some kind of
entity, they are generally interpreted against the background of the (nominal)
concept they modify. Note that certain semantic aspects of the modified

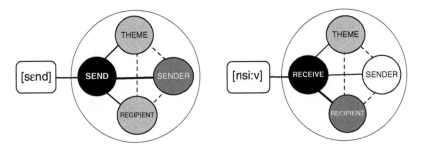

Figure 6.3 Transfer event frame evoked by the verbs *send* and *receive*

concept are implicit in the meaning of the adjective: *round*, for instance, specifies an object, *intelligent* specifies a person, *furry* specifies an animal and *disastrous* specifies an event. What is more, many adjectives evoke a frame in which the figure concept presupposes a contrastive term: *long*, for instance, is interpreted in contrast to *short*, and *old* in contrast to *young* or *new* (Fillmore 1982).

Since nouns typically designate things rather than relations (Chapter 8), they do not generally presuppose a particular base concept. However, like verbs and adjectives, nouns are interpreted in the context of a frame if the access node presupposes a particular conceptual relation. The noun *roof*, for instance, is interpreted relative to a particular base. Although *roof* itself does not explicitly refer to a building or shelter, it is impossible to define the meaning of *roof* without concepts such as *building, shelter, house, cottage, barn* or *tent*, indicating that these concepts are implicit in the meaning of *roof*.

The frame-semantic analysis of *roof* is based on the part-whole relationship, which is arguably one of the most important types of conceptual relations that are invoked by nominal expressions, but there are also other types of conceptual relations that underlie the semantic interpretation of certain nouns. Consider, for instance, the difference between *land* and *ground*, which is one of Fillmore's classic examples. Both terms, *land* and *ground*, refer to the "dry surface of the earth," but provide different conceptualizations: *land* contrasts with *sea* and *ground* contrasts with *air*, so that the conceptual figure (i.e., the dry surface of the earth) is presented from different perspectives that presuppose different base concepts. A similar analysis has been proposed for the nouns *shore* and *coast* (Fillmore 1982: 382).

6.4.2   Domains

The notion of domain is closely related to that of frame. In fact, some scholars use the terms frame and domain interchangeably (Croft and Cruse 2004: 17); but here we restrict the notion of frame to conceptual gestalts in which a particular figure concept entails a particular base, whereas the notion of domain is used for larger knowledge structures that are only loosely associated with the access node, that is, the figure concept, and its base.[2]

Consider, for instance, the meaning of the word *summer*. In its basic use, *summer* designates one of four seasons, falling between *spring* and *fall* and contrasting with *winter*. Although *summer* does not explicitly refer to *spring*, *fall* and *winter*, these concepts are entailed in the meaning of *summer*, as it

---

[2] Fillmore's use of the term "frame" is ambivalent in this regard. In some contexts, it is restricted to conceptual gestalts (defined by figure and base), but in other contexts, it seems to correspond to what is here called a domain.

would be impossible to explain what *summer* means without reference to other seasons. In other words, *summer* evokes a conceptual gestalt, a frame, that is, the frame of season.

Interestingly, there are two variants of the season frame: there is the meteorological frame, in which *summer* designates the time period from the beginning of June to the end of August, and there is the astronomical frame, in which *summer* lasts from summer solstice (June 20/21) to the fall equinox (September 22/23). Moreover, the frame varies with the hemisphere. What has been said thus far holds for the notion of *summer* in the northern hemisphere. In the southern hemisphere, the frame changes and *summer* designates the time period that corresponds to the period of *winter* in the northern hemisphere.

Crucially, in addition to the concepts that constitute the frame of season, *summer* is associated with a wide range of other concepts including *sunshine, heat, light, thunderstorm, vacation, beach, swimming, traveling, outdoors* and *Labor Day* (in the US). These concepts are more loosely associated with the meaning of *summer* than the concepts of *spring, fall* and *winter*.

Like *summer*, the three other seasons evoke conceptual domains including clusters of associated concepts that are parallel across seasons. All four seasons are associated with concepts concerning the domains of weather (*sunshine, snow, ice, rain, hail, fog*), vegetation (*fruits, blossom, ripeness*), light (*brightness, darkness*), seasonal activities (*planting, watering, harvesting, skating, heating*) and cultural events (*Easter, Thanksgiving, Christmas*). The network in Figure 6.4 seeks to capture the proposed analysis of *summer*.

Domains vary in size and are hierarchically structured (Langacker 2008: 147–182). Space, for instance, is an extensive domain that subsumes a large number of more specific domains such as country, forest or body, which in turn subsume even more specific domains such as city, tree and head. Crucially, many linguistic expressions evoke concepts of multiple domains. A noun such as *car*, for instance, is related to the domains of space, object, transportation, traffic, force, accident and many others, which together constitute what Langacker calls the "domain matrix" of a concept or lexeme (Langacker 2008: 47–48; see also Croft and Cruse 2004: 24–27). While lexical expressions are usually associated with concepts of multiple domains, the activation of domains varies with the context.

6.5   The Role of the Context

If we look at lexemes in isolation, the figure node entails one or more base nodes that are associated with general semantic information from particular domains (e.g., space, time); but apart from this information the base nodes are unspecified. Yet, if we look at the use of lexemes in a particular situation, the base nodes are (usually) elaborated by more specific information from the context. One can think of the base nodes of a frame (accessed by a particular

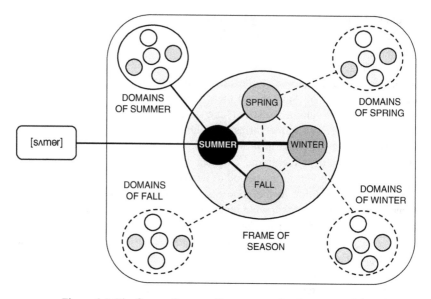

Figure 6.4 The frame of season: figure, ground and conceptual domains

relational expression) as "slots" for contextual information. The general idea is well known from the analysis of argument structure.

Every verb evokes a set of participant roles, or argument nodes, that are elaborated by information from the linguistic or nonlinguistic context. In English, the core arguments (i.e., subject and object) are obligatory so that the participant nodes of a verb are usually specified by linguistic elements that accompany the verb within the same clause, but in many languages arguments are not obligatory so that the participant nodes evoked by a verb are usually inferred from the discourse context or speech situation.

Since argument-structure constructions are based on very close conceptual relations, involving actions and their participants, it is generally accepted that verbs provide slots for particular referents. However, this does not only hold for verbs but also for other types of expressions. If we accept the hypothesis that lexemes provide access to networks, their meanings are generally elaborated by the context, both the linguistic context and the surrounding situation. Consider, for instance, the interpretation of the word *head* in the two following examples.

(3)   the head [of a person]

(4)   the head [of a snake]

Head designates a body part that evokes the concept of *body* as its base, but, as can be seen in (3) and (4), the base concept can be elaborated in different ways that affect the semantic interpretation of the access node. Combining *head* with *person* evokes the body concept of a human being, whereas the combination of *head* and *snake* evokes the body of a reptile. In other words, *person* and *snake* specify the base concept of *head* in the body frame in specific ways that affect the interpretation of *head*. Note that this does not only concern the physical attributes of *head* and *body* (e.g., shape, size, color, hair), but also a wide range of other concepts that are associated with *person* and *snake*. Intelligence, emotions and language, for instance, are concepts associated with *head* in the context of *person* but not in the context of *snake*, whereas *poison, danger* and *wildlife* are associated with *snake* but not with *person*.

One way of analyzing the composite structures in (3) and (4) would be to say that *person* and *snake* "add" meaning to a highly schematic body concept of *head*, but given that the semantic contrast between *head of a person* and *head of a snake* does not only concern the entities that are designated by *body* and *head* but also concepts of behavior, cognition and the living environments of human beings and snakes, it seems to be more appropriate to say that the meanings of these expressions are formed by integrating two complex knowledge structures, evoked by *head* and *person/snake*, into a coherent semantic representation.

Conceptual integration, also known as "conceptual blending" (Fauconnier and Turner 2002), is a general mechanism of language use and cognition. Since the conceptual network evoked by a lexeme is always elaborated by information of the linguistic and/or nonlinguistic context, word meanings are highly variable. In fact, if we follow this line of reasoning to its ultimate conclusion, we may say, with Langacker (2008: 50), that "a lexeme is never used twice with exactly the same meaning," as there are always some differences in the linguistic or situational contexts that affect the semantic interpretation of a lexeme in a unique way.

6.5.1   Conceptual Shifts

The effect of the context varies with the semantic compatibility of the various linguistic and nonlinguistic cues that have to be integrated into a coherent semantic interpretation. In examples (3) and (4), *person* and *snake* fit the semantic specifications of the body frame evoked by *head*, but in example (5) there is a semantic incompatibility that has profound consequences for the process of conceptual integration.

(5)   the head [of the department]

Since the meaning of *department* does not fit the body frame evoked by *head*, *head* is shifted together with its conceptual base to a different domain where it is semantically compatible with *department*. Cognitive linguists have characterized this phenomenon as "conceptual metaphor." Lakoff and Johnson (1980) define

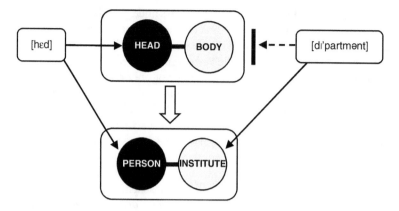

Figure 6.5 Conceptual shift caused by semantic incompatibility

conceptual metaphor as a process whereby a conceptual structure of one domain, the source domain, is mapped onto another domain, the target domain, where it receives a different semantic interpretation.

Lexical expressions that are routinely used in multiple domains are said to be polysemous. One can think of polysemy (and conceptual metaphor) as a particular case of inference triggered by the incompatibility of a lexeme and its context. Since the meaning of *department* is not compatible with the body frame of *head, head* is shifted together with its associated nodes to a different conceptual domain, that is, the domain of institution, where it can be integrated together with *department* into a coherent semantic unit (Figure 6.5).

Like nouns, adjectives and verbs are semantically elaborated by the context and shifted to different domains if they are not compatible with the context. Consider, for instance, the meaning of the adjective *long* in the following examples.

(6)   long [hair]

(7)   long [road]

(8)   long [game]

In its basic use, *long* contrasts with *short* and profiles the end point of a scale that serves to characterize the size or extension of a physical entity in the domain of space. Examples (6) and (7) illustrate the basic spatial sense of *long*. Note that while *long* evokes a scale in both examples, the conceptualization of the scale varies with the context, as the co-occurring nouns, *hair* and *road*, evoke scales of very different size. In example (8), the scale evoked by *long* is shifted from the domain of space to that of time, as *game* designates a temporally extended activity that does not match the default sense of *long* as a spatial adjective. A parallel analysis applies to verbs:

(9)   to sell [groceries]

(10)   to sell [a house]

(11)   to sell [an idea]

Sell evokes the commercial transaction frame, which includes a prominent node for the goods that are transferred (Fillmore et al. 2003). In examples (9) and (10), *groceries* and *house* match the semantic specifications of the commercial transaction frame as these two nouns designate typical goods. Note, however, that *selling groceries* and *selling a house* describe rather different events involving different actions (e.g., putting fruits into a cart vs. taking out a loan) and different locations (e.g., store vs. bank), suggesting that the conceptualization of *sell* is accommodated to the meanings of *groceries* and *house*. Still, *selling groceries* and *selling a house* pertain to the same general domain of commerce. In example (11), however, *sell* is shifted to a different domain, the domain of abstract concepts, as the noun *idea* is not compatible with the semantic specifications of the goods in the commercial transaction frame.

In general, we can distinguish two different ways in which the context affects the semantic interpretation of a lexeme. If the context is compatible with the semantic specifications of the base nodes of a particular frame, the access node is elaborated by contextual cues within its default domain; but if the context is not compatible with the semantic specifications of a particular frame, the whole system of concepts evoked by a lexeme is shifted to a different domain in order to construct a coherent semantic representation from the various cues that are co-present in a particular situation.

6.5.2   Polysemy

If a lexeme is routinely interpreted in light of different domains (due to its routine use in different contexts), it is said to be polysemous (Fillmore 1982). Polysemy involves conceptual shifts across domains that are commonly characterized in terms of metaphor (or metonymy)[3] (Lakoff and Johnson 1980; see also Bowdle and Gentner 2005). Since lexemes can undergo multiple metaphorical shifts, or multiple metaphorical mappings, some words are highly polysemous. Consider, for instance, the following examples of *head* (12a–j).

(12)   a. head of body
           b. head of department
           c. head of hammer
           d. head of flower

---

[3] In cognitive semantics, metaphor is commonly defined as a mapping across domains, whereas metonymy is defined as a mapping within one domain (Lakoff and Johnson 1980). Yet, as we will see shortly, there is no sharp distinction between mappings across domains and mappings within the same domain (see Barcelona 2015 for discussion).

     e. head of parade
     f. head of phrase
     g. to head a committee
     h. to head a list
     i. to head for town
     j. headline

Traditionally, the notion of polysemy refers to particular types of lexical expressions that are used with two or more related senses, but cognitive linguists have argued that most words are polysemous as they are used with multiple senses. The hypothesis is intriguing, but suffers from the fact that Lakoff and other cognitive linguists did not provide clear criteria for the distinction of different senses (Sandra and Rice 1995; Tyler and Evans 2001).

In the current framework, the notion of polysemy applies to lexical expressions that are routinely used in multiple domains. In the semantic literature, polysemy is (usually) treated as a classic category defined by a set of discrete senses, but if we think of polysemy in terms of domains, lexemes can be more or less polysemous depending on the distance and amount of overlap between domains. As pointed out in §6.5.1, domains are organized in hierarchies and overlap in manifold ways. Items that are used in clearly delineated, nonoverlapping domains are strongly polysemous, whereas items that are used in related and partially overlapping domains are weakly polysemous.

For instance, the expressions *head of a person* and *head of a phrase* are strongly polysemous because there is no (obvious) overlap between the domains of body and syntax. Other uses of *head* are not so clearly delineated. The expressions *head of a person* and *head of a hammer*, for instance, are polysemous in that *head of a person* evokes the domain of animate beings, whereas *head of a hammer* pertains to the domain of (inanimate) objects. However, assuming that the domains of animate beings and inanimate objects are both subsumed under the domains of entity and space, they appear to be less polysemous than the expressions *head of a person* and *head of a phrase* (which are not subsumed under a higher-level domain). Finally, the expressions *head of a person* and *head of a snake* are not polysemous because they both pertain to the domain of body. Note, however, that one could argue that the human body and the body of reptiles constitute distinct domains at a lower level of the hierarchy. On this view, *head of a person* and *head of a snake* would be (weakly) polysemous (Figure 6.6).

There is an ongoing debate about the notion of polysemy in cognitive semantics (see Evans and Green 2006: Chapter 10 for a review). Some researchers have claimed that polysemy is a rampant phenomenon as lexical expressions typically occur with a large number of distinct senses (Lakoff 1987), but other researchers have argued against the proliferation of word senses based on the distinction between polysemy and vagueness (Tyler and Evans 2003). Two general criteria can be used to distinguish polysemy from

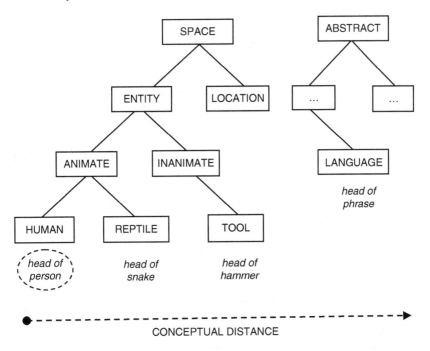

Figure 6.6 Conceptual domains of the various senses of *head*

vagueness: (i) the conceptual distance between distinct senses or uses, and (ii) the degree of conventionalization. On this view, an item is polysemous if it has multiple conventional uses that are associated with clearly delineated senses, and it is vague if its different senses concern subtle semantic nuances and/or if a particular sense is spontaneously derived from the context and thus nonconventional.

Both criteria, that is, conceptual distance and conventionalization, are important for the analysis of word meanings, but they are both gradient, making it very difficult (or even impossible) to draw a sharp distinction between polysemy and vagueness. As we have seen, conceptual distance varies with the degree of overlap between domains, and conventionalization varies with frequency of occurrence. The more often a word is used with a particular sense in a particular context by the members of a speech community, the more deeply entrenched is the path of interpretation, but there is no rigid division between conventional and nonconventional senses, suggesting that polysemy is a gradient concept.[4]

---

[4] Recall that conventionalization is not just a matter of frequency but also of social cognition (§5.1). Multiple word senses are conventionalized if they are frequent and shared by speakers of a speech community (see Schmid 2015 for discussion).

6.5.3   Polysemy Networks

Lexical items such as *head* that are used with a wide range of clearly delineated senses are said to form a "polysemy network" (Lakoff 1987). Polysemy networks are created by conceptual mappings, notably by metaphor (Lakoff and Johnson 1980). If we look at these networks of related senses from a diachronic perspective, they are (often) organized around a center, which is represented by the original use of a lexeme from which all other uses are historically derived. In the case of *head*, for instance, the body sense constitutes the diachronic center as it represents the oldest use of *head* (Figure 6.7).

Note, however, that synchronically, the oldest use is not always the basic or dominant one. Novel uses may increase in frequency and old uses may vanish. Moreover, the various senses created by metaphor (and/or other cognitive processes) may undergo subsequent semantic changes. It would thus be a mistake to assume that the various synchronic uses of a polysemous item such as *head* represent the various stages of its diachronic trajectory. Instead, the synchronic uses may constitute a set of senses that are only indirectly related, as some of the links and nodes that were created by conceptual metaphor have undergone additional changes.

In fact, the metaphorical mappings that are initially so prominent in metaphor tend to fade away in language change. Once a new sense is established, there are always two possible routes to access it. Initially, there is a strong bias to activate the new sense via the source domain along the metaphorical path that created it, but if the new sense is frequently used, it becomes autonomous in the sense that it can now be accessed directly. As a consequence, the metaphorical link that has given rise to a new sense fades away and the newly created sense turns into a frozen metaphor (Figure 6.8) (see Bowdle and Gentner 2005 for discussion).

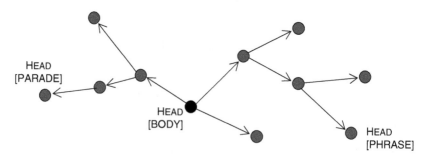

Figure 6.7 Polysemy network of *head*

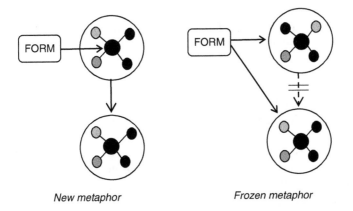

New metaphor   Frozen metaphor

Figure 6.8 Diachronic development of a polysemous item

To summarize the discussion thus far, we have seen that symbolic associations are derived from the use of phonetic cues in meaningful contexts. They are the joint product of social-cognitive skills, such as the ability to understand intentions, and conceptual processes, such as metaphor and conceptual integration. The latter explains why word meanings are generally influenced by the context. Since many lexemes are used across different contexts, they are usually associated with multiple paths of semantic interpretation that are strengthened by frequency of occurrence. The result of this is a linguistic sign or symbol that can guide a language user along various paths of semantic interpretation, contingent on the context.

6.6   The Meaning of Constructions

Concluding this chapter, let us consider the meaning of constructions. The construction-based literature has emphasized the parallels between lexemes and constructions (Croft 2001; Goldberg 2006; Hilpert 2014). Both are commonly analyzed as signs or symbols that combine a particular form with meaning. Yet, while constructions are symbolic, one must not overlook the differences between lexemes and constructions.

Like lexemes, constructions act as prompts for the construction of meaning, but the conceptual processes that are induced by constructions are different from those of lexemes. Lexical expressions provide access to an open-ended system of encyclopedic knowledge, but constructional meanings are only indirectly related to world knowledge. Since constructions are derived from lexical sequences with similar forms and meanings (Chapter 4), they do not directly tap into encyclopedic knowledge but generalize over linguistically invoked meanings. Specifically, we may say that constructional meanings reside in the way they guide the semantic interpretation of (multiple) lexemes. Consider, for instance, the following example of the resultative construction including two nonce words.

(13)   The toma meeked John dizzy.

Although the words *toma* and *meek* do not have conventional meanings, they receive particular semantic interpretations in example (13). *Toma* is interpreted as an agentive subject of an action, designated by *meek*, that causes somebody to feel *dizzy*. The meanings of *toma* and *meek* are derived from the resultative construction, which includes four structural positions for lexical expressions that are assigned to a particular semantic role or function. To put it another way, the resultative construction instructs a language user to interpret lexical expressions in a particular way (Figure 6.9).

Since the schematic representations of constructional meanings are derived from the meanings of lexical sequences (Chapter 4), there is a close connection between the meaning of constructions and that of lexemes. As we will see, grammatical and lexical meanings influence each other and develop in tandem. We will consider the interaction between lexemes and constructions in the two following chapters. Here we concentrate on the general claim that constructions provide processing instructions for the interpretation of lexical items.

The processing instructions that are provided by grammatical constructions can be more or less specific, more or less constrained. Some constructions guide a language user along a narrow path to a particular semantic interpretation, but others leave room for variation. In the latter case, listeners make more extensive use of semantic and pragmatic cues in order to integrate the various lexemes of a construction into a coherent semantic interpretation. Let us consider the processing of relative clauses to better understand how constructions constrain the processing of lexical items.

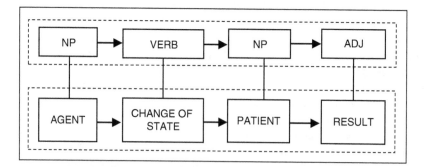

Figure 6.9 The resultative construction

In §4.2, it was said that relative clauses serve to modify the meaning of a nominal expression, the head noun, in the main clause (or in another subordinate clause). The head noun is interpreted as a semantic participant of the event expressed by the verb in the relative clause. In English, the head can serve a wide range of semanto-syntactic roles in the relative clause including the roles of agent [SUBJECT], patient [OBJECT], theme [OBJECT], location [OBLIQUE], instrument [OBLIQUE], source [OBLIQUE] and goal [OBLIQUE] (14a–g).

(14)   a. The person who helped me.   AGENT [SUBJECT]
       b. The house (which) the storm destroyed. PATIENT [OBJECT]
       c. The book she sent me.   THEME [OBJECT]
       d. The city where we live.   LOCATION [OBLIQUE]
       e. The key with which you unlocked the door. INSTRUMENT [OBLIQUE]
       f. The place they come from.   SOURCE [OBLIQUE]
       g. The restaurant we went to.   GOAL [OBLIQUE]

The various roles are indicated by a set of structural features (§4.2). Agent [subject] relative clauses, for instance, are distinguished from all other types of relative clauses by a particular word order and the obligatory use of a relative marker in front of the verb, and instrument [oblique] relative clauses are distinguished from other types of relative clauses by the preposition *with*. The various relative clauses provide specific processing instructions regarding the semanto-syntactic role of the head in the relative clause. Each role is expressed by a particular configuration of structural features that guides a listener to a particular semantic interpretation of the head noun. However, interestingly, in other languages the relativized role can often only be inferred from the context. Relative clauses in Japanese, for instance, are structurally much less constrained than relative clauses in English and most other European languages (Matsumoto 1997; Comrie 1998).

Japanese relative clauses precede the noun they modify and do not include a relative pronoun or any other grammatical marker that would directly indicate the relativized role. The most important feature that distinguishes Japanese relative clauses from main clauses is linear order.[5] As can be seen in (15a–b), main clauses include the verb at the end of the sentence in Japanese, but in relative clauses the verb is followed by a noun (i.e., the head noun), which serves a particular semanto-syntactic role in the event expressed by the relative verb.

(15)   a.   gakusei   ga   hon   o   katta.
            student   NOM   book   ACC   bought
            'A student bought the book.' (Matsumoto 1997: 4)

---

[5] In addition to word order, case marking and sentence particles can distinguish relative clauses from main clauses in Japanese, but since these features are not always present, they will not concern us here.

b. [[gakusei ga   katta]   hon]   wa   doko   desu ka.
    student NOM   bought   book   TOP   where   is   QP
    'Where is the book (which) a student bought?' (Matsumoto 1997: 4)

In the syntactic literature, it is often said that the relativized role is indicated by a "gap" in Japanese. In example (15b), for instance, the relative clause includes a transitive verb, but since the direct object is not overtly expressed in the relative clause, we may say that the relativized role is indicated by a gap. However, as Matsumoto (1997) and Comrie (1998) have pointed out, this analysis is problematic as the gap of the relativized role is indistinguishable from the roles of other arguments that may be missing in a relative clause. Since arguments are not obligatorily expressed in Japanese, relative clauses can include multiple gaps making it impossible to infer the role of the head from its absence in the relative clause. Consider, for instance, the following example from Matsumoto (1997: 39).

(16)   [yonde-iru] kodomo wa doko   desu ka.
        calling-is   child   TOP where   is   QP
        a. 'Where is the child who is calling someone?'
        b. 'Where is the child whom someone is calling?' (Matsumoto 1997: 39)

As Matsumoto explains, the noun *kodomo* 'child' is preceded by a verb that has the function of a relative clause, but since both subject and object are missing in the relative clause, *kodomo* 'child' could be either agent [and SUBJECT] or patient [and OBJECT] of the preceding verb; that is, the relative clause is structurally ambiguous and the relativized role can only be inferred from the context.

If the relative clause includes a case-marked nominal, as in (15b), the interpretation of the relativized role is structurally more constrained, as the head noun cannot serve the same role as an overtly expressed nominal in the relative clause, but even when the relative clause includes a case-marked nominal, Japanese relative clauses can be ambiguous. Consider, for instance, example (17).

(17)   [hon   o   katta]   gakusei
        book ACC bought student
        a. 'The student who bought a book.'   AGENT
        b. 'The student from whom someone bought a book.'   SOURCE
        c. 'The student for/to whom someone bought a book.' BENEFICIARY
        (Matsumoto 1997: 6)

According to Matsumoto (1997: 39), the head *gakusei* 'student' could be interpreted as agent (17a), source (17b) or beneficiary (17 c) of the buying event denoted by *katta*. The structural indeterminacy of Japanese relative clauses is not unusual. As Comrie (1998) and others (e.g., Haig 1998) have shown, there are many languages in which the semanto-syntactic role of the head is not fully determined by the structure of the relative clause (e.g., in Turkish, Korean, Mandarin).

If the interpretation of the relative-clause head is structurally underdetermined, as in Japanese, listeners must draw on contextual cues and general world knowledge in order to identify the relativized role. Of particular importance is the event frame that is evoked by the verb of the relative clause. For instance, while example (17) allows for at least three different interpretations, there is a tendency for speakers of Japanese to interpret *gakusei* 'student' as agent and subject of the relative clause because this is the most natural interpretation of an animate head in the event frame evoked by *katta* 'buy'. Other interpretations are possible (depending on the context), but there is a strong tendency to interpret an animate head noun as subject and agent of the relative verb, whereas inanimate heads are likely to be interpreted as objects and patients. Similar tendencies of semantic interpretation have been observed in other languages with structurally ambiguous relative clauses (e.g., in Turkish; see Haig 1998) and have also been noticed in psycholinguistic experiments with English relative clauses. Although subject and nonsubject relatives are structurally distinct in English, language users seem to associate particular semantic head nouns with particular structural types of relative clauses as evidenced by the fact that nonsubject relatives with animate heads cause prolonged reading times compared to nonsubject relatives with inanimate heads (Traxler et al. 2002, 2005; Mak et al. 2002, 2006).

In general, where speakers of English are usually guided by structural cues of particular relative-clause constructions, speakers of Japanese draw on frame-semantic considerations that are induced by lexical and contextual cues. In both languages, relative clauses provide processing instructions for the interpretation of the head noun, but the instructions of English relative clauses are more specific than those of relative clauses in Japanese.

6.7   Conclusion

To summarize, the current chapter has argued that symbolic links are created by domain-general processes of conceptualization and social cognition (or pragmatic inference). This concerns both lexemes and constructions. Both can be seen as signs or symbols that combine a particular form with meaning; but while cognitive linguists have often claimed that constructions are the same symbolic entities as lexemes, the current chapter has argued that the meanings of lexemes and constructions reside in different cognitive processes.

Lexical items provide access to an open-ended network of encyclopedic knowledge that reflects a language user's experience with objects and events in the world. One can think of lexemes as prompts or stimuli speakers use to manipulate hearers' knowledge or mental states. On this account, lexical expressions connect a particular phonetic form with certain paths of semantic interpretation that are determined by two general factors: the structure of the knowledge network and the context.

Every lexeme designates a concept that is interpreted against the background of a whole system of related concepts. This system has been characterized by the notions of frame and domain. A frame is a conceptual gestalt that involves a particular relationship between the access node, or figure concept, and one or more base nodes that are entailed by the figure concept; whereas the notion of domain applies to broader knowledge structures that are only loosely associated with figure (and base). If the context is not compatible with the semantic specifications of the frame and (default) domain evoked by a particular lexeme, the whole structure is shifted to a different domain where figure and base can be integrated into a coherent semantic representation. As a consequence of these shifts (or mappings), lexemes are usually associated with multiple paths of interpretation and are therefore polysemous. Note, however, that polysemy is a gradient notion that varies with the amount of overlap between domains and the degree of conventionalization (and entrenchment).

Since constructional schemas are extracted from lexical sequences, they do not directly tap into encyclopedic knowledge but represent generalizations over semantic interpretations that are invoked by strings of lexical expressions. These generalizations constitute a conceptual framework that constrains the interpretation of lexemes in specific ways. In particular, the chapter has argued that constructional schemas provide processing instructions for integrating the meanings of multiple lexemes into a coherent semantic representation.

Part III

Filler–Slot Relations

7   Argument Structure and Linguistic Productivity

7.1   Introduction

In the three previous chapters, we have been concerned with three basic types of links or relations: taxonomic relations (Chapter 4), sequential relations (Chapter 5) and symbolic relations (Chapter 6). Together, these relations define the various types of linguistic signs, that is, morphemes, lexemes, words, phrases and constructions. In the remainder of this book, we will take a closer look at syntactic categories and the overall organization of the grammar network. In order to analyze syntactic categories, we need three other types of relations: (i) lexical relations, which indicate associations between semantically and/or phonologically similar lexical items, (ii) constructional relations, which characterize relationships between constructions (at the same level of abstraction), and (iii) filler–slot relations, which specify associations between individual lexemes and particular slots of constructional schemas.

The latter (i.e., filler–slot relations) are of particular importance to the analysis of syntactic categories. In formal linguistic theory, syntactic analysis presupposes a toolkit of preestablished categories (Chapter 1), but in the current approach, syntactic categories are derived from the interaction between the various types of linguistic signs. It is the purpose of the subsequent analyses to explain how syntactic categories are shaped by the interaction between lexemes and constructions. In the current chapter, we will be concerned with categories of argument structure and in the two following chapters we will consider grammatical word classes (Chapter 8) and phrase structure categories (Chapter 9).

7.2   Theories of Argument Structure

The notion of argument structure refers to the way verbs and their semantic participants are formally expressed in a clause. In the previous chapter, we have seen that verbs designate relational concepts of an event frame that entails particular participants, commonly referred to as arguments. The verb *give*, for instance, evokes the transfer frame, which entails three arguments: an actor, a recipient and a theme (§6.4.1). The number of arguments that are entailed by a verb (or frame) constitutes its valency. Since the transfer frame includes three arguments, *give* has a valency of three.

Crucially, speakers do not only know the number of arguments and their semantic roles, they also know how the various arguments of a verb are expressed in a clause. *Give*, for instance, is commonly used in clauses in which the agent precedes the verb and functions as subject, whereas recipient and theme are designated by postverbal complements, which can be expressed in two different ways: either the recipient precedes the theme and both complements are encoded by simple NPs, or the theme precedes the recipient and the latter is expressed by a prepositional phrase (examples 1–2).

(1)   Sue gave her older brother the keys.

(2)   Sue gave the keys to her older brother.

This knowledge – that is, the knowledge of how semantic arguments are formally realized in a clause – constitutes the argument structure of a verb. There is general consensus that argument structure is an important aspect of speakers' grammatical knowledge, but the analysis of argument structure is controversial. To simplify, there are two main approaches: there is the lexicalist approach, in which argument structure is determined by lexical properties of the verb (Levin and Rappaport 2005), and there is the constructional approach, in which argument structure is primarily determined by constructions (Goldberg 1995). In what follows, I briefly describe the two approaches and then outline a network model of argument structure that builds on the constructional approach.

7.2.1   The Lexicalist Approach

Many linguists assume that basic aspects of clause structure are predictable from the meaning of verbs. Building on the traditional distinction between grammar and lexicon, these scholars argue that the "lexical entry" of a verb includes information about the syntactic encoding of arguments, which is mapped from the lexicon onto clause structure. In this account, syntactic clause structure is seen as a "projection" of lexical properties of the verb or predicator (Pinker 1989; Levin and Rappaport 2005).

Every verb selects particular participants, but, of course, there are also general principles of argument selection and argument projection that go beyond individual verbs. These principles are the focus of the lexicalist approach. There are two important generalizations. First, following Pinker (1989), it is widely assumed that verbs can be grouped together into particular semantic classes based on a limited set of (semantic) features that are immediately relevant to the encoding of arguments in syntax. And second, these researchers assume that there are general "linking rules" that explain how (lexical) representations of argument structure are mapped onto (syntactic) clause structure. To illustrate, consider the following sentences including the verbs *break* and *hit* (adopted from Fillmore 1970: 126).

(3)   a. John broke the window with a rock.
         b. John hit the fence with a rock.

(4)   a. The rock broke the window.
         b. The stick hit the fence.

(5)   a. The window broke.
         b. *The fence hit.

(6)   a. *I broke him on the leg.
         b. I hit him on the leg.

As can be seen, *break* and *hit* are used in several syntactic contexts. In some of these uses, they take the same general types of complements: Both verbs appear in transitive clauses with or without an explicit NP denoting an instrument (3a–b, 4a–b), but while *break* can also be used in intransitive clauses, this is not possible with *hit* (5a–b), and while *hit* can also be used with a locative *on*-phrase, this is not permissible with *break* (6a–b).

Fillmore (1970) showed that the syntactic behaviors of *break* and *hit* are characteristic of two distinct groups of verbs: verbs such as *bend, fold, shatter* and *crack* denote a change of state and pattern syntactically like *break*; whereas verbs such as *slap, strike, bump* and *stroke* involve contact with a concrete entity (but do not denote a change of state) and pattern syntactically like *hit*. Similar correlations between verb meaning and syntactic behavior have been observed with many other verbs and sentence types (Pinker 1989).

Given that verbs with similar meanings often exhibit the same or similar syntactic behaviors, it is a plausible assumption that clause structure is, to a large extent, projectable from lexical representations of verbs by general linking rules. There is a great deal of research on this topic (see Levin and Rappaport 2005 for a survey), but the approach has been criticized by Goldberg (1995) and other construction grammarians who have argued that argument structure is primarily determined by constructional schemas.

7.2.2   The Constructional Approach

In Chapter 4, we saw that constructional schemas are derived from strings of lexical expressions with similar semantic and syntactic properties. On this account, verb-argument schemas represent generalizations over lexical sequences that are organized around particular verbs with similar participants. However, while constructional schemas are based on lexical strings with overlapping properties, they are cognitive entities in their own right and at least partially independent of the expressions from which they are derived.

One crucial piece of evidence for this hypothesis comes from the fact that schemas can be applied to novel items. As many scholars of argument structure have pointed out (Goldberg 1995; Michaelis 2004), constructional schemas can be extended to verbs that were not previously used in this context, as illustrated by the following oft-cited examples from Goldberg (1995: 9; 2006: 6).

(7)   John sneezed the napkin off the table.

(8)   She smiled herself an upgrade.

Usually, *sneeze* and *smile* are used as intransitive verbs, which do not take a direct object, but in these examples, they occur in transitive clauses and receive a causative interpretation that is arguably invoked by the construction. This phenomenon, known as "coercion," provides good evidence for the role of constructional schemas in argument realization and challenges the lexicalist account. Since the lexical entries of *sneeze* and *smile* do not include transitive uses (on most accounts), it is unclear how the sentences in (7) and (8) can be explained by the projection of lexical properties of the verb onto clause structure. There is no obvious solution to this problem in the lexicalist approach, but in construction grammar the novel senses of *sneeze* and *smile* are readily explained by the extension of constructional schemas.

Note, however, that the innovative use of constructional schemas is fairly limited. While *sneeze* and *smile* can be accommodated to the conceptual constraints of the caused-motion construction, this is not always possible with other intransitive verbs. We will consider the factors that influence the innovative use of argument-structure constructions in the second part of this chapter. Here we note that the extension of constructional schemas to novel verbs is only possible if the verb can be construed in a way that fits the conceptual profile of the schema. This is explicitly expressed in Goldberg's "Semantic Coherence Principle," which holds that verbs and schemas can "fuse" if their roles are "semantically compatible" with each other (Goldberg 1995: 50). More precisely, the principle states that "the more specific participant role of the verb must be construable as an instance of the more general argument role" of the constructional schema in order to fuse (Goldberg 2006: 40). In the default case, verbs and schemas specify the same (general) roles, but in the case of coercion, the argument frame of the verb is adapted to the conceptual specifications of the constructional schema.

Coercion is one phenomenon that supports the construction-based approach to argument realization. In addition, Goldberg claims that constructions help to avoid "rampant verb polysemy," which she regards as a problem (Goldberg 1995: 10–13). Since most verbs occur in several syntactic contexts (e.g., *break* and *hit* in 3a–b to 6a–b), one has to stipulate a large number of verb senses in order to explain argument realization in the lexicalist approach (as every projection needs a separate lexical representation). However, if we assume that argument structure is ultimately determined by constructions, the polysemy of verbs is, at least in part, a consequence of their use in different syntactic contexts (§6.5.2).

7.2.3   Lexical Specificity and "Valency Constructions"

Goldberg's research on argument-structure constructions had a strong impact on the development of the usage-based model of grammar. In accordance with other usage-based linguists, she adopted an exemplar-based approach and emphasized the importance of particular tokens for the study of grammar and grammatical development. Note, however, that Goldberg's focus of analysis is on high-level schemas. Like most other scholars of grammar, she is primarily interested in generalizations that abstract away from the properties of particular lexical items. This approach has been criticized, however, by corpus linguists who have stressed the lexical-specific nature of argument structure (e.g., Boas 2008; Faulhaber 2011; Herbst 2014).

If we look at the actual use of verbs in linguistic corpora, we find an enormous amount of lexical idiosyncrasy. Verbs that are closely related in terms of their meaning can show very different syntactic behaviors. For instance, although the verbs *reply* and *respond* are semantically very similar to *answer*, they do not occur with a nominal object referring to a question (9a–c; Faulhaber 2011), and although the verbs *inform* and *notify* are fairly close in meaning to *tell*, they do not occur with two postverbal NPs (10a–c; Boas 2010).

(9)   a. She answered the question.
         b. *She replied the question.
         c. *She responded the question.

(10)   a. She told John a fairy tale.
         b. *She informed John all the beers she had.
         c. *She notified John her thought on the subject.

Similar idiosyncrasies have been observed with many other verbs and argument-structure constructions (Goldberg 1995; Boas 2003; Herbst 2014). Consider, for instance, the verbs of the double-object construction, which according to Goldberg (1995) denotes an act of transfer or giving (e.g., *He gave him the keys*).[1] The double-object construction occurs with a wide range of verbs including *give, send, offer, tell* and *teach*. Note that the use of some of these verbs involves a metaphorical mapping from the domain of physical transfer to the domains of

---

[1] Goldberg (1995) refers to the double-object construction as the "ditransitive construction," but in accordance with most other studies, we use the term "double-object construction" instead.

communication (cf. *He told me a story*) and social interaction (cf. *He offered me a beer*).

The double-object construction is closely related to the *to*-dative construction, in which the recipient is expressed by a prepositional *to*-phrase after the theme. The two constructions differ in terms of information structure (Bresnan et al. 2007), but have very similar meanings. Since both constructions evoke a notion of transfer, it does not come as a surprise that many verbs occur in both constructions; but there are some well-known idiosyncrasies (Goldberg 1995: 129–132):

- First, a significant number of transfer verbs are exclusively found in the *to*-dative construction, which subsumes a much larger number of verb types than the double-object construction. Interestingly, some of the verbs that are restricted to the *to*-dative construction were originally also used in the double-object construction. The verbs *whisper, shout* and *mumble*, for instance, were used with a dative NP preceding the theme in Early Modern English, but are now exclusively found in the *to*-dative construction (Colleman and De Clerck 2011).

- Second, most Latinate verbs denoting transfer (e.g., *contribute, present, transform, remit, explain, inform*) do not occur in the double-object construction, and speakers of English are aware of this. As Gropen et al. (1989) showed, polysyllabic verbs with Romance affixes (e.g., *per-, con-, -mit, -sume*) and/or stress on the noninitial syllable are not (fully) acceptable for English native speakers in the double-object construction.

- And third, the double-object construction occurs with a few verbs that do not encode any sense of transfer. These verbs include both Latinate verbs, such as *envy*, and verbs of Germanic origin, notably *ask* and *forgive*. Interestingly, if we look at the semantic histories of *envy* and *forgive*, we find that both verbs once had a transfer meaning. As Goldberg (1995: 132) noted, *envy* used to mean "to give grudgingly" and *forgive* used to mean "to give or grant."

While most of these restrictions are readily explained by the diachronic developments of individual verbs and the two constructions (Colleman and De Clerck 2011; Zehentner 2018), it must be emphasized that they are not consistent with the (synchronic) generalizations that are expressed by high-level schemas (or general verb classes and linking rules).

Goldberg (1995: 129–132) characterized the above-mentioned restrictions on the use of particular verbs as (synchronic) "exceptions" to the generalizations that are expressed by verb-argument schemas, but other researchers have argued that the lexical idiosyncrasies of argument-structure constructions are so pervasive that high-level schemas are not really useful for explaining the syntactic behaviors of individual verbs (Boas 2003, 2008; Faulhaber 2011; Herbst 2014). While these scholars do not deny the existence of fully schematic argument-structure constructions, they stress the importance of verb-specific information for argument realization. Specifically, they claim that argument realization is primarily determined by "valency constructions" (Herbst 2014) or "mini-constructions" (Boas 2003) that are organized around particular verbs (or very narrow verb classes).

7.3   The Network Approach to Argument Structure

Lexical-specific constructions provide a plausible explanation for the many idiosyncrasies that occur in the domain of argument structure. But do they also account for coercion?

Boas (2003: 260–284) argued that the innovative use of verbs in novel syntactic contexts can be explained by "item-based analogy," which is motivated by local similarities between particular verbs. For instance, considering Goldberg's example of *She sneezed the napkin off the table*, Boas argued that *sneeze* is readily acceptable in this context because the meaning of *sneeze* is related to that of *blow*, which is well established in the caused-motion construction. Like *sneeze*, *blow* denotes a process of "air emission," and since *blow* is conventionally used with a causative meaning, it provides a model for the construal of *sneeze* in the caused-motion construction (11a–b; Boas 2003: 261–262).

(11)   a. The wind blew the leaves off the street.
         b. She sneezed the napkin off the table.

Interestingly, while *sneeze* is easily construable as a causative verb, this is more difficult with other air emission verbs. Consider, for instance, the use of *breath* and *wheeze* in the following examples, which, according to Boas (2003: 272–273), are less acceptable than the use of *sneeze*.

(12)   a. ?Kristin breathed the napkin off the table.
         b. ??Julio wheezed the napkin off the table.

Analyzing the frame-semantic specifications of *breath* and *wheeze*, Boas showed that there is less semantic overlap between *blow* and these two verbs than between *blow* and *sneeze*. In particular, he argued that, while *sneeze* is readily construed as a causative verb in analogy with *blow*, this is not so easily possible with *breath* and *wheeze* because the (air) force that is emitted by breathing and wheezing is usually not strong enough to cause an object (such as a napkin) to move, as in the case of *sneeze*.

Boas's analysis provides good evidence for the role of item-based analogy in the innovative use of argument-structure constructions but says very little about two other factors which, according to Goldberg and others, have a significant impact on the extension of constructional schemas: type frequency and the coherence of a constructional schema (Barðdal 2008; Suttle and Goldberg 2011; Perek 2015).

We return to this issue below (§7.5 and §7.6). Here we note that an adequate account for argument realization must take into consideration that speakers' knowledge of argument structure involves both constructional schemas and a large amount of lexical-specific information, which must not be ignored in grammatical analysis (Diessel 2016).

Moreover, we note that argument realization has an important probabilistic component that is not adequately explained by any account. While it is often recognized that many verbs are biased to occur in particular constructions, this is largely ignored in current theories of argument realization. In fact, in the construction-based literature, it is commonly assumed that constructions include "open slots" that can be filled by any item as long as the item can be construed according to the semantic specifications of the construction (§7.2). Very often, however, lexical items are statistically biased to appear in particular slots (or conversely, slots are biased to be filled by particular items); that is, the co-occurrence of lexemes and constructions is statistically skewed (Manning and Schütze 1999; Stefanowitsch and Gries 2003).

7.3.1   Filler–Slot Relations

Stefanowitsch and Gries (2003) developed a corpus method, known as "collo-structional analysis," to analyze the statistical biases in the distribution of lexemes and constructions. Collostructional analysis is not the only method available for investigating the (statistical) relations between lexemes and con-structions – there are alternative approaches (see Schmid and Küchenhoff 2013 for some discussion), but since collostructional analysis has been used in a large number of studies (e.g., Gries and Stefanowitsch 2004; Gries et al. 2005; Hampe 2011; Hilpert 2013), we will use this method to explain, in general terms, how lexemes and constructions are related.

In order to determine the associations between verbs and argument-structure constructions (or verb-argument schemas) we need the following four frequen-cies: (i) the frequency of a particular verb v_1 in construction c_1, (ii) the frequency of all other verbs in c_1, (iii) the frequency of v_1 in other (related) constructions ($c_2, c_3, c_4 \ldots$) and (iv) the frequency of other (relevant) construc-tions that do not include v_1 (Gries and Stefanowitsch 2004).

Consider, for instance, the following frequencies of *give* in the double-object and *to*-dative constructions in the International Corpus of English (adopted from Gries and Stefanowitsch 2004). Overall, *give* appears 461 times in the double-object construction and 146 times in the *to*-dative construction. In addition, the double-object construction occurs 574 times with other verbs, and the *to*-dative construction occurs 1733 times with other verbs. If we enter these numbers into a two-by-two table, we can calculate (by means of a simple statistical formula) if and to what extent *give* appears more or less frequently than statistically expected in the

Table 7.1 *Distribution of* give *in the double-object and the* to-*dative constructions*

	give	Other verbs	Total
Double-object	461 (213)	574 (822)	1035
to-dative	146 (394)	1773 (1.525)	1919
Total	607	2347	2954

Source: Gries and Stefanowitsch (2004: 102)

two constructions (in Table 7.1 the expected frequencies are indicated in parentheses), and we can use the distance between observed and expected frequencies to calculate (by means of a statistical association measure) how strongly *give* is "attracted" or "repelled" by the two constructions.

As can be seen in Table 7.1, *give* occurs more frequently than expected in the double-object construction, and less frequently than expected in the *to*-dative construction. In other words, *give* is "attracted" by the double-object construction and "repelled" by the *to*-dative construction, but for other verbs, it is the other way around. *Bring*, for instance, is more frequent in the *to*-dative construction than one would expect if the distribution of *bring* were random, and it is less frequent in the double-object construction than statistically expected. Other verbs that are statistically biased to occur in the double-object construction are *tell, show, offer, cost, teach* and *wish*, whereas *play, take, pass, make, sell* and *supply* are biased to appear in the *to*-dative construction (Gries and Stefanowitsch 2004: 104–107).

Stefanowitsch and Gries devised collostructional analysis in order to explore the meanings of constructions. Specifically, they argued that the meaning of a construction is reflected in the meanings of their "collexemes," which are the verbs that are attracted by a particular construction. But this is where I disagree with their analysis. While the meanings of collexemes are usually compatible with the meaning of the construction, this is not always the case. As we have seen, the co-occurrence of verbs and argument-structure constructions exhibits a great deal of semantic idiosyncrasy. The double-object construction, for instance, occurs with verbs such as *envy* and *forgive* that do not evoke any sense of transfer, and the *to*-dative construction occurs with a large number of verbs that are semantically very similar to *give* (and other collexemes of the double-object construction), but are exclusively found in the *to*-dative construction. *Donate*, for instance, is semantically compatible with both constructions, but for most speakers of American English, *donate* is not acceptable in the double-object construction (**She donated the Red Cross 100 Dollars*) (Gropen et al. 1989).

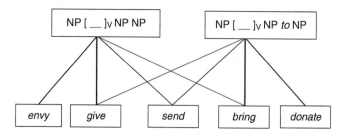

Figure 7.1 Argument-structure network of the double-object and *to*-dative constructions

Similar semantically unmotivated restrictions occur with other verbs and other constructions, suggesting that the co-occurrence of verbs and argument-structure constructions is not fully predictable from general semantic factors. In fact, I suggest that in addition to the semantic fit, it is language users' experience with an established pattern that determines the co-occurrence of lexemes and constructions. Of course, the semantic fit affects speakers' and listeners' linguistic behaviors – their syntactic decisions and lexical choices – which in turn determine their experience with particular lexemes and constructions, so that the two factors are likely to reinforce each other over time; however, as we have seen, language users' linguistic decisions are not always semantically motivated, suggesting that the two factors, that is, semantic fit and experience, are in principle independent of each other (Diessel 2015).

Considering everything that has been said thus far, I conclude that what is needed in order to account for the interaction between verbs and schemas is a probabilistic theory of argument realization. Specifically, I suggest that the relationships between lexemes and constructions are most adequately analyzed in the framework of a dynamic network model that is shaped by language use. On this account, verbs and argument-structure constructions are related to each other by particular types of associations, to which we refer as filler–slot relations, that reflect the combined effect of general semantic factors and language users' experience with particular lexemes and constructions. Figure 7.1 seeks to capture this analysis.

7.3.2   Experimental Evidence

Experimental evidence for the probabilistic nature of argument structure comes from psycholinguistic research on sentence comprehension. There is a large body of results indicating that the processing of argument-structure constructions is influenced by speakers' experience with particular verbs and constructions (Ford et al. 1982; MacDonald et al. 1994; Spivey-Knowlton and Sedivy

1995; Garnsey et al. 1997). Most of this research uses syntactic ambiguity resolution to investigate the effect of (linguistic) experience on sentence comprehension (see MacDonald and Seidenberg 2006 for a review).

For instance, if the direct object of a transitive verb is followed by a prepositional phrase, there are two possible interpretations: either the prepositional phrase is interpreted as a noun modifier of the preceding NP, or it is interpreted as an immediate constituent of the verb or verb phrase. For example, in the sentence *The boy hit the man with a stick*, the *with*-phrase denotes either an instrument of the verb *hit* (i.e., NP V NP PP$_{INST}$) or it functions as a prepositional attribute of the noun *man* (i.e., NP V [NP PP$_{ATTR}$]). Crucially, several studies have found that the interpretation of the ambiguous PP varies with the relative frequency with which particular verbs occur with certain types of adjuncts. Consider, for instance, the two following sentences from a seminal study by Ford et al. (1982: 729), in which participants had to perform a forced choice task to distinguish the two meanings.

(13)   a. The women discussed the dogs on the beach.
         b. The women kept the dogs on the beach.

Although these sentences have the same surface structure, they received very different interpretations: 90 percent of all participants interpreted the sentence in (13a) as a simple transitive clause (in which the prepositional phrase modifies the preceding nominal), but 95 percent of all participants interpreted the sentence in (13b) as a structure with two immediate constituents of the verb. While this contrast seems to reflect, at least in part, a contrast in meaning (Ford et al. 1982), there is evidence that participants' responses were also influenced by their experience with the two verbs in these constructions. As it turns out, three out of four instances of *discuss* occur in simple transitive clauses (i.e., V [NP PP]), but four out of five instances of *keep* occur in constructions with two postverbal constituents (i.e., V [NP] [PP]) (Jurafsky 1996). In other words, *discuss* and *keep* are associated with different argument-structure constructions (Figure 7.2) and this affects the way they are processed.[2]

Parallel effects have been observed with other verbs (Spivey-Knowlton and Sedivy 1995) and other argument-structure constructions (Garnsey et al. 1997). We will return to this research in Chapter 9. Here we note that most (English) verbs are associated with multiple argument-structure constructions and that the strength of these associations is determined by two general factors: (i) the

---

[2] Interestingly, Tanenhaus et al. (1995) showed that in addition to semantics and entrenchment, the situational context can influence the interpretation of an ambiguous PP. If the visual context includes multiple entities that could be interpreted as the referent of the NP before the PP, listeners tend to interpret the PP as a restrictive noun modifier that helps to identify the referent of the previous nominal; but if the visual context is unambiguous, there is a tendency to interpret the PP as an adjunct or adverbial.

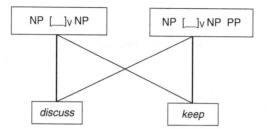

Figure 7.2 Argument-structure network of *discuss* and *keep*

semantic fit of lexemes and constructions, and (ii) the relative frequency with which particular verbs and schemas co-occur. Every time a verb is used in a particular construction, it strengthens the associations between verb and schema. In this way, frequency is also an important determinant for speakers' knowledge of argument structure. Verbs that are frequently used in a particular schema are likely to be reused in that schema in similar situations.

Nevertheless, while there is a tendency to reuse established patterns, it is not uncommon that verb-argument schemas are extended to novel items, as in Goldberg's famous example *She sneezed the napkin off the table*. What motivates the extension of a constructional schema to verbs that were not previously licensed by a particular schema? This is one of the most hotly debated questions in the usage-based literature on argument structure and is immediately related to the usage-based analysis of linguistic productivity.

In the remainder of this chapter, we will consider three general factors that influence the extensibility or productivity of verb-argument schemas: (i) semantic similarity (§7.4), (ii) type and token frequency (§7.5) and the relationships between different argument-structure constructions in the grammar network (§7.6).

7.4   Semantically Motivated Extensions of Verb-Argument Schemas

Let us begin with semantic similarity. Above, we have seen that item-based analogy plays an important role in the analysis of coercion. Specifically, Boas argued that a verb-argument schema is readily extended to a new verb if this verb is semantically similar to one or more verbs that are routinely used in that schema (as in the case of *sneeze* and *blow* in the caused-motion construction). Boas's analysis is based on corpus data, but there is also experimental evidence that item-based analogy affects the innovative use of argument-structure constructions (Suttle and Goldberg 2011). Whatever speakers do in language use is ultimately based on their experience with particular lexical expressions, but while the extension of verb-argument schemas is often motivated by lexical-specific processes (i.e., by item-based analogy), it is also influenced by general semantic features.

According to Pinker (1989), the syntactic behavior of verbs is largely predictable from semantic verb classes that are defined by a limited set of "grammatically relevant" features. Ambridge and colleagues tested this hypothesis in a series of experiments in which child and adult speakers were asked to rate the use of novel verbs of different semantic verb classes in different types of argument-structure constructions (Ambridge et al. 2008, 2012). In accordance with Pinker's hypothesis, these scholars found that their participants' rating scores vary with the degree of semantic overlap (or semantic similarity) between novel verbs and semantic verb classes. If a novel verb is semantically similar to a class of verbs that is routinely used in a particular construction, participants are willing to accept the new verb in the context of this construction, but if there is no semantic overlap (or similarity) between the novel verb and a semantic verb class, participants are reluctant to accept the innovative use.[3]

The influence of semantic features on the productivity of verb-argument schemas is not only evident from people's responses in experiments, it is also reflected in the diachronic developments of argument-structure constructions. Like all other aspects of linguistic knowledge, argument structure is subject to continuous change. This does not only concern the strength of filler–slot relations, but also the type of verbs that are associated with a particular schema. To simplify, we may distinguish between the creation of new filler–slot associations and the loss of established connections. Both developments are influenced by semantic factors. Here are two examples from the recent history of English.

7.4.1   The way-*Construction*

A construction that has acquired a large number of new verb types is the *way*-construction (Israel 1996; Mondorf 2010; Traugott and Trousdale 2013: 76–90). In Present-Day English, the *way*-construction combines the following structural pattern [NP$_i$ V POSS$_i$ *way* OBL] with a particular semantic interpretation, in which an agentive subject performs an action that entails movement

---

[3] The research by Ambridge and colleagues provides good evidence for the effect of semantic verb classes on the productivity of verb-argument schemas. Note, however, that it can be difficult to distinguish the role of semantic verb classes from item-based analogy. Since semantic verb classes are based on particular verbs (with similar semantic properties), it is not always obvious if and to what extent the extension of a verb-argument schema is motivated by the meaning of a particular verb or the semantic features of a whole class of verbs.

along a path even if the action designated by the verb does not directly invoke any sense of motion or path, as in the following examples.

(14)   a. John dug his way out of prison.
        b. Sam joked his way into the meeting.
        c. Sue whistled her way to the front door.

Synchronically, the *way*-construction is highly idiosyncratic, but, as Israel (1996) showed, the construction evolved in Middle English from a more regular pattern in which a general motion verb such as *go* was accompanied by a possessive noun denoting a path (15–16).

(15)   Þe   kniht   tok   leue   and wente his wei.
        The   knight   took   leave   and went   his way
        (Trousdale and Traugott 2013: 80)

(16)   Tho   wente   he   his   strete ...
        Then   went   he   his   street
        (Israel 1996: 223)

As can be seen, *way* was not the only path-denoting noun that appeared in the source constructions. In example (16), the possessed path is denoted by *strete*, but in the course of development, *way* superseded all other nouns in this position and was regularly combined with an oblique phrase denoting the direction of the designated path.

Crucially, while the early instances of the *way*-construction appeared with a few general motion verbs (e.g., *go, ride, run, pass*), the construction was later extended to a wide range of other semantic types of verbs including verbs of laborious motion (*plod, crawl, grind*), verbs of fighting (*fight, force, push*), verbs of clearing and cutting (*cut, dig, poke out*), verbs of road building (*pave, smooth, bridge*) and verbs of noise creation (*crash, crunch, snarl*) (Israel 1996). While some of these verbs are only distantly related to the notions of motion and path, Israel showed that the development of the *way*-construction is motivated by many local semantic extensions between individual verbs and verb classes.

7.4.2   The Double-Object Construction

A construction that has lost a significant number of verb types is the double-object construction. In Old English, ditransitive verbs were commonly used with two case-marked NPs in different case frames and different orders (e.g., V $NP_{DAT} NP_{ACC}$). A few verbs were also used with prepositional objects, but this was relatively rare (Zehentner 2018). In the course of the development, however, the prepositional dative construction has become increasingly more frequent, whereas the double-object construction has been gradually confined to certain semantic verb types. Crucially, the development proceeded in a lexical-specific fashion that was only partially predictable from general semantic criteria (Colleman and De Clerck 2011; Zehentner 2018).

Concentrating on the time period between 1710 and 1920, Colleman and De Clerck (2011) found that a significant number of verbs that occurred with two postverbal NPs at the beginning of the eighteenth century are now exclusively used in the prepositional dative construction, as for instance the verbs *banish* and *whisper* (17–18).

(17)   And a man that could in so little a space, first love me, then hate, then *banish* me his house. (Richardson 1740) (Colleman and De Clerck 2011: 192)

(18)   At her departure she took occasion to *whisper* me her opinion of the widow, whom she called a pretty idiot. (Fielding 1751) (Colleman and De Clerck 2011: 198)

Interestingly, as Colleman and De Clerck showed, the majority of verbs that have lost their connection to the double-object construction pertain to one of three semantic classes: (i) verbs denoting banishment (*banish, dismiss, expel, discharge*), (ii) verbs denoting a particular manner of communication (*whisper, shout, yell, mumble*) and (iii) verbs that entail a beneficiary who is not the intended recipient of a transfer event but who benefits from some other type of event in a particular way (e.g., *She cleaned me my windows).

Another interesting observation of this study is that the double-object uses of *envy* and *forgive* decreased in frequency after they had lost their transfer meanings (§7.2.3). Both the disappearance of entire semantic verb classes and the decreasing frequencies of *envy* and *forgive* suggest that the development of the double-object construction is influenced by general semantic features.

Colleman and De Clerck do not indicate how many verbs the double-object construction has lost during the past 300 years, but judging from their examples, the number must be substantial. Note, however, that the double-object construction also acquired some new category members during the same time period. Specifically, verbs denoting an instrument of communication, such as *fax, email* and *wire*, have been added to the class of verbs that are now routinely used in the double-object construction (e.g., *I emailed him a message*). Needless to say that the extension of the double-object construction to these verbs is also motivated by general semantic features, notably by the semantic similarity between *fax, email* and *wire* and verbs of communicative transfer, such as *tell* and *send*, which are routinely used in the double-object construction. As a consequence of these developments, the double-object construction has now a more specific meaning than it had a few centuries ago (Colleman and De Clerck 2011; Zehentner 2018).

In general, there is abundant evidence that semantic similarity (both the similarity between individual verbs and the similarity between verbs and verb classes) affects the extension of constructional schemas to novel verbs. Yet, the productivity of argument-structure constructions is not only motivated by semantic similarity (which is ultimately a matter of categorization; see §3.5.2), it is also influenced by frequency.

7.5   Frequency and the Internal Structure of Verb-Argument Schemas

Two general types of frequency must be distinguished (§2.4.3): type frequency, which refers to the number of different verb types that appear in a particular schema, and token frequency which refers to the frequency of particular verbs in one or multiple argument-structure constructions. Both types of frequency affect the productivity of verb-argument schemas.

7.5.1   Type Frequency

That type frequency correlates with productivity has been observed in a large number of studies (Bybee 1985; Goldberg 1995; Dąbrowska 2008, among others). According to Bybee (1995: 430), type frequency strengthens the representation of a constructional schema in memory, which in turn determines the availability of that schema for categorizing novel items. In accordance with this view, it has been repeatedly argued that argument-structure constructions that are associated with a large number of verb types are more easily extensible to new items than argument-structure constructions that are only associated with a few verb types (Goldberg 1995: Chapter 5; Barðdal 2008: Chapter 2). There is good evidence that type frequency affects the availability of constructional schemas (Wonnocatt et al. 2008), but note that the effect of type frequency on linguistic productivity is also influenced by the way the various (verb) types are related.

Imagine a verb-argument schema with 20 verb types. In the simplest case, all 20 verbs express the same general semantic concept (e.g., the concept of physical transfer), but there are other possibilities. The 20 verbs could also express several related concepts that are instantiated by particular types of verbs or verb clusters (physical transfer, transfer of communication, etc.). What is more, the conceptual distance between verb clusters is variable and individual clusters can include different numbers of verb types (Goldberg 1995; Barðdal 2008). More generally, the conceptual organization of verb-argument schemas varies with the particular semantic relationships between the verbs that are licensed by a schema. This is illustrated by the three schemas in Figure 7.3, in which individual verbs are represented by colored circles that cluster in certain conceptual areas.

As can be seen, the three schemas "subsume" the same number of verb types, but their internal structures are different. The verbs of schema A form a

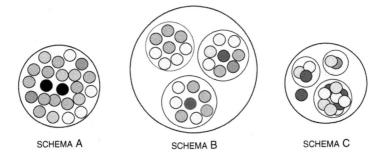

Figure 7.3 Internal structure of three different verb-argument schemas with 20 verb types

homogeneous concept, whereas the two other schemas include verb clusters of semantically related verb types that are more distantly related to the verbs of other clusters within the same schema.

Needless to say, type frequency correlates with the internal (conceptual) organization of verb-argument schemas. Other things being equal, the more verb types are associated with a particular schema, the smaller the distance between individual types and type clusters. Schemas that subsume a very large number of (verb) types are sometimes so densely populated that they lack an internal structure. Bybee (1995: 430) characterized schemas of this type as "open schemas," as they place "few restrictions to the items to which they can apply." Open schemas are generally associated with a large number of types, but the effect of type frequency on productivity is not just a function of "openness," it is also influenced by the overall arrangement of (verb) types and type clusters that define the conceptual space of a constructional schema. There is little research on this topic, but Barðdal (2008) and Suttle and Goldberg (2011) present data and analyses that illustrate how the arrangement of verb types can affect the productivity of verb-argument schemas (see also Madlener 2016).

7.5.2 Token Frequency

Like type frequency, token frequency affects the productivity of verb-argument schemas, but the effect of token frequency is (in some sense) the opposite of that of type frequency, as token frequency typically restricts, or constrains, the extension of constructional schemas to new items. There are two important points to note.

First, since linguistic expressions with high token frequency are deeply entrenched in memory, they often resist the pressure of analogical change or analogical leveling. There is copious evidence for the "preserving effect" of high token frequency in morphology (Bybee 1985, 1988) and the same effect occurs in syntax (Bybee and Thompson 2000). The double-object uses of *envy* and *forgive*, for instance, can be explained by token frequency (§7.2.3). Although these two verbs are no longer semantically compatible with the transfer meaning of the double-object construction, they are still used with two postverbal NPs because these uses are so deeply entrenched in memory that they have survived even after the semantic motivation for using them in the double-object construction disappeared (i.e., after they lost their transfer meaning).

The second important point to be noted about token frequency concerns its role in L1 acquisition. As pointed out in Chapter 4, children overgeneralize the use of verb-argument schemas, as in the following examples of the double-object construction (adopted from Bowerman 1988).

(19)   a. I'll brush him his hair. (2;3)
        b. I said her no. (3;1)
        c. Button me the rest. (3;4)

How do children learn to avoid overgeneralization errors of this type? Pinker (1989) argued that semantic verb classes help to constrain the use of verb-argument schemas. There is some experimental evidence for this hypothesis (Ambridge et al. 2008, 2012), but in addition to semantic verb classes, it is the frequency of particular co-occurrence patterns that restricts the extension of argument-structure constructions. Other things being equal, children are more likely to (over-)extend the use of a verb-argument schema to an infrequent verb than to a frequent one. For instance, Brooks et al. (1999) showed that preschool children are less reluctant to apply the transitive SVO-schema to an infrequent intransitive verb such as *vanish* than to a frequent intransitive verb such as *disappear* (20a-b).

(20)   a. He vanished the rabbit.
        b. He disappeared the rabbit.

Since *vanish* and *disappear* have the same or very similar meanings, it is a plausible hypothesis that children's greater reluctance to extend the transitive schema to *disappear* is related to the fact that *disappear* is more frequent and thus more strongly tied to the intransitive schema than *vanish*. Parallel results were obtained in several related studies (e.g., Stefanowitsch 2008; Ambridge et al. 2012; Robenalt and Goldberg 2015), indicating that the entrenchment effect of token frequency provides an important constraint on the productivity, or extensibility, of argument-structure constructions.

7.6   Grammatical Ecology

Finally, in addition to semantic similarity, type and token frequency and the conceptual organization of verb-argument schemas, we have to consider the ecology of the grammar network to fully understand the cognitive mechanisms that determine the productivity of argument-structure constructions. Thus far, the discussion has concentrated on filler–slot relations, but the productivity of argument-structure constructions is also influenced by constructional relations (i.e., associations between schemas or constructions). In the construction-based literature, it is commonly assumed that every construction has particular semantic and/or pragmatic properties that distinguish it from other constructions in the network (Goldberg 2002); however, although constructions are never fully equivalent (in terms of their functions and meanings), speakers can often choose among several competing argument-structure constructions to express a particular communicative intention. For instance, although the double-object construction and the *to*-dative construction have different information-structure properties, there is an area of overlap between them where both constructions are appropriate to describe a particular event or situation.

If speakers can choose between alternative constructions, there is competition between schemas, which can influence the productivity of argument-structure constructions. Few studies have examined this factor (Wonnacott et al. 2008; Perek 2015; Perek and Goldberg 2015), but they all suggest that the ecology of the grammar network is of central significance to the extension of verb-argument schemas.

7.6.1 Alternating and Nonalternating Verbs

The associations between verbs and constructions typically involve many-to-many relations. As we have seen, many (English) verbs appear in multiple argument-structure constructions. *Give*, for instance, is an alternating verb that occurs in both the double-object and *to*-dative constructions. Likewise *bring*, *lend* and *send* are used in both constructions of the "dative alternation," but there are also nonalternating verbs, such as *donate* and *ask*, that are exclusively found in one or the other construction.

In an important study, Wonnacott et al. (2008) investigated the effect of speakers' experience with alternating and nonalternating verbs on the productivity of argument-structure constructions. In order to control for speakers' experience with particular co-occurrence patterns, these researchers used an artificial language learning paradigm, in which participants were taught a new language consisting of a small set of novel nouns and verbs and two novel transitive constructions (denoting similar scenes). Both constructions occurred with a clause-initial verb, but were distinguished by case marking and word order. In one construction, there was no case marking and the subject preceded the object (VSO), but in the other construction, the subject was marked by *-pa* and followed the object (*VOS-pa*). After five days of training, participants were tested in a series of experiments under various conditions.

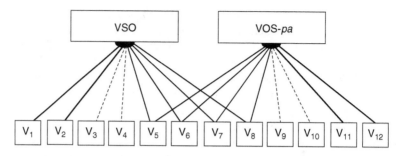

Figure 7.4 Constructional network of an artificial language: experiment 1 of Wonnacott et al. (2008)

In the first experiment, participants were exposed to three different types of verbs: (i) four verbs that occurred exclusively in the VSO construction, (ii) four verbs that occurred exclusively in the VOS-*pa* construction and (iii) four verbs that appeared in both constructions. In addition, token frequency was manipulated: two of the nonalternating verbs were frequent, but the two other non-alternating verbs were infrequent. The four alternating verbs occurred with the same frequency. Figure 7.4 represents the language of experiment 1 in the form of a network in which verbs and constructions are connected by filler–slot relations with different strengths that reflect their frequency during training.

Using three experimental tasks (i.e., a sentence completion task, an online comprehension task and a grammaticality judgment task), Wonnacott et al. made two important observations: First, they found that participants were reluctant to extend the co-occurrence patterns they had encountered during training. Specifically, they observed that while the four alternating verbs appeared in both constructions, the nonalternating verbs were mostly used in the constructions in which they had occurred during training. And second, the researchers found that token frequency had a significant impact on novel uses. While high-frequency verbs were almost exclusively used in the pattern that subjects had heard during training, low-frequency verbs were occasionally extended to the other construction.

Crucially, when Wonnacott et al. increased the proportion of alternating verbs, there was a much stronger tendency to go beyond the learned patterns. In a second experiment, participants were exposed to eight alternating verbs and four nonalternating verbs (Figure 7.5). Under this condition, participants used all 12 verbs alternatingly regardless of their prior distribution, that is, even the non-alternating verbs appeared in both constructions. Moreover, the difference between frequent and infrequent verbs disappeared. In the first experiment, token frequency placed a significant constraint on the use of nonalternating verbs, but, surprisingly, in the second experiment, the constraining effect of

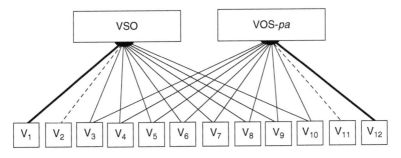

Figure 7.5 Constructional network of an artificial language: experiment 2 of Wonnacott et al. (2008)

token frequency vanished and all 12 verbs were freely used in both constructions, irrespective of their prior frequency and distribution.

Building on these results, a third experiment was designed to compare the responses of two different groups of participants that were exposed to different languages. One group of participants learned a language in which all verbs were exclusively found in only one of the two constructions, and the other group of participants learned a language in which all verbs alternated between constructions. In accordance with the results of experiments 1 and 2, the first group of subjects was lexically conservative with all verbs, that is, there were almost no extensions under this condition, but the second group of subjects used all verbs in both constructions proportional to their frequency in the training phase.

Taken together, this research provides compelling evidence for the hypothesis that the productivity of argument-structure constructions is influenced by the proportions of alternating and nonalternating verb types. If the majority of verbs are exclusively used in one of several competing constructions, speakers are lexically conservative, especially with frequent verbs, but if a large proportion of verbs alternates between constructions, speakers tend to generalize across all verbs and use them in both constructions irrespective of their prior distribution and prior frequency.

7.6.2   Type Frequency versus the Proportion of Alternating Verb Types

Inspired by these findings, Perek (2015) devised an experiment that investigated the effect of alternating verb types on the extensibility of existing argument-structure constructions. Specifically, he examined how the proportion of shared (or alternating) verbs affects the productivity of the double-object construction and *to*-dative construction.

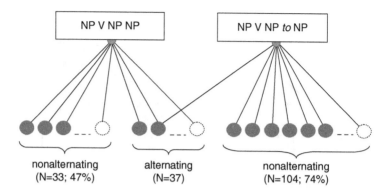

Figure 7.6 Proportion of alternating and nonalternating verbs in the English double-object and *to*-dative constructions (based on data from Perek 2015: 203)

A corpus analysis revealed that the *to*-dative construction does not only occur with a much larger number of verb types than the double-object construction, it also occurs with a much larger proportion of nonalternating verbs. Overall, there were 37 alternating verbs in Perek's data, but, as can be seen in Figure 7.6, the double-object construction includes a much larger proportion of alternating verbs than the *to*-dative construction. In fact, more than half of the verbs in the double-object construction are alternating (53 percent), whereas the vast majority of verbs in the *to*-dative construction are nonalternating (74 percent).

The asymmetry is especially striking in the case of physical transfer verbs. With one exception (that is, *throw*), all verbs of this class alternate in the double-object construction (in Perek's corpus data), but the *to*-dative construction occurs with a large number of nonalternating transfer verbs (e.g., *play, take, return*). Verbs of other semantic classes (e.g., communication verbs) are less strongly skewed in this regard, but the asymmetry goes in the same direction (Perek 2015: 200–203).

Considering these distributions, we may hypothesize that speakers are more productive with the *to*-dative than with the double-object construction. Perek tested this hypothesis in an experiment in which participants listened to a short story including a novel verb, such as *pell*, in one of the two variants of the dative alternation, referring either to a process of physical transfer (21a) or to an act of communication (21b).

(21)   a. Sam *pelled* Susan a package.
       b. Sam *pelled* Susan the news.

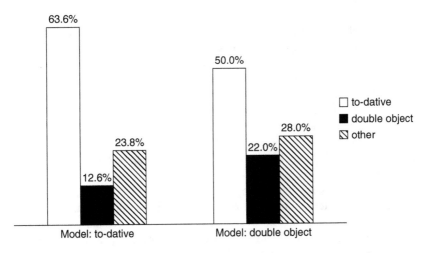

Figure 7.7 Percentage of *to*-dative and double-object responses after *to*-dative and double-object constructions with novel verbs (based on data from Perek 2015: 186)

When the story ended, participants had to complete a sentence prompt consisting of a subject and a nonce verb (e.g., *Sam pelled . . .*) in order to answer a question about the story (e.g., *What did Sam do?*). As expected, there was a striking asymmetry in participants' use of the two constructions: When the novel verb had occurred in the *to*-dative construction, participants overwhelmingly used the same construction (i.e., the *to*-dative) to answer the question, but when the novel verb had occurred in the double-object construction, they did not favor the same construction, but often applied the *to*-dative to the novel verb. As can be seen in Figure 7.7, while the *to*-dative was especially frequent when the novel verb was introduced in the *to*-dative construction (model: *to*-dative), it was also more frequently used when the novel verb was introduced in the double-object construction (model: double-object): only 22 percent of the participants' responses involved the double-object construction with verbs that had appeared in that construction, whereas 50 percent of their responses involved the *to*-dative construction (the remaining 28 percent involved other responses). In other words, there was a general preference for the *to*-dative construction (in both conditions) and a strong tendency to extend the use of the *to*-dative to novel verbs (in condition 2). This tendency was especially prominent in the case of physical transfer verbs, but was also evident with verbs of communication (Perek 2015: 186; see also Conwell and Demuth 2007 and Arunachalam 2017 for parallel results with preschool children).

Since the *to*-dative construction includes a much larger number of verb types than the double-object construction, one might hypothesize that type frequency accounts for the greater productivity of the *to*-dative construction, but there is reason to believe that participants' responses were also (or even primarily) determined by the different proportions of alternating and nonalternating verb types. As Perek points out, if a construction includes a large proportion of alternating verb types (like the double-object construction), a language user is likely to assume that a novel verb is also alternating; but if a construction includes only a small proportion of alternating verbs (like the *to*-dative construction), it is less likely that a novel verb is alternating (see also Wonnocatt et al. 2008).

This hypothesis is supported by data from a second experiment on the so-called locative alternation (Perek 2015: 177–194). As can be seen in (22) and (23), the locative alternation involves two semantically related constructions that are distinguished by word order and the occurrence of different prepositions (Levin and Hovav 2005: 17–18).

(22)   Pat sprayed paint on the wall.
(23)   Pat sprayed the wall with paint.

Like the two variants of the dative alternation, the two variants of the locative alternation occur with both alternating and nonalternating verbs, but the proportion of nonalternating verb types is much smaller than in the case of the dative alternation. In Perek's data, 21.3 percent of the verbs in the double-object and *to*-dative constructions are alternating, but only 5.3 percent of the verbs of the locative alternation occur in both constructions; that is, the vast majority of verb types are nonalternating in the locative alternation (94.7 percent).

What is more, both constructions of the locative alternation are primarily used with nonalternating verbs. As can be seen in Figure 7.8, the *on*-variant includes a much larger number of verb types than the *with*-variant. The asymmetry is even more pronounced than in the case of the dative alternation; however, more important is the fact that both constructions (of the locative alternation) are primarily used with nonalternating verbs, whereas one of the variants of the dative alternation (i.e., the double-object construction) occurred with a larger number of alternating verbs than with nonalternating verbs (see Figure 7.6 above).

Using the same experimental paradigm as in the above-described study of the dative alternation, Perek found that participants were lexically conservative with both variants of the locative alternation. Although the *on*-variant subsumes an even larger number of verb types than the *to*-dative, participants were reluctant to extend the *on*-construction to verbs that were introduced in the *with*-construction (and vice versa). This suggests that the high degree of

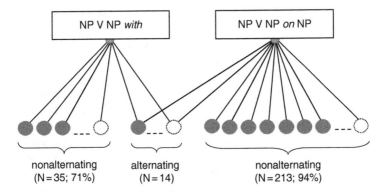

Figure 7.8 Proportion of alternating and nonalternating verbs in the two constructions of the locative alternation (based on data from Perek 2015: 204)

productivity that characterizes the *to*-dative construction is not primarily a function of type frequency but of the particular distribution of alternating and nonalternating verb types in the dative alternation. Since speakers know that most verbs of the double-object construction are also used in the *to*-dative construction, they tend to assume that novel verbs allow for the same alternation and extend the *to*-dative construction to verbs which they (first) witnessed in the double-object construction.

7.6.3   Constructional Relations

Finally, Perek and Goldberg (2015) showed that speakers' choice of construction is not only influenced by the proportion of alternating verb types, but also by constructional relations between competing schemas. Adopting the approach of Wonnocatt et al. (2008), these researchers exposed participants to a set of novel verbs that appeared in two transitive constructions with different word orders: SOV and OSV. The experimental design was very similar to that of Wonnocatt et al., but there was one important difference: The constructions Perek and Goldberg used were not functionally equivalent, as in the Wonnocatt study, but had different information-structure properties. Specifically, the OSV-construction included a pronominal object, which typically refers to a familiar (or topical) entity, whereas the SOV-construction occurred with two lexical NPs (which typically refer to nontopical entities).

What the researchers wanted to find out is how learners deal with nonalternating verbs if the discourse context motivates the extension of a learned pattern to a novel combination of verb and argument-structure construction. Will they be lexically conservative as in the Wonnocatt study? Or will the discourse pressure increase their willingness to apply a constructional schema to a new item?

After several days of training, participants were asked two different questions: (i) *What happened to the patient?*, which is biased to elicit the OSV-construction with a pronominal object, and (ii) *What happened here?*, which is biased to elicit the SOV-construction, as transitive clauses typically begin with an agentive subject (unless the discourse context favors a different order).

As expected, the researchers found that the pragmatic bias of the question had a significant impact on participants' responses. When the researchers asked *What happened to the patient*, participants were likely to use the OSV-construction to answer the question, but when they asked *What happened here*, the vast majority of participants responded by using the SOV-construction. Crucially, while participants' experience with alternating and nonalternating verbs had a noticeable effect on their responses, there was a clear tendency to use the pragmatically appropriate construction with all verbs (even when the verb had not occurred in that construction during the training phase), suggesting that the productivity of competing verb-argument schemas is influenced by their semantic and/or pragmatic relationships to other constructions in the network. We will return to this issue in Chapters 10 and 11.

7.7   Conclusion

Building on research in construction grammar, the current chapter has proposed a network model of argument structure in which verbs and verb-argument schemas are connected by filler–slot associations. These associations are shaped by two general aspects of language use: (i) the semantic fit between verbs and schemas (which is ultimately a matter of categorization), and (ii) language users' experience with particular co-occurrence patterns (which reflects the effect of automatization and conventionalization).

The network approach sheds new light on the analysis of linguistic productivity. While speakers are generally inclined to reuse frequent co-occurrence patterns (§10.3), there are situations in which they extend the use of verb-argument schemas to novel items. Considering evidence from research on L1 acquisition, language change and language use, the chapter has shown that the productivity of argument-structure constructions is determined by an intricate interplay between semantic, pragmatic and statistical aspects of language use. Specifically, we have seen that the following factors affect the extension of verb-argument schemas:
- the semantic similarity between individual verbs and verb classes,
- the conceptual organization of verb-argument schemas,
- the proportion of alternating and nonalternating verb types,
- the token frequency of particular co-occurrence patterns,

- and the semantic-pragmatic relations between competing argument-structure constructions.

Note that type frequency is not included in this list as a separate factor. However, since type frequency is an important aspect of the conceptual organization of argument-structure constructions and the proportion of alternating and nonalternating verb types, it is implicit in two of the five above-mentioned factors.

8   A Dynamic Network Model of Parts of Speech

8.1   Introduction

In most grammatical theories, word classes, also known as parts of speech, have the status of primitive concepts. They are generally included in the toolkit of linguistic categories that structural and generative linguists use for the analysis of syntactic structure (Chapter 1). However, in the usage-based approach, grammatical word classes are emergent categories that evolve from the interaction between lexemes and constructions.

This chapter presents a dynamic network approach to the analysis of grammatical word classes parallel to the network analysis of argument structure proposed in Chapter 7. Specifically, the chapter argues that the major parts of speech are best analyzed in terms of associative connections between lexemes and particular semantically and pragmatically specified slots of constructional schemas.

The proposed analysis builds on studies by Langacker (1991: 59–100) and Croft (1991: 36–148; 2001: 63–107), which in turn are based on earlier accounts by Dixon (1977) and Hopper and Thompson (1984). Yet, while all of these studies are related to the current approach, the present chapter emphasizes more strongly than any previous account that word class systems are dynamic and shaped by language use.

Two basic types of linguistic expressions are commonly distinguished in the analysis of parts of speech: content words, which subsume the major word classes of nouns, verbs and adjectives;[1] and grammatical function words, which are commonly divided into a set of minor word class categories including adpositions, auxiliaries and conjunctions (Schachter and Shopen 2007). The two types of expressions (i.e., content words and grammatical function words) serve very different functions in discourse and grammar but are diachronically related. As research on grammaticalization has shown, most grammatical function words are derived from content words, notably from nouns and verbs (Hopper and Traugott 2003) or from demonstratives (Diessel 2012a). In this chapter, the main

---

[1] In addition, (most) adverbs are content words, but adverbs will not be considered in this chapter.

focus of analysis is on the three major parts of speech – that is, nouns, verbs and adjectives – but at the end of the chapter, we will also take a look at some of the minor word class categories and their relationship to content words.

8.2   The Network Approach to Grammatical Word Classes

There are two main approaches to the study of parts of speech: the semantic approach and the structural or distributional approach. In the semantic approach, the major word classes are defined by particular semantic criteria. Traditionally, it is said that nouns designate entities, verbs designate actions and adjectives designate properties. The semantic word classes correlate with structural features such as case and tense inflection or the occurrence of particular function words. However, since the structural features of nouns, verbs and adjectives are not fully predictable from semantic criteria, many linguists have abandoned the semantic approach in favor of a purely structural analysis of parts of speech. On this account, word class categories are defined by a set of distributional criteria that are easily identified by linguistic scholars (or automatic speech taggers). The distributional method groups lexemes with the same or similar properties into formal classes that are more consistent in their grammatical behavior than the semantic word classes of traditional grammar (§4.4). However, as Croft (2001: 29–47) showed in an important study, the distributional method is not without problems.

One of these problems is that it does not help the linguist to identify nouns, verbs and adjectives (see also Croft 1991: 45–46). In practice, many linguistic scholars take the occurrence of particular grammatical morphemes as evidence for a certain category. The occurrence of case markers, for instance, is commonly interpreted as evidence for the category of noun, and the occurrence of tense-aspect markers is taken as evidence for the category of verb. This approach is problematic, however, as the occurrence of case markers and tense-aspect markers is not restricted to items that qualify as nouns and verbs by other criteria (§8.3.2).

What is more, in order to be able to characterize grammatical morphemes as markers of case, tense-aspect or any other category, one must take semantic factors into account (Croft 2001: Chapter 2). It is only when we consider the meaning of a particular function word (or affix) in conjunction with the meaning of its lexical hosts that we are able to distinguish case markers from tense-aspect markers and other grammatical morphemes. In other words, the distributional method cannot do away with semantic criteria in order to define nouns, verbs and adjectives.

Both approaches, the semantic approach and the distributional method, can be used to group lexemes into classes with the same or similar properties, but they need to be combined in order to analyze the major parts of speech. In what follows, we will consider an approach in which the correlations between the semantic and formal properties of nouns, verbs and adjectives emerge from the interaction between lexemes and constructions in a dynamic network.

Traditionally, the morphosyntactic properties of nouns, verbs and adjectives are seen as properties of particular lexical items, but they can also be seen as properties of particular slots of constructional schemas. In English, for instance, nouns are commonly defined by distributional criteria such as the occurrence of a determiner, the plural suffix -*s* and a subsequent or preceding verb, which together specify a set of "noun slots" in morphological and syntactic schemas (1a–d).

(1)   a. [DET [___]$_N$]
       b. [___]$_N$-*s*
       c. [ADJ [___]$_N$]
       d. [[___]$_N$ VERB [___]$_N$]

Crucially, while the slots of grammatical word classes are commonly defined by distributional criteria, they are not merely structural positions. As we have seen in previous chapters, the slots of constructional schemas evoke particular semantic specifications. The double-object construction, for instance, includes a verb slot for certain semantic types of action words denoting transfer and three associated noun slots for referring terms (§7.3). Each slot has a particular semantic profile that is ultimately derived from language users' experience with strings of lexical expressions in particular communicative situations (§4.5).

In accordance with this view, the current chapter argues that the major word classes are best analyzed by associative connections between lexemes and particular semantically (and pragmatically) specified slots of constructional schemas. The gist of the analysis is the same as in the previous analysis of argument structure: Grammatical constructions attract lexemes that match the conceptual profile of a particular slot, and they repel lexemes that do not match their semantic specifications. However, as we have seen in Chapter 7, while the associations between lexemes and constructions (or slots) are semantically motivated, they are also influenced by language users' experience with particular items and constructions. Lexemes that are frequently used in particular slots become associated with certain word class categories irrespective of any semantic criteria.

8.3   Nouns and Verbs

Having outlined the general approach, let us now turn to the analysis of particular word class categories. We begin with nouns and verbs and then turn to adjectives.

There are many different ways in which content words can be grouped together to form semantic classes. Word meanings are extremely rich and diverse, but when we look at the use of lexemes in a sentence, we find that, while content words are semantically diverse, they are consistently used with particular communicative functions: A sentence usually includes at least one item that is used to identify a referent, and one item that is used to say something about the identified referent. As Sapir (1921: 119) observed: "There must be something to talk about and something must be said about this subject of discourse once it is selected."

Building on this observation, Croft (1991) proposed a theory of parts of speech that crucially relies on the pragmatic functions of lexemes in a sentence or speech act. Specifically, Croft argued, based on Searle (1969: Chapters 4 and 5), that speech acts include two basic "propositional act functions" that are performed by content words: the "act of reference" and the "act of predication":

The act of reference is that of identifying some entity, that is, the entity that the speaker intends to talk about (Searle 1969: 85). The act of predication is the act of ascribing a property to the referred-to entity. (Croft 1991: 110)

The two propositional acts determine the basic structure of a sentence (or speech act) and provide a foundation for the analysis of nouns and verbs. In a first step, we may say that nouns are used for reference and verbs for predication (Croft 1991, 2001; Hengeveld 1992, among others), but this statement must be qualified. As pointed out above, traditionally word class categories are assumed to be determined by inherent properties of lexical items, but in what follows we will see that the speech act functions of reference and predication do not immediately apply to lexical items but to particular slots of constructions to which we refer to as "N/V-schemas."

8.3.1 N/V-Schemas

Lexical items that occur in the noun slot of a constructional schema are used for reference regardless of their semantic content. For instance, although an item such as *talk* designates an action, it serves as a referring term, if it precedes a verb at the beginning of a sentence (e.g., *His talk was boring*), but if it follows a referring term, it serves as a predicating expression (e.g., *John talked about his new book*). Crucially, while the slots for nouns and verbs are characterized by speech act functions, they also provide particular conceptualizations (Langacker 1991: 59–100; Croft 1991: 107–109; see also Searle 1969: §3.2.2). Consider, for instance, the two uses of *walk* in (2a–b).

(2)   a. They walked to school.
       b. Their walk to school

In both examples, *walk* designates an action, but the designated action is conceptualized in different ways. In (2a), where *walk* is used for predication, the action is conceptualized as a process, but in (2b), where *walk* is used for reference, it is conceptualized as some kind of thing. Langacker (1991: 59–100) argues that nouns and verbs can be seen as constructional schemas that "construe" the "semantic content" of a lexeme in a particular way. Nouns, or N-schemas, construe (or conceptualize) the semantics of a lexeme as a time-stable entity, which Langacker calls a "thing," whereas verbs, or V-schemas, construe the semantics of a lexeme as a transitory event, which Langacker calls a "process." The distinction between "things" and "processes" involves two conceptual properties: things are nonrelational and atemporal, and processes are relational and temporal (Langacker 2008: 103–112).

There is a close connection between communication and conceptualization. As Croft (1991: 108–109) explains: "We organize our experience, encoded by the semantics of lexical items, in a particular way in order to communicate it to our interlocutors." Specifically, we may say that in the current case, speakers conceptualize the meaning of a lexeme as a "thing" in order to perform the act of reference, and they conceptualize the meaning of a lexeme as a "process" in order to perform the act of predication.

The different conceptualizations that are evoked by N/V-schemas are reflected in the linguistic properties of the items whose meaning they structure. For instance, a lexeme that is conceptualized as a "thing" by an N-schema becomes available for reference tracking even if the designated referent is an event, as in the case of *talk* (in 3a); and a lexeme that is conceptualized as a "process" by a V-schema has valency even if the (basic) lexical meaning of the item is nonrelational, as in the case of *spoon* (in 3b). Table 8.1 provides a summary of the previous discussion.

(3)   a. I heard three *talks*$_i$. They$_i$ were all very interesting.
        b. He *spooned* the ice cream into a bowl.

Table 8.1 *Pragmatic and conceptual properties of N/V-schemas*

	Propositional act functions	Conceptual properties
N-schemas	reference	thing (= nonrelational and atemporal)
V-schemas	predication	process (= relational and temporal)

8.3.2   The Hierarchical Organization of N/V-Schemas

N/V-schemas occur in various constructions, which may be divided into three basic types: (i) morphological constructions, which are marked by a particular affix (e.g., [__-SG], [__-PST]), (ii) phrasal constructions, which include a free function word (e.g., [DET __], [AUX __]), and (iii) syntactic constructions, which include at least two content words. Argument-structure constructions, for instance, include at least two N/V-schemas that are distinguished either by linear order or the co-occurrence of morphological or phrasal constructions. The three types of constructions are hierarchically related: morphological constructions are embedded in phrasal constructions, and phrasal constructions are embedded in syntactic constructions (Figure 8.1).

The hierarchical organization of N/V-schemas constitutes an important aspect of speakers' word class knowledge and is the product of grammaticalization. As we will see in Chapter 9, morphological constructions are derived from phrasal constructions, which in turn are derived from syntactic constructions (§9.3–§9.6). These developments are crucial for understanding why nouns and verbs tend to occur with certain types of grammatical markers. As we will see, although nouns and verbs can occur with a wide range of grammatical markers, there are cross-linguistic tendencies in the encoding of the major word classes that result from cross-linguistically similar developments of N/V-schemas.

Note that while there is a tendency to use N/V-schemas consistently across the three levels in Figure 8.1, this is not generally the case. English makes a fairly rigid division between N-schemas and V-schemas across levels, but other languages are more flexible in this regard. In Tagalog, for instance, it is not uncommon that a fully inflected verb marked for voice and mood is

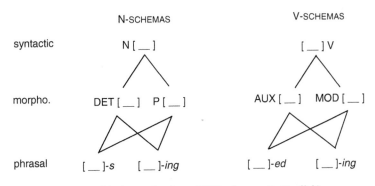

Figure 8.1 Hierarchical organization of N/V-schemas (in English)

accompanied by the specific indefinite article *ang*, as in example (4), which converts the whole structure into an N-schema at the phrasal level.

(4)   iuuwi   nya   [**ang** àalaga'-**an**   nya]
       VOICE.returned.home 3SG.POSS ART cared.for-VOICE 3SG.POSS
       'He would return the ones he was going to care for.' (Himmelmann 2008: 13)

Constructional inconsistencies of this type are characteristic of subordinate clauses (Cristofaro 2003). Since subordinate clauses designate actions or events, they often include inflected verb forms, as in Tagalog; but since subordinate clauses also serve as arguments (or attributes) in the main clause, they often fill the N-slot at a higher level of syntactic organization, which is reflected in the occurrence of grammatical morphemes that are characteristic of N-schemas. The following examples from Japanese (5), Lakhota (6) and Diegueño (7) include subordinate clauses with finite verbs that are accompanied by nominalizers, demonstratives and case affixes (which is cross-linguistically very frequent).

(5)   Taroo=wa [Hanako=ga   hasittekita=**no**]=**o**   tukamaeta.
       Taro=TOP   Hanako=NOM   came running=NML=ACC caught
       'Taro caught Hanako who came running.' (Ohara 1992: 102)

(6)   Wičháša ki [[šúka ki igmú   wą   ø-ø-yaxtáke]   **ki**   **he**]
       man   the dog the cat   a   3SG.P-3SG.A-bite the   DEM
       wą-ø-ø-yáke   yelo.
       3SG.P-3SG.A-see   DEC
       'The man saw the cat which the dog bit.' (Van Valin and LaPolla 1997: 499)

(7)   'nʸaː-c '-iːca-s   [puy ta-'-nʸ-way]-**pu-Ø**.
       I-SUBJ I-remember-EMPH   there ASP-I-be-there-DEM-OBJ
       'I remember that we were there.' (Jany 2008: 46)

8.3.3   N/V-Lexemes

Having analyzed the conceptual and communicative properties of N/V-schemas, let us now turn to the lexical items that are associated with these schemas. To repeat the general hypothesis: The associative connections between lexemes and word class schemas are semantically motivated and shaped by frequency of language use. Let us begin with the semantic motivations for the associations between lexemes and N/V-schemas.

If we look at the items that are used as nouns and verbs (for reference and predication), we find that while N/V-schemas are not restricted to particular semantic types of lexical expressions, there is a strong tendency for N-schemas to occur with items that designate objects and animate beings, whereas V-schemas tend to occur with items that designate actions and events. Consider,

Table 8.2 *Correlations between propositional act functions and semantic word classes*

		Objects	Actions	Others	Total
Quiché	Reference	**176**	0	13	189
	Predication	0	**108**	12	120
Nguna	Reference	**254**	10	0	264
	Predication	15	**113**	51	179
Soddo	Reference	**183**	8	1	192
	Predication	7	**75**	13	79
Ute	Reference	**161**	2	1	164
	Predication	2	**156**	82	240

Source: Croft (1991: 88–90)

for instance, the data in Table 8.2, which Croft (1991: 87–93) collected from text samples of four languages (Quiché, Nguna, Soddo and Ute) in order to examine the semantic properties of lexical expressions that are used for reference and predication.

As can be seen, in all four languages, the act of reference typically involves lexical expressions that designate "objects" (e.g., Engl. *stone, car, boy*), whereas the act of predication typically involves lexical expressions that designate "actions" (e.g., Engl. *run, kick, give*). Assuming that the two propositional act functions, that is, reference and predication, are expressed by particular N/V-schemas, the data in Table 8.2 provide strong evidence for the hypothesis that the major word class schemas attract particular semantic types of lexical expressions: N-schemas attract items that denote time-stable entities, which Croft called "objects," and V-schemas attract items that denote transitory events, which he called "actions." The cognitive mechanism behind this correlation is arguably the same as in the case of verbs and argument-structure constructions: There is a tendency to combine schemas and lexemes that are semantically compatible with each other. This is in essence Goldberg's Semantic Coherence Principle (§7.2.2), which does not only account for the interaction between verbs and argument-structure constructions, but also for the oft-noted correlation between semantic word classes and syntactic categories. A revised version of the Semantic Coherence Principle is given in (8).

(8)   Semantic Coherence Principle (revised version)
        Constructional schemas attract lexical items that are compatible with the semantic specifications of particular slots.

The Semantic Coherence Principle is of central significance to the analysis of syntactic categories, but in order to fully understand how lexemes and schemas are related, we have to consider a second factor that interacts with the Semantic Coherence Principle. As we have seen (Chapter 7), the relationship between verbs and argument-structure constructions is not fully predictable from semantic criteria. There are many idiosyncrasies that must be stored in memory and that can only be explained by language users' experience with particular verbs and constructions. The same argument applies to the analysis of parts of speech. The interaction between lexemes and N/V-schemas is semantically motivated but not fully predictable from semantic criteria. For instance, although the English word *hammer* designates an object, it is also used as a predicating term (in V-schemas), and although the lexeme *game* designates an action, it is primarily used as a referring term (in N-schemas).

Lexical items of this type challenge purely semantic analyses of nouns and verbs, but provide indirect support for an experience- or usage-based analysis of syntactic categories, as they arguably reflect the effect of memory and entrenchment on speakers' grammatical knowledge. Although lexemes do not always match the semantic profile of a certain word class schema, speakers have no difficulties with semantically nonmatching items, as they know (from their experience with particular items) if and how commonly a lexeme is used in a particular schema as a particular category. While this is usually ignored in linguistic studies, there is good evidence that language users associate individual lexemes with particular word class schemas based on their experience with certain co-occurrence patterns.

One piece of evidence for this hypothesis comes from psycholinguistic research on multifunctional expressions that are associated with different categories (MacDonald et al. 1994; Trueswell 1996). Consider, for instance, an item such as *kissed*, which can be a verb in past tense or a passive participle. After nouns, both uses are possible (9a–b), but the past tense use is much more frequent in this position.

(9)   a. The boy kissed ... the girl. PAST
        b. The boy kissed ... by the girl (... fell in love with her). PARTICIPLE

This explains why a sentence such as *The horse raced past the barn fell* is difficult to process. As Bever (1970) and others demonstrated, there is a very strong tendency to interpret *raced* (or some other V-*ed* form) as a past tense verb after nouns, but this can create comprehension problems when the parser encounters another verb (as in 9b), as the initial interpretation of *raced* as a past tense verb must now be changed to an interpretation in which it serves as the past participle of a reduced relative clause. Crucially, while this has been interpreted as evidence for a syntactic strategy of sentence processing (Frazier 1985), there is now abundant evidence that the strength of the garden-path effect correlates with language users' experience with particular lexical items. Verbs such as *raced* which are primarily used in active voice

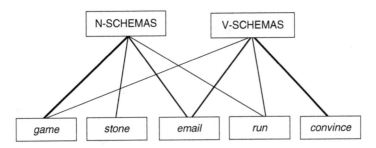

Figure 8.2 Word class network of lexemes and N/V-schemas (in English)

create a strong garden-path effect in relative clauses; but the effect is much less pronounced with verbs such as *kissed* or *named* that are frequently used in passive voice (cf. *A horse named Bill fell*) (Trueswell 1996; MacDonald and Seidenberg 2006).

Similar results have been obtained in many other psycholinguistic studies with other multifunctional expressions (for reviews, see MacDonald et al. 1994; MacDonald and Seidenberg 2006). In general, there is compelling evidence that frequency of language use creates associative connections between individual lexemes, categories and constructions. If a lexeme is frequently used as a particular category in a certain context, or construction, it becomes associated with that category, or construction, even if the associative link is not specifically motived by semantic factors (Chapter 7).

To summarize the discussion thus far, I have argued that constructions include slots, or N/V-schemas, for reference and predication that attract lexical items with particular semantic properties. Lexemes and N/V-schemas are associated with each other by probabilistic links, or filler–slot relations, that are determined by two general factors: (i) the semantic fit of lexemes and N/V-schemas (i.e., the Semantic Coherence Principle), and (ii) the frequency with which individual items (or classes of similar items) are experienced in particular positions. Figure 8.2 illustrates this analysis with a few selected examples from English.

Some items are exclusively found with one or the other type of schema (e.g., *convince*), other items are linked to both word class schemas but are statistically biased to occur in one of them (e.g., *stone, run*), and yet others are about equally frequent in both schemas (e.g., *email*). Not all associations are semantically motivated. *Game*, for instance, designates an action but is primarily used in N-schemas. However, the vast majority of lexical items match the conceptual profile of the associated schema. What is more, Croft (1991) showed that the nonmatching items are often accompanied by an extra morpheme, which he interprets as an instance of "structural markedness" (see also Croft 2003: 87–101).

Structural markedness refers to an encoding asymmetry between related grammatical categories or constructions such as singular and plural nouns. If we look at the encoding of these categories from a cross-linguistic perspective, we find that the more frequent category is usually "unmarked," whereas the less frequent category member often occurs with a particular morpheme. For instance, while plural nouns are commonly "marked" by a plural suffix, the corresponding singular forms are frequently "unmarked" or "zero-coded" (Bybee 2011: 144). We will consider encoding asymmetries of this type in detail in Chapter 11. Here we concentrate on a few general aspects of structural markedness in the encoding of word classes.

As Croft (1991: 51–87) observed, if there is an asymmetry in the encoding of the major word classes, it usually involves a formal contrast between the dominant and the less frequent use of a lexeme. Specifically, we find that lexemes denoting actions often occur with a nominalizing morpheme if they are used for the act of reference, whereas lexemes denoting objects may occur with a verbalizing morpheme if they are used for the act of predication. To illustrate this with examples from English, lexemes denoting actions are (often) nominalized by a derivational morpheme if they occur in an N-schema. Some nominalizing affixes add a particular semantic feature to the lexical host (e.g., *kill-er*), but others have no other function than to reify the denoted action in order to make it available for its referring use in a (syntactic) N-schema (10a–b). Action nominalizations of this type are very common across languages and are usually expressed by an extra morpheme (Koptjevskaja-Tamm 1993).

(10)   a. destruct → destruct-*ion*
        b. govern → govern-*ment*

Items denoting objects can often be used without an additional marker in a V-schema (e.g., *They bridge the gap*). English is very flexible in this regard (Clark and Clark 1979). There are few verbalizing affixes in English (11a), but note that expressions denoting objects or animate beings are accompanied by the copula *be* if they are used for the act of predication in presentational or identificational constructions (11b). Both the occurrence of nominalizing and verbalizing affixes and the use of copular verbs in predicate nominal constructions are consistent with Croft's hypothesis that content words are frequently accompanied by an extra morpheme if their meaning does not match the semantic profile of an N/V-schema.

(11)   a. hospital → hospital-*ize*
        b. author → *is* author

Excursus: Are Nouns and Verbs Universal?   The distinction between nouns and verbs is foundational to the organization of grammar. It constitutes the center of the word class network and provides a basis for the organization of phrase structure (Chapter 9). In accordance with this view, it is widely assumed that the categories of noun and verb are universal (e.g., Hopper and Thompson 1984). However, some recent studies in linguistic typology have questioned this view, arguing that every language has its own syntactic categories that cannot be adequately analyzed by a universal set of grammatical concepts (Dryer 1997; Croft 2001; Haspelmath 2010).

These studies have launched an intensive debate about the nature of "cross-linguistic categories," including the categories of noun and verb (e.g., Broschart 1997; Croft 2001; Evans and Osada 2005; Chung 2012; Van Lier and Rijkhoff 2013). The debate has shed new light on language universals but suffers from terminological confusion. In what follows, we will consider the status of nouns and verbs as cross-linguistic categories in the context of the current network model. To this end, we will consider three hypotheses about the universality of nouns and verbs.

Hypothesis 1. All languages have constructions that combine the act of reference with the act of predication.

Hypothesis 1 should be uncontroversial. Since reference and predication are foundational to human communication, the two propositional act functions are very likely to be universal. Note, however, that not all communicative acts involve the distinction between reference and predication. As pointed out in Chapter 4, the first utterances children produce are holophrases that do not formally distinguish between reference and predication. For example, when a child says "cookie," the word "cookie" serves a double function: it directs a hearer's attention onto a particular referent and indicates a particular communicative intention (e.g., that the child would like to have the cookie). In other words, one-word utterances of this type entail both reference and predication, but the propositional acts are not expressed by distinct elements.

The same holds true for animal communication. While some nonhuman primates appear to have a limited capacity to combine signs (gestures or calls) (Clay and Zuberbühler 2011), their communicative acts are not structured by propositional act functions (Tomasello 1999: 153). It seems that the distinction between reference and predication is a unique trait of adult human communication.

Building on this view, Arbib (2012: 252–269) argues that the development of holophrases to multiword utterances does not only mark a milestone in L1 acquisition but also in language evolution. Specifically, he claims that the communicative acts of early human language, which he calls "protolanguage," involved "unitary utterances," or "holophrases," that developed into multiword expressions through "fractionation" (Arbib 2012: 180, 254). While this hypothesis is difficult to verify, it does not seem to be implausible that the distinction between reference and predication in speech acts marks the result of an important step in language evolution, which ultimately led to the development of syntactic word classes. A crucial step in this development would have been the emergence of N/V-schemas, which leads us to the second hypothesis about the universality of nouns and verbs.

Hypothesis 2. All languages have (some) formally distinct N/V-schemas.

Above, we have seen that English has a rich inventory of hierarchically organized N/V-schemas that are characterized by particular structural properties. The morphosyntactic properties of N/V-schemas are language-particular. English, for instance, has morphological N-schemas that indicate number (cf. [N-*s*]) and morphological V-schemas that indicate tense (cf. [V-*ed*]). Number and tense inflection are also found in many other languages, but they are not universal. In Vietnamese, for example, nouns (i.e., referring terms) and verbs (i.e., predicating expressions) are entirely uninflected; that is, Vietnamese does not have morphological N/V-schemas, but referring and predicating expressions are distinguished by word order and free grammatical function words. In (12), for instance, the past tense particle *đã* indicates that the ensuing content word serves as a predicating expression, and the demonstrative *này* indicates that the preceding lexeme serves as a referring term. In other words, while Vietnamese lacks morphological N/V-schemas, it has syntactic and phrasal schemas for reference and predication.

(12)   tôi   [**đã**   biết]   [thằng   **này**]   không   thật thà
       1SG   PST   know   guy   this   NEG   honest
       'I (already) knew this guy was dishonest.' (native speaker informant)

There is a great deal of cross-linguistic variation in the encoding of N/V-schemas, making it impossible to define nouns and verbs by a universal set of morphosyntactic features. However, while nouns and verbs are NOT structurally uniform across languages, it seems that all languages have some formally distinct schemas for reference and predication. That does not mean that the two major propositional act functions (i.e., reference and predication) are generally expressed by distinct formal properties. There are structural ambiguities at all levels of morphosyntactic organization and propositional act functions can also be inferred from the pragmatic context (Gil 2013). Nevertheless, while the distinction between reference and predication is not contingent on particular structural properties, I am not aware of any language in which the major propositional act functions do not correlate with some formal properties.

Finally, some typologists have argued that N/V-schemas are generally linked to sets of lexical expressions that are exclusively used in one or the other schema. This is, in essence, the third hypothesis about the universality of nouns and verbs.

Hypothesis 3. All languages have two separate classes of lexical expressions that occur in N-schemas or V-schemas.

The third hypothesis has been at the center of the debate about nouns and verbs in linguistic typology. Above, we have seen that in English lexemes such as *talk* and *walk* occur in both N-schemas and V-schemas. English has a very large number of lexical expressions that can be used for both reference and predication, but many other languages are more constrained in this regard. In German, for instance, N-schemas and V-schemas are often tied to distinct lexical roots with similar meanings. The predicating use of English *walk*, for instance, corresponds to German *gehen*, whereas the referring use of *walk* corresponds to *Gang* (or *Spaziergang*).

The flexibility of lexical roots in English is remarkable in the context of other European languages, but outside of Europe, there are languages that are even more flexible than English in this regard. Consider, for instance, the following oft-cited examples from Nootka.

(13)   a. mamu:k=ma   qu:ʔas-ʔi
           working=PRES.IND   man-DEF
           'The man is working.' (Evans and Osada 2005: 368)

        b. qu:ʔas=ma   mamu:k-ʔi
           man=PRES.IND   working-DEF
           'The working one is a man.' (Evans and Osada 2005: 368)

In (13a), *mamu:k* occurs in a V-schema (marked by the present indicative clitic *=ma*) and *qu:ʔas* occurs in an N-schema (marked by the definite suffix *-ʔi*), but in (13b) it is the other way around: *mamu:k* is formally a noun and used for reference, and *qu:ʔas* is formally a verb and used for predication. Since this type of variation is very common and productive in Nootka, it has been argued that Nootka does not distinguish between nouns and verbs. Specifically, the claim is that while Nootka has N/V-schemas (marked by morphemes such as *-ʔi* and *=ma*), it lacks a distinction between "lexical nouns and verbs" (see Croft 2001: 76–81 for discussion).

This claim is problematic for several reasons. There are three important points to note. First, it is true that Nootka (and other languages of the same family) have lexical items that are very flexible with regard to their use in N/V-schemas; but contrary to what is sometimes said in the literature, these items are not entirely free in their distribution. As it turns out on closer inspection, lexical roots denoting objects and lexical roots denoting actions do NOT have exactly the same distribution. For instance, while it is possible to use action roots such as *mamu:k* 'work' in N-schemas, this use is not entirely unconstrained. As Jakobsen (1979) showed, action roots can freely occur in definite N-schemas including the definite suffix *-ʔi* (as in 13a), but action roots cannot occur in indefinite N-schemas. As can be seen in (14a–b), if referring terms are indefinite in Nootka, they are not accompanied by a particular grammatical morpheme, but while the (unmarked) indefinite schema is readily available for object roots (14a), it is not possible to use action roots in this way (14b). Similar lexeme-specific restrictions have been found in other languages that have been claimed to lack the distinction between lexical nouns and verbs (e.g., Mundari; see Evans and Osada 2005).

(14)   a. mamuːk=ma   quːʔas
            working=PRES.INDIC   man
            'A man is working.' (Evans and Osada 2005: 375)
        b. *quːʔas=ma   mamuːk
            man=PRES.INDIC   working
            'A working one is a man.' (Evans and Osada 2005: 375)

Second, there are always semantically motivated biases in the distribution of lexical roots. Even in languages in which lexical roots are very flexible with regard to their use in N/V-schemas (as for instance in Nootka), there is a strong tendency to use object roots in N-schemas and action roots in V-schemas (for quantitative evidence, see Mosel and Hovdhaugen 1992: 17–18; Broschart 1997; Evans and Osada 2005; Chung 2012). The statistical biases can be explained by the Semantic Coherence Principle and language users' experience with particular lexical expressions. While semantic coherence and frequency (or experience) are usually excluded from the analysis of grammatical word classes in formal syntax, they are of central significance to the analysis of nouns and verbs in the network approach.

Third, we have to ask how lexical items are represented in memory if they occur in both N-schemas and V-schemas. There are two opposing views. Some researchers have argued that multicategorical items such as Nootka *mamuːk* 'work' are semantically vague. On this account, lexical expressions receive different interpretations in N/V-schemas, but these interpretations are not part of their lexical meanings (Hengeveld 1992; Hengeveld et al. 2004; Van Lier and Rijkhoff 2013; Gil 2013).

The vagueness analysis accords with the claim that N/V-schemas construe the semantics of lexemes in different ways (§8.3.1), but this does not mean that speakers do not also associate the different construals evoked by N/V-schemas with particular lexical items. Proponents of the vagueness analysis have referred to parsimony in order to defend their view. According to Van Lier and Rijkhoff (2013: 22), "the key argument in favor of flexible, uncategorized or category-neutral roots is that it is the most parsimonious option." In the usage-based approach, however, parsimony is not an important factor. As pointed out in Chapter 4, it is a standard assumption of the usage-based approach that the same information is often stored redundantly.

More important than parsimony is psychological adequacy. The crucial question is: Do speakers "know" that multicategorical expressions such as Nootka *mamu:k* 'work' or English *walk* have different meanings in N/V-schemas? The answer is: If both uses are frequent, both meanings are entrenched in memory. For instance, there is good reason to assume that speakers of English store the nominal and verbal uses of *head* in (long-term) memory (§6.5.2). One piece of evidence for this hypothesis comes from the fact that the various senses of multicategorical expressions such as *head* are often idiosyncratic. Clark and Clark (1979) showed that there are systematic semantic relationships between deverbal nouns and verbs (in English), but these relationships are not fully predictable from general principles. For instance, that *head* can be used with several distinct senses in V-schemas (e.g., *to head for the door, to head the parade, to head the ball*) cannot be predicted from general cognitive processes, suggesting that these senses are also stored in memory. If this is correct, multicategorical expressions such as English *head* (and Nootka *mamu:k*) are polysemous items that speakers associate with distinct senses (Evans and Osada 2005).

To sum up the previous discussion, all languages have multiword constructions in which lexemes are used for reference and predication (Hypothesis 1). Moreover, all languages have some formally distinct N/V-schemas for reference and predication (Hypothesis 2) (though propositional act functions can also be inferred from the pragmatic context). And finally, it seems that the general network architecture of the word class system, consisting of associative connections between lexical roots and N/V-schemas, is also universal (Hypothesis 3). Thus, although the recent literature in linguistic typology has downplayed the importance of language universals, there is good reason to assume that one of the most fundamental concepts of grammar, namely, the distinction between nouns and verbs, is truly universal.

8.4   Adjectives

The network analysis of nouns and verbs can be extended to adjectives. In Chapter 2 we saw that (English) adjectives occur in two major constructions: Either they occur in attributive constructions before a noun (e.g., *a rich man*), or they occur in copular constructions after certain types of verbs, notably after *be* (e.g., *the man is rich*). There are some well-known semantic differences between the two types of constructions. In the attributive construction, adjectives typically denote stable and inherent properties, but in the copular construction, they tend to denote temporary or circumstantial properties (Bolinger 1967).

What is more, according to Croft (1991: 105), copular constructions serve basically the same propositional act function as (intransitive) verbs: both verbs and predicative adjectives are used for the act of predication, which is reflected in the fact that predicative adjectives are often marked by grammatical morphemes that are associated with V-schemas. Across languages, there are two main strategies to form predicative adjective constructions: (i) either predicative adjectives are accompanied by a copular verb (cf. *He is tall*), or (ii) they are inflected like (intransitive) verbs, as illustrated by the following examples from Bororo, in which the property root *kuri* 'tall' is marked by the same person and tense affixes as the action root *mago* 'speak' (see Stassen 2005 for a cross-linguistic survey of these constructions).

(15)   a. i-mago-re
            1SG-speak-NEUTRAL
            'I speak/spoke' (Stassen 2005: 478)

        b. i-kuri-re
            1SG-tall-NEUTRAL
            'I am/was tall.' (Stassen 2005: 478)

Attributive adjectives are different. They modify referring expressions and are integrated into a noun phrase. Croft (1991: 52) argues that attributive adjectives serve a particular propositional act function, distinct from reference and predication, which he calls "modification." In accordance with this view, we will say that (most) languages have particular adjective constructions, or A-schemas, that are used for modification.

Like N/V-schemas, A-schemas conceptualize the content of a lexeme in a particular way. Recall that Langacker distinguished "things" and "processes" by two conceptual features: relationality and temporality. Things are nonrelational and atemporal, whereas processes are relational and temporal. A-schemas evoke a conceptual profile that shares properties with both things and processes. According to Langacker (2008: 112–117), attributive adjectives are construed as being relational and atemporal (see also Croft 1991: 108). Table 8.3 shows the conceptual specifications that are evoked by the three major word class schemas.

Above, we have seen that N-schemas typically occur with object roots and V-schemas tend to occur with action roots (§8.3.3). Croft (1991: 90–91) presents parallel data for adjectives. Analyzing texts from Quiché, Nguna, Soddo and Ute, he found that A-schemas typically attract "property roots."

Lexemes that are not immediately compatible with the meaning of a particular schema are semantically restructured in accordance with the features in Table 8.3. In other words, these items are coerced into an interpretation that accords with the conceptual profile of the schema. For instance, when property roots are used in N-schemas, they are conceptualized as things (e.g., *the poor*), and when they are used in V-schemas they are conceptualized as processes (e.g., *to open*). Likewise, when object roots and action roots are used in A-schemas, they are conceptualized as properties (e.g., *childish, inspiring*) (Figure 8.3).

Table 8.3 *Conceptual properties of the three major word class schemas*

	N-schemas	A-schemas	V-schemas
Relationality	– relational	+ relational	+ relational
Temporality	– temporal	– temporal	+ temporal

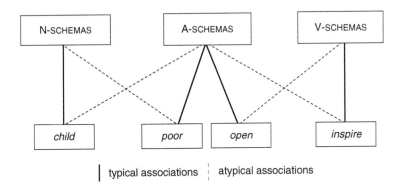

Figure 8.3 Typical and atypical associations between four (English) lexical roots and the three major word class schemas

In general, there is a cross-linguistic tendency to combine lexemes and schemas that are semantically compatible with each other, but not all combinations are semantically motivated. Lexical items that do not match the meaning of a particular word class schema are construed in accordance with the conceptual specifications of the licensing schema, and if the nonmatching use is frequent, it becomes entrenched and conventionalized, as in the case of *the poor* and *to open*. One can think of the major parts of speech as an encompassing network in which the categories of noun, verb and adjective emerge from the use of particular lexical roots and certain schemas (Figure 8.4).

Note, however, that in many languages the scope of A-schemas is more limited than that of N/V-schemas. Nouns and verbs are licensed by word class schemas that are always associated with an open class of lexical roots. That is, across languages, N/V-schemas are linked to large classes of lexical items that can be extended through borrowing, conversion or the creation of new lexical roots. In contrast, A-schemas do not generally occur with an open class of lexical items. As Dixon (1977) showed in a seminal study, some languages have adjective constructions, or A-schemas, that are only associated with a very

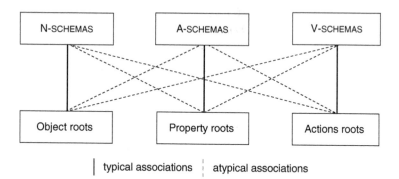

Figure 8.4 Typical and atypical associations between three semantic classes
of lexical items and the three major word class schemas

small and closed class of expressions. In these languages, most property roots
are linked to N-schemas or V-schemas.

There are two common strategies to express the semantic equivalent of an
attributive adjective in these languages. Either the property term occurs in the
noun slot of a nominal attribute construction, or it occurs in the verb slot of
some kind of relative clause (or participle clause). For instance, as can be seen
in (16a), in Hausa, property roots appear in the same construction as object
roots denoting possession (16b), and in Mojave, they occur in the same position
as action roots in relative clauses (17a–b).

(16)   a. mutum   mai   [alheri]
           person   having   kindness
           'a kind person' [= A person having kindness] (Schachter and Shopen
           2007: 15)
        b. mutum   mai   [doki]
           person   having   horse
           'a person's horse' [= A person having a horse] (Schachter and Shopen
           2007: 15)

(17)   a. ʔiːpa   [(kʷ)-homiː-nʸ-č]   ivaːk
           man   (REL)-tall-DEM-SUBJ   is.here
           'The tall man is here.' (Schachter and Shopen 2007: 19)
        b. ʔiːpa   [kʷ-suːpaw-nʸ-č]   ivaːk
           man   REL-know-DEM-SUBJ   is.here
           'The man who knows is here.' (Schachter and Shopen 2007: 19)

Since nominal attributes and relative clauses are used to modify nouns, similar
to adjectives, languages like Hausa and Mojave can do without a (productive)
A-schema. As a consequence, most property roots are associated with
N-schemas or V-schemas in these languages (cf. Figure 8.5).

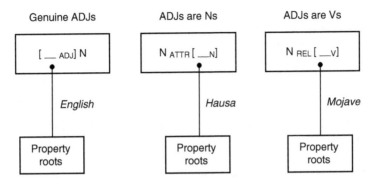

Figure 8.5 Associations between property roots and different word class schemas in languages with open and closed classes of adjectives

Interestingly, Dixon (1977) observed that the encoding of property roots in N/V/A-schemas correlates with the meaning of the property root. Analyzing data from a large number of languages, he distinguished seven semantic classes of property items: items denoting age (e.g., new, young), color (e.g., blue, white), value (e.g., good, bad), dimension (e.g., big, short), physical property (e.g., head, heavy), human propensity (e.g., kind, happy) and speed (e.g., fast, quick). What Dixon's analysis showed is that items denoting age, color, value and dimension are usually expressed by A-schemas, but items denoting physical properties, human propensity and speed are frequently expressed by N/V-schemas. Since the three latter classes are semantically more similar to object roots and action roots than adjectives denoting age, color, value and dimension, it is a plausible hypothesis that their frequent occurrence in N/V-schemas is semantically motivated (see also Dixon 2004).

8.5 Subclasses

The major word classes can be divided into subclasses. In what follows, we will consider some nominal and verbal subclasses that will elaborate the network approach.

8.5.1 Count Nouns and Mass Nouns

Two basic types of common nouns are commonly distinguished: count nouns such as *house* and *cat,* and mass nouns such as *water* and *music.* Count nouns refer to physical entities and animate beings, whereas mass nouns denote liquids and substances. In many languages, the semantic distinction between count nouns and mass nouns correlates with certain structural properties. In

English, for instance, mass nouns do not inflect for number and are not accompanied by indefinite articles (as opposed to count nouns). In other languages, mass nouns and count nouns are formally distinguished by case inflection (e.g., Finnish).

Traditionally, the count/mass noun distinction is seen as a property of lexical items. On this view, lexemes are members of a particular subclass regardless of their use in a particular context. The problem with this view is that many nouns can be used in both ways. Very often, one use is dominant and the other use is derived, but there is much flexibility in the system. For instance, it is well known that nouns denoting liquids or sounds can be used as grammatical count nouns if they are construed as countable entities (18a–b).

(18)   a. I have *two waters* please.
        b. This is *a music* (that) I like.

Likewise, many (count) nouns denoting objects or animate beings can be construed as undifferentiated concepts, or mass nouns, as in the following examples (from Langacker 1987: 72–73):

(19)   a. Since the bank crisis, you get a lot of *house* for your money.
        b. There is *cat* all over the driveway.

Parallel to the distinction between the three major parts of speech, the count/mass noun distinction can be analyzed in the framework of a dynamic network model consisting of particular word class schemas and associated lexical roots. Specifically, we may say that the distinction between count nouns and mass nouns emerges from the interaction between two particular subtypes of N-schemas and certain semantic types of object roots. The two subschemas inherit the two conceptual features of the general N-schema, that is, they are both nonrelational and atemporal, but they are differentiated by a third feature, that is, boundedness.

According to Talmy (2000: 50–55), count nouns designate conceptually bounded entities, whereas mass nouns specify unbounded quantities (see also Langacker 2008: 128–132). Note that this is primarily a property of schemas, rather than of lexemes. Of course, the two types of N-schemas are associated with items that are semantically compatible with their conceptual specifications. Count noun schemas attract items that designate discrete entities (e.g., physical objects and animate beings), whereas mass noun schemas attract items that designate undifferentiated quantities (e.g., substances and liquids). However, as we have seen, the associations between lexemes and schemas are variable and shaped by language use. Figure 8.6 illustrates the interaction between the two types of N-schemas and different semantic types of object roots with a few selected examples from English.

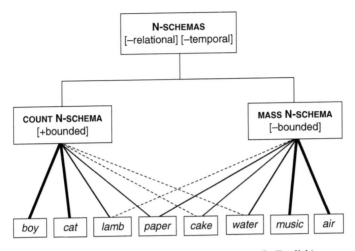

Figure 8.6 Network of count nouns and mass nouns (in English)

Items that are linked to both schemas are polysemous. *Paper*, for instance, has two senses. A *sheet of paper* profiles a bounded entity (licensed by the count noun schema), but if *something is wrapped in paper, paper* designates an unbounded entity (and is licensed by the mass noun schema). Items that are linked to only one schema are stored with only one sense (e.g., *cat*), but can be coerced into a novel interpretation if they are used in the other type of schema (as in examples 18–19 above). The links are semantically motivated and reinforced by frequency of language use. Novel links become entrenched through repetition, and existing links may disappear if they are no longer used.

8.5.2   Aspectual Subclasses

Like nouns, verbs can be divided into grammatical subclasses. Let us consider the English progressive construction to illustrate the network approach to the analysis of verbal subclasses. It is a standard assumption that the progressive construction construes the meaning of a verb in a particular way (§3.4). The construal varies with the meaning of the verb. For instance, if a durative verb such as *run* is used in the progressive, the denoted action is construed as being in progress at a particular point in time (20a), and if a punctual verb such as *knock* is used in the progressive, it designates a repeated action that extends over a certain period of time (20b).

(20)   a. Peter is running in the park.
        b. Peter is knocking on the door.

Since these construals (or conceptualizations) are not immediately compatible with the semantics of stative verbs, the English progressive construction is primarily used with dynamic verbs (Stefanowitsch and Gries 2003: 230–231). However, as Comrie (1976: 32–40) and others have pointed out, while the English progressive construction was once limited to dynamic verbs, it is now also (occasionally) used with stative verbs that have developed particular semantic interpretations. Very often, stative verbs are construed as being nonpermanent when they occur in the progressive construction (cf. *He is silly* vs. *He is being silly*). Conversely, dynamic verbs are construed as abilities when they occur in the simple present tense construction (e.g., *He plays the piano* vs. *He is playing the piano*). There are, however, many lexical idiosyncrasies. For instance, as Comrie (1976: 38) noted in 1976, while *look* can be used in both the simple present tense and the progressive (21a), *sound* was banned from the progressive at that time (21b) (though, interestingly, it can be used in the progressive today).

(21)   a. You look well.   Or: You are looking well.
         b. You sound hoarse. But not: *You are sounding hoarse.

What is more, if we look at the aspectual use of verbs from a cross-linguistic perspective, we find that individual verbs denoting the same action (or state) are often used in very different ways across the various aspect constructions that are employed in a particular language, indicating that while the interaction between verbs and aspect schemas is motivated by general conceptual processes, it is not fully predictable from semantic criteria. Speakers "know" how individual verbs are used in different aspect schemas based on their experience with particular co-occurrence patterns. In order to account for the combined effect of semantic motivation and experience, we may propose a network model in which individual verbs are linked to particular aspect schemas by probabilistic associations (Figure 8.7).

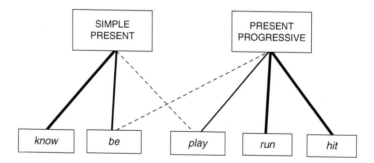

Figure 8.7 Network of stative/dynamic verbs and two different aspect schemas (in English)

8.5.3   Regular and Irregular Past Tense Verbs

Interestingly, the interaction between lexemes and constructions is not only motivated by semantic factors, it is also influenced by formal features. Consider, for instance, the formation of the English past tense, which involves two major strategies. The vast majority of English verbs form the past tense by means of the V-*ed* schema (e.g., *walk* → *walked*), but there are about 180 "irregular verbs" that form the past by stem internal changes (or no changes) licensed by particular phonetic schemas. As can be seen in (22), the irregular verbs can be divided into several classes that form the past tense in similar ways, e.g., verbs in which the past tense is marked by a changing stem vowel (22a–b), verbs that indicate the past by a final [d] or [t] in addition to a changing stem vowel (22c), and verbs that do not change at all (22d).

(22)   a. sing/sang   b. cling/clung   c. feel/felt   d. hit/hit
        ring/rang   swing/swung   lose/lost   cut/cut
        drink/drank   wring/wrung   tell/told   beat/beat

Crucially, the irregular past tense schemas are productive. As Bybee and Slobin (1982) demonstrated, when speakers are given a nonce verb that is phonetically similar to the verbs of one of the irregular verb classes, they are likely to accommodate the given nonce form to an irregular past tense schema. For instance, given an invented form such as *slink*, speakers may produce an irregular past form such as [slʌŋk] or [slæŋk] instead of the regular *slinked*.

Concentrating on verbs of the *sing/sang* and *cling/clung* class, Bybee and Moder (1983) observed that the likelihood of using an irregular past tense schema correlates with the degree of phonetic similarity between a given nonce verb and existing verbs. Other things being equal, the larger the amount of phonetic overlap between a given nonce verb and existing verbs, the higher the proportion of irregular past tense responses. The results are complex, but Table 8.4 shows how participants responded when they were given present tense forms with the vowel /ɪ/ and certain types of consonants in onset and coda.

As can be seen, the highest percentage of irregular past tense responses occurred with verbs including /s/ and two other consonants in the onset and a velar nasal in the coda. The proportion of irregular past tense responses correlates with the phonetic features of the segments before and after the vowel. The more features are shared, the higher the rate of irregular responses. Generalizing across these results, Bybee and Moder argued that the past tense of verbs such as *sing/sang* and *cling/clung* constitutes a prototype that is organized around a phonetic template, or schema, consisting of /sCC/ in the onset and /ŋ(k)/ in the coda (Figure 8.8).

Thirty years ago, Steven Pinker argued that the use of regular and irregular verbs involves different cognitive mechanisms (Pinker and Prince 1988; Pinker 1991).

Table 8.4 *Percentage of irregular responses to different nonce verbs*

Manipulation of the onset with constant vowel and coda (i.e., /ɪŋ/)		Manipulation of the coda with constant vowel and onset (i.e., /sCC/)	
Given present tense	Percentage of irregulars	Given present tense	Percentage of irregulars
sCC ɪ ŋ	44	sCC ɪ ŋ/ŋk	44
sC ɪ ŋ	37	sCC ɪ k/g	25
CC ɪ ŋ	27	sCC ɪ n/m	21
C ɪ ŋ	22	sCC ɪ C	4

Source: Bybee and Moder (1983: 139)

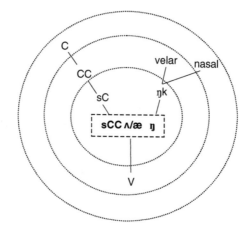

Figure 8.8 Past tense schema of *sing/cling* verbs

Specifically, he claimed that while irregular past tense forms are created by schemas (as proposed by Bybee and Modor 1983; Rumelhart and McClelland 1986b), the regular past is produced by an "algebraic rule" (see also Marcus 1999). However, later research disproved all of the arguments Pinker and colleagues presented in support of the "dual mechanism account" (see Seidenberg and Plaut 2014 for a review of the "past tense debate"). For instance, Pinker and Prince (1988) claimed that the use of regular past tense forms is NOT influenced by frequency (like the use of irregular past tense forms), but there is now ample evidence that frequency affects both irregular and regular verbs (Hare et al. 2001). Moreover, they claimed that phonetic similarity is irrelevant to the formation of regular past tense forms, but, as Albright and Hayes (2003) demonstrated, verb

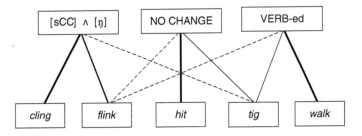

Figure 8.9 Associations between existing and novel base forms and three English past tense schemas

stems ending in a voiceless fricative are always licensed by the (regular) past tense schema (e.g., *mi*[*s*]*ed, wi*[*ʃ*]*ed, lau*[*f*]*ed*).

Assuming that regular and irregular verbs are subject to the same cognitive processes, we may analyze the English past tense in terms of a dynamic network model in which several past tense schemas are associated with particular base forms (Figure 8.9).

The various past tense schemas function as "attractors" that are in competition with each other. Real, existing verbs are tied to specific past tense forms if they are frequent, but infrequent verbs may lose their connection to a particular schema and may be recategorized, as for instance the verb 'laugh', which used to be irregular in Old English (*low* 'laughed') but is now licensed by the V-*ed* schema. What is more, novel verbs can often be assigned to multiple schemas depending on their phonetic form. The past tense of *tig*, for instance, could be *tig, tug* or *tigged*, reflecting the associative connections between the various present and past tense forms. On this account, category membership is gradient and shaped by language use.

8.6   Grammatical Function Words

Concluding this chapter, let us take a look at grammatical function words, which are commonly divided into a number of minor word classes. English has several minor word class categories including auxiliaries, adpositions, articles (or determiners), pronouns and conjunctions. In contrast to the major parts of speech, notably nouns and verbs, the minor word classes are NOT universal. There are, for instance, many languages that do not have articles and auxiliaries (e.g., Russian, Dyirbal, Zapotec). The inventory of the minor parts of speech is language-particular and there is a great deal of cross-linguistic variation.

One reason for this is that grammatical function words are generally derived from other types of expressions, notably from nouns and verbs (Hopper and Traugott 2003) and from demonstratives (Diessel 2012a). We have considered some of these developments in previous chapters (under the notion of grammaticalization) (Chapter 5). There is a very rich literature on this topic, which cannot be reviewed in this chapter; but here are some of the grammaticalization processes that are cross-linguistically very frequent.[2]

- Auxiliaries are commonly derived from certain semantic types of verbs (§4.6.1). Future tense auxiliaries, for instance, are often based on motion verbs (cf. Engl. *is going to* > *gonna;* see Hilpert 2007), and aspectual auxiliaries are sometimes based on phrasal verbs (e.g., Engl. 'finish' > 'completive/perfective'). Auxiliaries that fuse with the co-occurring verb develop into tense, aspect and mood affixes (Bybee et al. 1994).

- Adpositions have two common sources (§9.5). Very often, adpositions are derived from aspectual verbs or verbs of motion (cf. Mandarin *dào* 'arrive/ reach' > *dào Zhōngguó* 'to China') or they are based on nouns denoting body parts (e.g., Engl. 'back' > 'behind') or abstract relations (cf. Engl. *in front of*). Both "verbal" and "nominal adpositions" can further develop into case markers (Heine et al. 1991: 123–147).

- A grammatical category that is frequently derived from a demonstrative is the definite article. English *the*, for instance, has evolved from an adnominal demonstrative (§4.6.2). Parallel developments have occurred in many other languages including French, Swedish, Basque and Hungarian (Diessel 1999: 128–129). Once demonstratives are used as definite markers, they are often extended to nondefinite nouns and then (sometimes) reanalyzed as noun class markers (Greenberg 1978).

- Another type of function word that is frequently derived from a demonstrative is the third-person pronoun (e.g., Lat. *ille* 'that' > Fr. *il* 'he'). In fact, in many languages, unstressed demonstrative pronouns are used in the same way as third-person pronouns in languages that have a separate class of anaphoric pronouns (Givón 1984: 356–360). Anaphoric pronouns that are routinely used to track nominal referents, may lose their status as independent words and may turn into agreement markers (§5.3.3).

- Copular verbs are sometimes based on verbs (cf. Lat. *sĕdēre* 'to sit' > Sp. *ser* 'to be') and sometimes on demonstratives or third-person pronouns derived from a demonstrative (cf. Hebrew *ze*). The development of the latter originates from a topicalization construction in which a topicalized noun is resumed by a demonstrative pronoun of a nonverbal clause that is reanalyzed as a copular verb [the.man$_i$ [*that/he$_i$* my.friend]] > [the.man *is* my.friend]) (Diessel 1999: 143–159). Moreover, Givón (1979: 246–248) argued that demonstrative copulas can develop into focus markers.

---

[2] Readers who are not familiar with the grammaticalization literature may consult the following sources: Heine et al. (1991), Bybee et al. (1994), Lehmann ([1995] 2015), Diessel (1999: §6), Heine and Kuteva (2002), Hopper and Traugott (2003), and Narrog and Heine (2011).

- Finally, conjunctions and complementizers are derived from a wide range of sources including both content words and demonstratives (Kortmann 1996). The Swahili complementizer *kwamba*, for instance, has developed from a verb meaning 'say' (Güldemann 2008: 271), and the German complementizer *dass* has evolved from a demonstrative pronoun (Diessel 1999: 123–125). Once a complementizer is in place, it is often extended to other types of subordinate clauses.

Figure 8.10 provides an overview of the described developments. Needless to say that there are many other pathways of development and that the shown trajectories are much more complex and diverse than indicated in this diagram.

Crucially, while the older literature on grammaticalization has focused on the diachronic developments of lexical items, the more recent literature has emphasized that the diachronic developments of grammatical function words involve entire constructions rather than just isolated words (Traugott and Trousdale 2013). If we look at the rise of grammatical function words from a construction-based perspective, we find that grammaticalization does not only explain where auxiliaries, articles and other function morphemes come from, it also accounts for the diachronic development of N/V-schemas. We will consider this aspect of grammaticalization in Chapter 9. Here we note that grammaticalization gives rise to constructional schemas that include particular slots for certain types of function words.

Like content words, grammatical function words are associated with particular structural positions of constructional schemas that interact with their meaning or function. To illustrate, English *in, on, after, since, if* and *when* are associated with adpositional constructions and/or subordinate clauses (Figure 8.11). Some items are linked to both types of constructions (*after, since*), but others are associated with only one type (*in, on, if, when*).

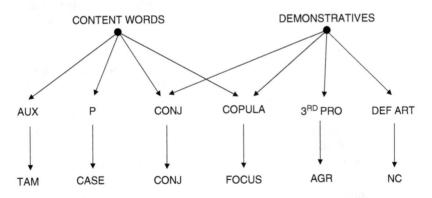

Figure 8.10 Some frequent diachronic paths leading from content words and demonstratives to grammatical function words and bound morphemes

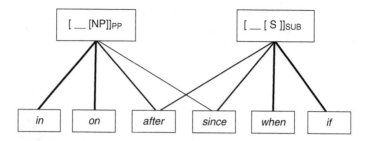

Figure 8.11 Network of relational expressions linked to schemas of adpositional phrases and subordinate clauses

The associative connections between grammatical function words and constructional schemas are shaped by the same cognitive mechanisms as the associations between content words and N/V/A-schemas: They are semantically motivated and reinforced by frequency of language use. For instance, both constructions in Figure 8.11 specify particular semantic types of relations and attract expressions that designate relations in particular semantic domains. Adpositional phrases attract primarily relational expressions of space and time, whereas subordinate clauses (also) attract relational expressions of more abstract domains such as cause and condition.

Like content words, grammatical function words tend to occur in constructional schemas that are consistent with their meaning, but in addition to the semantic fit, it is a language user's linguistic experience that has a significant impact on the associative connections between grammatical items and schemas. One piece of evidence for this hypothesis comes again from the analysis of multicategorical expressions.

Consider, for instance, the English word *that*, which can be a demonstrative (e.g., *That book is interesting*) or a complementizer (e.g., *She said that she would come*). Overall, the demonstrative use of *that* is more frequent than the complementizer use, but the frequency of the two uses varies with the syntactic context. As Juliano and Tanenhaus (1993) showed, at the beginning of a sentence *that* is primarily used as a demonstrative and only rarely as a complementizer, but after verbs it is the other way around: 89 percent of all instances of *that* are demonstratives at the beginning of a new sentence, but after verbs, 93 percent of all *that* tokens function as complementizers in Juliano and Tanenhaus's data.

Considering this asymmetry, the researchers hypothesized that the skewed distribution of *that* will have an impact on sentence processing. The hypothesis was confirmed by a reading time experiment in which participants' response times were significantly longer with sentences in which the use of *that* deviated from the dominant pattern. When *that* appeared at the beginning of a sentence, reading times were short with the demonstrative and long with the complementizer, but after verbs it was the other way around, suggesting that speakers associate the use of *that* in different positions with different word class schemas.

8.7   Conclusion

In conclusion, this chapter has outlined a dynamic network approach to the study of grammatical word classes parallel to the network approach to the analysis of argument structure proposed in Chapter 7. Like argument structure, grammatical word classes are defined by associative connections between lexemes and constructions, or more specifically, they are defined by associations between lexemes and particular word class schemas.

At the heart of every word class system is the distinction between nouns and verbs, or N/V-schemas. Building on Langacker and Croft, it has been argued that constructions include particular slots that conceptualize the meanings of content words as things or processes in order to use them for certain communicative functions. More precisely, N-schemas conceptualize the content of a lexeme as a time-stable entity so as to perform the act of reference, and V-schemas conceptualize the content of a lexeme as a transitory event so as to perform the act of predication.

Schemas attract lexical items that are semantically compatible with the constructional meaning. N-schemas attract lexical roots that designate objects (or time-stable entities), whereas V-schemas attract lexical roots that designate actions (or transitory events). The co-occurrence of lexemes and schemas is thus semantically motivated, but not all lexemes that occur in N/V-schemas are consistent with the constructional meaning. Lexemes that do not fit the semantic specifications of a particular schema are coerced into a novel interpretation. If such nonmatching uses are frequent, they become entrenched in memory, indicating that the associative connections between lexemes and N/V-schemas are determined by two general factors: (i) the semantic fit of lexemes and schemas (i.e., the Semantic Coherence Principle) and (ii) language users' experience with particular co-occurrence patterns.

The network analysis of nouns and verbs can be extended to other word class categories including the categories of grammatical function words. Like nouns and verbs, grammatical function words are associated with semantically specified slots in constructional schemas. However, in contrast to the major parts of speech, the minor word classes are based on roots that are generally derived from other types of expressions, notably from certain semantic types of nouns and verbs and from demonstratives.

9 Phrase Structure

9.1 Introduction

The two previous chapters have outlined a dynamic network model for the analysis of argument structure and parts of speech. The current chapter extends the network approach to the analysis of phrase structure, also known as constituent structure or constituency. Specifically, the chapter argues that hierarchical phrase structure involves probabilistic links, or filler–slot relations, between syntactic schemas and phrasal (or lexical) fillers.

In formal grammar, phrase structure is derived from a finite set of syntactic categories (e.g., N, P, NP, PP) and combinatorial rules (e.g., PP → P NP) (Chomsky 1965: 63–127). There are various ways of analyzing phrase structure in formal syntax, but in many theories, it is analyzed in terms of "phrase structure trees," such as the tree in Figure 9.1.

Phrase structure trees consist of nodes and links that one could interpret as some kind of network. The nodes represent particular syntactic units and the links specify how these units are related in a sentence. What is more, phrase structure trees can be analyzed from a psychological perspective in terms of memory chunks. Recall that, according to Miller (1956) and other cognitive psychologists, memory involves a cognitive mechanism of chunking whereby individual pieces of information are bound together into a single unit or chunk (§5.1). Since chunks are hierarchically organized in long-term memory, they can increase the amount of information that is simultaneously available for processing. It is only because linguistic information is packaged into chunks (i.e., words, phrases and clauses) that listeners are able to integrate the many pieces of information they encounter in an unfolding sentence into a coherent interpretation (Miller 1956; Gobet et al. 2001; see also Bybee 2010: 34–37).

However, while phrase structure graphs are useful to explain certain aspects of syntactic structure, they suffer from the same general problem as many other theoretical concepts of formal syntax. If we think of grammar as a dynamic system, traditional phrase structure analysis is inadequate to explain syntactic structure, as it presupposes a predefined set of discrete categories and categorical rules that are independent of language use. Moreover, the traditional approach is

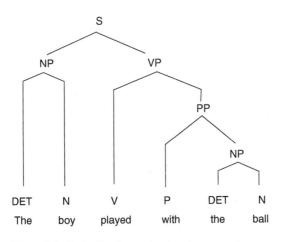

Figure 9.1 Syntactic phrase structure tree

problematic as it concentrates on abstract representations of syntactic structure; but, as we have seen, there is good evidence that syntactic representations are always associated with particular lexical items (Chapters 4, 5, 7 and 8).

In accordance with this view, the current chapter outlines a dynamic network approach to syntactic constituency that builds on the analysis of item-specific constructions and constructional schemas in previous chapters (notably in Chapters 4 and 5). Specifically, the chapter argues that phrase structure emerges from the interaction of several domain-general processes, including conceptualization, automatization, analogy and abstraction, which together account for both the syntactic generalizations that are expressed in constructional schemas and the many idiosyncrasies that reflect the influence of speakers' experience with particular co-occurrence patterns.

9.2   Constituent Types

Before we consider the various cognitive processes that underlie constituency, let me briefly introduce the different constituent types to be considered in this chapter. There are two important distinctions. First, in accordance with traditional phrase structure analysis, we distinguish between noun phrases (NPs), verb phrases (VPs) and various other types of phrases based on the so-called head. In the syntactic literature, heads are commonly defined by structural criteria, but in accordance with Langacker (2008), we define the head of a phrase as the linguistic element that determines the conceptual profile and function of a constituent. An expression such as *an old man*, for instance, is "headed" by the noun *man* as the phrase inherits the conceptual and functional properties of *man*. Like the noun *man*, the NP *an old man* designates a thing (in Langacker's sense of the term) and serves to perform an act of reference (as defined by Croft). Parallel analyses apply to other types of phrases (e.g., verb phrases, adjective phrases, adpositional phrases and subordinate clauses).

Second, we distinguish between "compound phrases" and "grammatical phrases." Compound phrases combine two lexical units (i.e., units that include at least one content word) as immediate constituents. For instance, an expression such as *a friend of my father* is a compound NP consisting of a noun and a nominal attribute, and an expression such *saw my friend* is a compound VP consisting of a verb and a nominal complement. Grammatical phrases, in contrast, combine a grammatical function word with a lexical component as immediate constituents. Adpositional phrases, for instance, are grammatical phrases as they combine a particular grammatical morpheme (i.e., an adposition) with a noun or noun phrase. Likewise, subordinate clauses are grammatical phrases that combine a function word (i.e., a conjunction or complementizer) with a lexical component (i.e., a clause). Moreover, NPs and VPs are grammatical phrases if one of their immediate constituents is a grammatical marker, e.g., a determiner or auxiliary. Table 9.1 provides examples of compound phrases and grammatical phrases in English. Similar types of constituents occur in many other languages.

The distinction between NPs, VPs and other types of phrases has been at center stage in phrase structure grammar, but the distinction between compound phrases and grammatical phrases is only rarely considered in the syntactic literature. However, in what follows we will see that the latter distinction is of central importance to the usage-based analysis of constituency, as compound phrases and grammatical phrases are shaped by different processes. In particular, we will see that compound phrases are created by general conceptual processes of frame semantics, whereas grammatical phrases are not only motivated by certain conceptual processes but are also shaped by grammaticalization. We begin with compound phrases and then turn to grammatical phrases.

Table 9.1 *Examples of compound phrases and grammatical phrases*

Compound phrases (lex & lex)		Grammatical phrases (gram & lex)	
V – NP	[*saw*] [*a man*]	P – N(P)	[*at*] [*school*]
V – PP	[*walk*] [*into the room*]	AUX – V(P)	[*has*] [*done*]
V – CC	[*notice*] [*that she is leaving*]	DET – N(P)	[*the*] [*tree*]
A – N	[*beautiful*] [*day*]	COP – NP/AP	[*is*] [*my friend*]
G – N	[*John's*] [*brother*]	COMP – S	[*that*] [*she will come*]
N – REL	[*people*] [*I met*]	SUB – S	[*when*] [*they left*]

9.3   The Conceptual Foundations of Compound Phrases

In traditional phrase structure grammar, syntactic constituents are derived from primitive categories by particular phrase structure rules, but syntactic constituency is not just a structural phenomenon. There is good evidence that syntactic constituents, or phrases, are semantically motivated. To begin with, as many scholars of grammar have pointed out, there is a general tendency to place semantically related elements next to each other. An early statement of this is Behaghel's "first law":

Geistig eng Zusammengehöriges wird auch eng zusammengestellt. [Conceptually related entities are placed close to each other.] (Behaghel 1932)

Evidence for this "law" can be found in every language. For instance, across languages, attributive adjectives tend to occur adjacent to the noun they modify, and object complements tend to occur next to the associated verb (or predicate). What is not immediately clear from Behaghel's first law is the nature of the conceptual relations that motivate the adjacency of particular expressions. In the case of compound phrases, these relations are established by the conceptual properties of particular content words.

In Chapter 6 it was said that the meaning of a word resides in a network of conceptually related nodes that are accessed or activated by an expression. In many cases, this network includes a conceptual gestalt, or frame, consisting of a figure node that is directly accessed by a particular expression and one or more base nodes that are entailed by the figure node or figure concept (§6.2). Verbs, for instance, are interpreted against the background of an event frame consisting of the action node that is directly activated by a verb and one or more participant nodes that are entailed by a verb and elaborated by referring expressions (§6.4.1).

A similar analysis applies to adjectives. As pointed out in Chapter 6, adjectives evoke a frame that entails an entity, or referring term, in addition to the property concept that is accessed by an adjective. The adjective *bitter*, for instance, evokes a frame that includes a base concept for something to eat (e.g., *bitter melon*), and the adjective *furry* evokes a frame that includes a base concept of an animal (e.g., *furry dog*) (Fillmore 1982).

Like verbs and adjectives, nouns provide access to an open-ended network of related concepts (§6.4), but unlike verbs and adjectives, nouns do not generally evoke a conceptual gestalt, or frame, with a particular base concept. Since nouns construe an experience as a "thing," they are usually nonrelational (§8.3). For instance, while a noun such as *tree* is arguably associated with concepts such as 'green', 'grow', 'wood' and 'nature', *tree* does not immediately entail any of these concepts as a particular base node. This explains why nouns are conceptually more autonomous than verbs and adjectives. The two latter (i.e., verbs and adjectives) are relational expressions that provide slots for particular referring terms, but most nouns are nonrelational expressions, which (usually) function to elaborate the base concepts evoked by verbs and adjectives (1a–b).

(1)   a.   hit [__]ɴ   b.   bitter [__]ɴ

Note that the nominal fillers serve different functions in (1a–b). If the noun elaborates a participant slot of an event frame, it functions as a "dependent category" (of a VP), but if it elaborates the entity slot of a property frame, it functions as "head" (of an NP). In other words, the conceptual relations of compound phrases are evoked by different categories: There are compound phrases with relational heads (e.g., verbs) that take a complement as filler; and there are compound phrases with relational dependent categories, known as "modifiers," that take a head filler. Figure 9.2 seeks to capture this analysis by two distinct network graphs.

As can be seen, in the head-complement construction, the relational expression is the head of the composite structure that provides a slot for a (dependent) filler (i.e., the complement), but in the head-modifier construction, the relational term is a dependent category that provides a slot for a filler as head.

The distinction between complements and modifiers does not only concern verbs and adjectives but also various other types of phrasal constructions. In particular, the modifier construction is very common. Manner adverbs, for instance, are relational expressions that modify a verbal head (Figure 9.3). Likewise, nominal attributes and relative clauses are relational expressions that modify a nominal head, similar to adjectives (Figure 9.4).

In all of these constructions, compound phrases are organized by relational expressions that create a conceptual link between two lexical elements

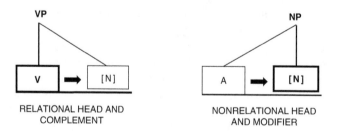

Figure 9.2 Complement and modifier constructions

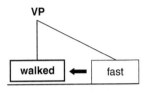

Figure 9.3 VP consisting of a head verb and a manner adverb

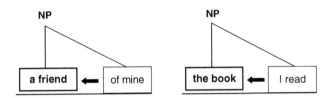

Figure 9.4 NPs consisting of a head noun and a prepositional/clausal modifier

(indicated by the arrow). In English, relational expressions are usually accompanied by a filler, but there are also languages in which relational expressions do not require an overt filler. In particular, the subject slot of verbs is often left empty (a phenomenon that is known as "pro drop" in generative grammar). In contrast to the subject slot, the object slot is usually filled by a referring term, but note that there are languages in which not only the subject but also the object can be omitted. In Mandarin Chinese, for instance, transitive verbs are NOT generally accompanied by an object complement. As can be seen in (2), the verb *xǐhuān* 'like' can occur without an object filler.

(2) nèi-kē   shù   yèzi   dà;   (suǒyǐ) wǒ   bu   xǐhuān.
     that-CL tree   leaf   big   (so)   I   not   like
     'That tree, the leaves are big; (so) I don't like it (the tree).' (Li and Thompson
     1981: 102)

Like verbs, adjectives are NOT generally accompanied by a filler. In German, for instance, adjectives can occur without a noun as in example (3).

(3) Ich nehme das rote.
     I   take   the red
     'I take the red one.'

What these examples show is that while relational expressions are generally associated with a conceptual base (or slot), the base concept is not always elaborated by a linguistic filler. To be sure, there is a cross-linguistic tendency to combine relational expressions with linguistic fillers, but the probability that a (conceptual) slot is filled by a constituent varies across both languages and constructions. In English, relational expressions are almost always elaborated by referring terms, but in other languages, they are often used without an overt filler.

Thus, while compound phrases are semantically motivated by the conceptual properties of relational content words, the conceptual properties alone are not sufficient to explain the structure and use of compound phrases. In addition to semantic factors, it is language users' experience with certain co-occurrence patterns that affects the use of compound phrases in a particular language. To put it another way, while relational expressions evoke the same or similar frames across languages, there are significant cross-linguistic differences in the use of compound phrases that reflect language users' experience with particular constructions and language-specific conventions.

9.4   Grammatical Phrases

Like compound phrases, grammatical phrases are semantically motivated. As many scholars of grammar have pointed out, grammatical function words elaborate the meaning of related content words. Auxiliaries, for instance, specify the meaning of a co-occurring (main) verb (Bybee et al. 1994), and determiners elaborate, or "ground," the meaning of a co-occurring nominal (Langacker 2008: 272–296). However, the coherence of grammatical phrases is not only motivated by general conceptual processes, it is also the product of grammaticalization. Consider, for instance, adpositional phrases (short PPs).

In the syntactic literature, PPs are usually analyzed on a par with NPs, VPs and APs, but in contrast to the three latter, PPs are generally derived from other phrasal patterns, notably from compound phrases headed by particular types of content words. As pointed out in Chapter 8, across languages, adpositions are historically derived from two major sources: (i) motion, transfer and aspectual verbs such as 'go', 'give' and 'finish', and (ii) relational nouns, including body part terms, such as 'back', 'front' and 'belly' (Heine et al. 1991: 123–147; Hagège 2010: 151–172).[1] Consider, for instance, the meaning and use of the item *dào* in the two following examples from Mandarin Chinese.

(4)   a. wŏmen   **dào**-le   Xiānggǎng.
          we   arrive-ASP Hong Kong
          'We have arrived in Hong Kong.' (Li and Thompson 1981: 365)

       b. tā   **dào**   Lúndūn   qù   le.
          3SG   to   London   go   SFP
          'S/he has gone to London.' (Li and Thompson 1981: 366)

---

[1] Another source for adpositions are adverbs (Lehmann [1995] 2015: 98–99).

As can be seen, in (4a) *dào* is a verb meaning 'arrive' that carries the perfective aspect marker -*le*, but in (4b) *dào* is a preposition meaning 'to'. Other verbs that also serve as prepositions in Mandarin Chinese include *gēn* ('follow' > 'with'), *bèn* ('go to' > 'toward'), *gěi* ('give' > 'for/by') and *cháo* ('to face' > 'facing') (Li and Thompson 1981: 362–369). Similar types of verbal adpositions occur in other East Asian languages (e.g., Lao, Thai, Vietnamese) and in many other languages across the world (e.g., Ijo, Ewe, Yoruba, Ute, Haitian Creole; see Hagège 2010: 151–172). Like verbal adpositions, nominal adpositions are derived from relational expressions, e.g., from nouns denoting body parts. Consider, for instance, the item *bu* in the following examples from Baka.

(5)   a. ʔé   à   kὲ   à   **bú-ὲ**.
         3SG   ASP   hurt   LOC   belly-3.SG.POSS
         'His stomach is aching.' (Heine and Kuteva 2002: 53)

      b. ʔé   à   nɔɔ̀   à   **bu**   ngo.
         3SG   ASP   run   LOC   belly[=in]   water
         'He is running in the water.' (Heine and Kuteva 2002: 53)

In (5a), *bu* is a noun meaning 'belly' or 'stomach' that is accompanied by a possessive suffix, but in (5b), *bu* serves as a preposition meaning 'in'. Similar extensions of body part nouns to adpositions have been found in many other languages including Mixtec (e.g., *nuù* 'face' > 'in front of'), Ewe (e.g., *megbé* 'back.N' > 'back.P'), Shona (e.g., *musoro* 'head' > *musoro pa* 'on top of' [lit. 'at head of']) and Icelandic (e.g., *bak* 'back.N' > *(að) bak(i)* 'behind/after') (consider also English *back, ahead*). Figure 9.5 summarizes the described developments of verbal and nominal adpositions.

Like adpositional phrases, grammatical NPs and VPs (consisting of a noun or verb and a grammatical function word) are derived from other phrasal patterns by grammaticalization. For instance, VPs including an auxiliary or

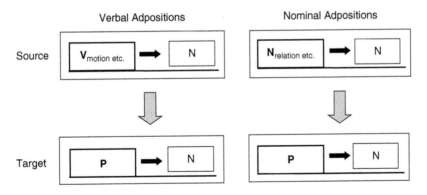

Figure 9.5 Diachronic developments of adpositional phrases from VPs and NPs

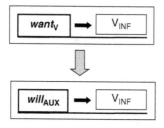

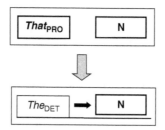

Figure 9.6 Diachronic development of Aux-V phrase from V-V phrase

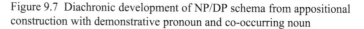

Figure 9.7 Diachronic development of NP/DP schema from appositional
construction with demonstrative pronoun and co-occurring noun

modal verb are commonly derived from compound phrases consisting of two
verbal elements: a verbal head that is downgraded to an auxiliary and a verbal
complement that is promoted to the main verb of a periphrastic verb form
(Bybee 2010: 111). The English auxiliary *will*, for example, has evolved from a
main verb meaning 'want' that was accompanied by an infinitive as object
complement (Figure 9.6).

The development of grammatical NPs including a determiner (e.g., *the man,
a car*) is somewhat different. In this case, the source construction does not
(usually) include a relational term (as in all previous examples). As it turns out,
determiners are commonly derived from pronouns that accompany another
nominal. For instance, as we have seen in Chapter 4, the simple noun phrase of
Modern English has evolved from some kind of appositional construction
consisting of a noun and a co-occurring referring term, e.g., a demonstrative,
a possessive or quantifier, that could also be used as an independent pronoun
(§4.6.2). However, in the course of the development, some of these terms have
been so frequently combined with other referring expressions that they now
appear to be incomplete without a co-occurring nominal. As a consequence,
English has acquired a new class of relational expressions (e.g., *the __, my __*)
that provide a slot for nouns, or NPs, similar to verbs, adjectives and adpositions (Figure 9.7).

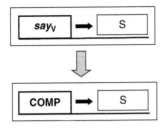

Figure 9.8 Diachronic development of complement clause from quotative construction

Finally, subordinate clauses are grammatical phrases that are commonly derived from other syntactic constituents. There are many different pathways of development leading from both compound phrases and (other) grammatical phrases to subordinate clauses. Complement clauses, for instance, are sometimes derived from quotative constructions consisting of a general speech verb and a quote clause that have merged into a subordinate clause in which the speech verb is reanalyzed as a complementizer. The Swahili complementizer *kwamba,* for instance, has developed from a verb meaning 'say' that has been reanalyzed as a grammatical marker of a complement clause (Figure 9.8; see §8.6).

In other cases, subordinate clauses are based on grammatical phrases. There are, for instance, many languages in which certain types of adverbial clauses are introduced by adpositions, suggesting that the development of adverbial clauses is influenced by adpositional constructions. For example, in many languages, purpose clauses are closely related to adpositional phrases (Schmidtke-Bode 2009: 187–198), as illustrated by the following examples from Turkish, in which purpose clauses are expressed by infinitive constructions marked by the postposition *için* 'for' (6a), which also appears after (pro) nouns in postpositional phrases (6b).

(6)   a. Hasan   kitab-ı   [[san-a   ver-mek]   **için**]   al-dı
         Hasan   book-ACC   you-DAT   give-INF   for   buy-PST
         'Hasan bought the book in order to give (it) to you.' (Kornfilt 1997: 73)

      b. bu   kitab-ı   [sen-in   **için**]   al-dı-m
         this   book-ACC   you-GEN   for   buy-PST-1SG
         'I bought this book for you.' (Kornfilt 1997: 226)

To sum up the discussion thus far, we have seen that syntactic constituents are motivated by general conceptual properties of relational expressions, but compound phrases and grammatical phrases are organized by different types of relational expressions. Compound phrases are organized around content words whose relational properties are due to general conceptual processes of frame semantics, whereas grammatical phrases are organized around function words whose relational properties are due to grammaticalization. In §9.5, we will see that the distinction between compound phrases and grammatical phrases is not only important for understanding the conceptual organization of syntactic constituents, it is also important for understanding the order of head and dependent categories and the occurrence of word order correlations.

9.5   Word Order Correlations

Word order correlations have been studied intensively in both formal and functional linguistics (see Song 2012 for a review). They are of fundamental significance to the analysis of phrase structure and have crucially influenced syntactic theory. The principles-and-parameters model of generative grammar, for instance, was motivated, at least in part, by the need to explain word order correlations. According to Chomsky (1981), there is a cross-linguistic tendency to arrange head and dependent categories in consistent orders because some aspects of word order are predetermined by the "head-direction parameter" of the language faculty.

Challenging the parameter account, linguistic typologists have argued that the Greenbergian word order correlations reflect the influence of three general factors: (i) genetic inheritance, (ii) language contact and (iii) general cognitive processes of language use (e.g., Dryer 1992; Hawkins 2004). There is ample evidence that genetically and geographically related languages tend to have the same or similar word orders because they inherited these orders from a common ancestor language or because they influenced each other through bilingualism and L2 acquisition (Thomason and Kaufman 1988; Nichols 1992). In what follows, however, we concentrate on the potential influence of cognitive processes on word order. Specifically, this section argues that word order correlations are due to two general factors: analogy and grammaticalization.

9.5.1   Grammaticalization and the Position of Grammatical Function Words

Most functional explanations for word order correlations revolve around particular cognitive processes of language use, but a number of studies have argued that some of Greenberg's word order universals do not need a functional or cognitive explanation, as they involve constructions that are related by grammaticalization (e.g., Givón 1975; Anderson 1979; Bybee 1988; Collins 2012; Dryer 2019). Consider, for instance, the correlation between the order of verb and object and that of auxiliary and verb. As Dryer (1992: 100) showed, tense-aspect auxiliaries precede the main verb in languages in which the object follows the verb, as for instance in English (e.g., *He is writing a letter*), but

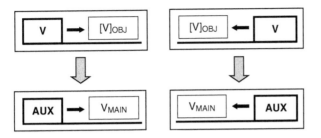

Figure 9.9 Diachronic relationship between V-O/O-V and Aux-V/V-Aux

they tend to follow the main verb if the object precedes the verb, as for instance in Burmese (7).

(7)   htamin: hce'   **pi**.
        rice   cook   ASP.PUNCTUAL
        '(I) have (finally) started to cook rice.' (Soe 1999: 134)

On the face of it, there is no reason why the position of auxiliaries correlates with that of object NPs, but this is readily explained by grammaticalization (Bybee 2010: 111). As pointed out above, across languages, tense-aspect auxiliaries are often derived from constructions in which a verb is accompanied by a verbal complement (e.g., an infinitive). In the course of the development, the complement-taking verb is downgraded to an auxiliary and the verbal complement is reanalyzed as the main verb of a periphrastic VP. Since verbal complements tend to occur in the same position as nominal complements, we find that in languages in which the verb precedes the (object) complement, auxiliaries also precede the main verb, whereas in languages in which the verb follows the (object) complement, auxiliaries are commonly postposed to the main verb (Figure 9.9).[2]

    A parallel analysis applies to the correlation between the order of adposition and noun and that of verb and object (Dryer 1992: 83). As we have seen, in many languages, adpositions are derived from certain types of verbs that are accompanied by an object complement (or adjunct). If the verb precedes the object, it gives rise to the order adposition-noun, but if it follows the object, it gives rise to the order noun-adposition (Figure 9.10). As a consequence of these

---

[2] There are two additional points to note here. First, auxiliaries can be "moved away" from the position of their diachronic source (for semantic or phonetic reasons) and this can disrupt the harmonic word order patterns that are created by grammaticalization (Harris and Campbell 1995: 220–224). And second, unlike tense-aspect auxiliaries, tense-aspect particles (indicating the same semantic features) do not pattern with other dependent categories of the verb, which may be related to the fact that tense-aspect particles do not usually originate from verbs of verbal complements like tense-aspect auxiliaries (Dryer 1992).

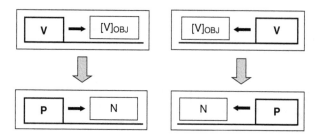

Figure 9.10 Diachronic relationship between V-O/O-V and P-NP/NP-P

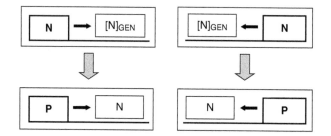

Figure 9.11 Diachronic relationship between N-G/G-N and P-NP/NP-P

developments, we find that some VO languages have acquired prepositions from verbs that precede the object (e.g., Yoruba), whereas some OV languages have acquired postpositions from verbs that follow the object (e.g., Korean).

What is more, the order of adposition and noun does not only correlate with that of verb and object but also with that of genitive and noun. In languages with postnominal genitives, adpositions tend to precede the noun, whereas in languages with prenominal genitives, adpositions usually follow the noun (Hawkins 1983: 53). Once again, the correlation can be explained by grammaticalization (Anderson 1979; Collins 2012; Dryer 2019). As we have seen, apart from verbs, body part terms and relational nouns can develop into adpositions if they are accompanied by a (genitive) attribute. If the relational noun precedes the (genitive) attribute, it develops into a preposition (as for instance some adpositions in Baka), but if the relational noun follows the attribute, it develops into a postposition (as for instance some adpositions in Mandarin Chinese) (Figure 9.11).

Interestingly, the diachronic developments of grammatical function words do not only account for certain word order correlations, they also explain some word order anomalies (Croft 2003: 76–77). Mandarin Chinese, for instance, has both prepositions and postpositions that developed from different source constructions. As it turns out, the prepositions are derived from so-called coverbs that precede a semantically associated noun, whereas the postpositions are derived from the nominal heads of an attributive construction in which a nominal attribute precedes the head noun (8a–b) (for more examples, see Dryer 2019).

(8)   a. [*dào*]$_V$ N 'reach N' → 'to N'
        b. N [*biān*]$_N$ 'N side' → 'N by'

In general, there can be no doubt that grammaticalization affects the development of word order correlations, but as Dryer (2019) and others have pointed out, grammaticalization is unlikely to provide a universal account for word order correlations. In particular, word order correlations between compound phrases cannot be (directly) attributed to grammaticalization, as compound phrases do not involve grammatical function words as immediate constituents (Diessel 2019). But how then do we account for ordering correlations between compound phrases?

9.5.2   The Linear Arrangement of Compound Phrases

Disregarding grammaticalization, there are two basic explanations for word order correlations in the functional-typological literature. First, some researchers have argued that word order correlations are due to general principles of syntactic processing. On this account, speakers tend to arrange syntactic categories in parallel orders across different types of constructions because structures with "consistent branching directions" have "short recognition domains" that are easier to process, and thus more highly preferred, than structures with "inconsistent branching directions" and "long recognition domains" (e.g., Dryer 1992, 2009; Hawkins 1994, 2004). Second, other researchers have claimed that word order correlations are best explained by similarity or analogy. On this account, speakers tend to arrange syntactic categories in parallel orders across constructions because they categorize similar constituents as instances of the same type (e.g., Krifka 1985; Justeson and Stephens 1990; Diessel 2019).

Both approaches explain word order correlations by speakers' preference for parallel orders in language use, but syntactic processing and analogy make somewhat different predictions as to how the various pairs of constructions are related (Justeson and Stephens 1990). In the processing approach, linear order is determined by universal syntactic principles such as "consistent left- or right-branching" (Dryer 1992) or "minimize domains" (Hawkins 2004) that apply to all constituents and are assumed to create global ordering patterns such as the distinction between "head-initial" and "head-final" structures. If word order correlations are due to analogy, however, one would expect to find local correlations between individual word order pairs, rather than two global patterns, as analogy is determined by the degree of similarity between particular constructions (Diessel 2019).

Although the distinction between head-initial and head-final languages is very prominent in the theoretical literature, it is not really supported by the typological data. While there are cross-linguistic tendencies to arrange syntactic constituents in particular orders across phrases, the ordering patterns cannot be subsumed under two global word order types. As Justeson and Stephens (1990) showed (based on data from 147 languages), a statistical model with local ordering correlations provides a much better fit for the typological data than a model with a global division between head-initial and head-final languages.

In accordance with this finding, one might think of the Greenbergian word order correlations as a network of locally related constructions. In what follows, I will explain this hypothesis based on a few selected word order pairs. As a starting point, let us consider the correlation between the order of verb and object and that of noun and relative clause (cf. Table 9.2).

As can be seen, there is a very strong tendency for relative clauses to follow the noun in VO languages, but in OV languages we find both pre- and postnominal relative clauses. Asymmetric correlations of this type are commonly explained by competing motivations (Croft 2003: 59–69). In the current case, it is widely assumed that the predominance of postnominal relatives is due to a general tendency to place long and heavy constituents after short ones (e.g., Dik 1997). We will consider the "short-before-long preference" in §9.6, but here we concentrate on the question of why the order of noun and relative clause correlates with that of verb and object.

If the correlation in Table 9.2 is due to analogy, noun phrases including relative clauses should be similar, in one way or another, to verb phrases including direct objects. However, on face value, NPs including a relative clause seem to be very different from VPs including a nominal object. Of course, at some level of analysis, one can always find some properties that are

Table 9.2 *Correlation between the order of verb and object and of noun and relative clause*

	V-O	O-V
N-RC	**415**	113
RC-N	5	**132**

Source: Dryer (2013)

shared by two (or more) constructions, but with no further information given, V-O and N-RC do not seem to have much in common.

Since there is no obvious overlap between these constructions, a number of studies have argued that the ordering correlation between V-O and N-RC is likely to be motivated by syntactic processing rather than by analogy (cf. Hawkins 2004; Dryer 2009). However, if we broaden the perspective and include complement clauses in the analysis, we can easily explain this correlation by analogy or structure mapping. While relative clauses do not have much in common with object NPs, they share important properties with object complement clauses. Consider, for instance, the following examples from English.

(9)   a. Paul noticed a truck [that crossed the street].
        b. Paul noticed [that a truck crossed the street].

Like relative clauses, complement clauses are subordinate clauses that are introduced by a complementizer (or relativizer) and both types of subordinate clauses are associated with a lexical head. The main difference is that relative clauses are headed by a noun, whereas complement clauses are headed by a verb; but, as can be seen in (9a–b), there is considerable overlap between relative and complement clauses in English. Similar kinds of overlaps occur in many other languages, suggesting that complement clauses may provide a link between relative clauses and nominal objects that explains why the order of noun and relative clause correlates with that of verb and object (Diessel 2019). Since complement clauses function as direct objects, there is analogical pressure to align them with object NPs, and since complement and relative clauses are similar types of subordinate constructions, there is also analogical pressure to place them in parallel positions. As a consequence, the order of noun and relative clause also correlates with that of verb and object, but this is likely to be an epiphenomenon of the tendency to place relative clauses and complement clauses in parallel positions.

Another set of word order correlations that is readily explained by analogy involves the order of adjective and noun. In the theoretical literature, it is often assumed that the order of adjective and noun correlates with that of verb and object, but as Dryer (1988) demonstrated (based on data from more than 600 languages), while there are certain geographical areas in which N-A/A-N correlates with V-O/O-V, this correlation is not universal. If we look at the positional patterns of adjectives from a cross-linguistic perspective, we find that adjectives tend to follow the head noun in both VO and OV languages, which is, of course, at odds with the global distinction between head-initial and head-final languages.

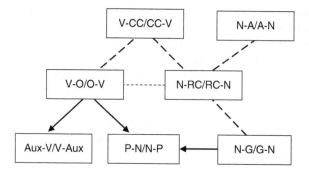

Figure 9.12 Network of locally related word order pairs

Nevertheless, while the order of adjective and noun is not part of the traditional VO/OV typology, there is a cross-linguistic tendency to align the position of adjectives with that of other noun modifiers. Adjectives and relative clauses, for instance, tend to occur on the same side of the head noun (Dryer 1988). Both categories are overall more frequent after the head, but if relative clauses precede the noun (in a particular language), adjectives are also usually preposed.[3] Moreover, as we have seen in §8.4, in many languages, attributive adjectives are morphologically similar to (reduced) relative clauses, suggesting that the relationship between adjectives and relatives is crucially influenced by analogy, which affects both the position and structure of these constructions.

Generalizing across these findings, we may characterize the Greenbergian word order correlations as a network of constructions that are created by two general factors: analogy and grammaticalization. Figure 9.12 summarizes the previous discussion in terms of such a network, in which arrows indicate connections that are primarily created by grammaticalization, whereas dotted lines indicate connections that are primarily created by analogy (for some discussion, see Diessel 2019).

In sum, in this section we have considered some new hypotheses as to how word order correlations are shaped by language use. These hypotheses can be tested with psycholinguistic methods;[4] but in §9.6, we turn to factors that can disrupt the preference for harmonic word order patterns.

---

[3] The eastern Tibeto-Burman languages are an exception: they have prenominal relative clauses and postnominal adjectives due to language contact (see Dryer 2003 for discussion).

[4] A number of psycholinguistic studies have examined the cognitive processes behind word order correlations with experimental and computational methods (e.g., Kirby 1999; Christiansen 2000; Culbertson et al. 2012, 2015).

9.6   Other Cognitive Processes That Influence Word Order

One factor that has been known for a long time to influence constituent order is length or "grammatical weight" (Wasow 2002). There is a well-known tendency to place short constituents before long ones. Otto Behaghel called this "das Gesetz der wachsenden Glieder," that is, 'the law of increasing constituents':

Von zwei Satzgliedern geht, wenn möglich, das kürzere dem längeren voran. [Given two phrases, when possible, the shorter precedes the longer.] (Behaghel 1932)

Evidence for this law comes from both language-particular corpus studies and cross-linguistic research on word order correlations. For instance, Hawkins (2000) showed that, given an English sentence with two postverbal prepositional phrases (10a–b), there is a preference to place the shorter PP before the long one (though other factors can also influence the order; see Wiechmann and Lohmann 2013).

(10)   a. He talked [to me]$_{PP}$ [about his new book]$_{PP}$.
         b. He talked [about his new book]$_{PP}$ [to me]$_{PP}$.

Parallel trends have been found in other corpus studies with other syntactic constituents in English and several other languages (e.g., Siewierska 1993; Wasow 2002; Bresnan et al. 2007). We will consider some of this research in §9.7. Here we note that constituent length may account for certain asymmetries in word order correlations. For example, above we saw that while the position of relative clauses correlates with that of other dependent categories, there is a cross-linguistic tendency for relative clauses to follow the head noun. Since relative clauses are usually longer than the noun they modify, it seems reasonable to assume that the predominance of postnominal relative clauses is related to the short-before-long preference (e.g., Dryer 2009).

The same line of reasoning applies to the dependent categories of compound VPs. For example, although object complement clauses serve the same syntactic function as object NPs, object clauses are more often postposed to the verb than nominal objects (Schmidtke-Bode and Diessel 2017). In Persian, for instance, nominal objects precede the verb, whereas object clauses follow it (11), which is, of course, consistent with the tendency for long constituents to follow short ones.

(11)   (mæn)   fekr-mi-kon-æm   [(ke)   mæryæm se-ta   mæjele
         (I)   think-DUR-know-1SG (that) Maryam three-CL magazine
         xær-id].
         bought-2PL
         'I think that Maryam bought three magazines.' (Mahootian 1997: 13)

That length has an impact on constituent order is uncontroversial (e.g., Hawkins 1994; Dik 1997; Wasow 2002), but the cognitive processes behind the length effect are not entirely clear. There are two general explanations.

Some scholars have argued that short constituents precede long ones because speakers are prone to express given information, which is easily accessible, before new information, which is more difficult to retrieve. Since new information needs more explicit coding than old or given information, long constituents typically follow short ones (Chafe 1994).

Other researchers have argued that processing accounts for the short-before-long preference. For instance, in Diessel (2005) I have argued, based on Hawkins (1994), that subordinate clauses tend to follow the associated element because preposed subordinate clauses create long "dependency domains" that are difficult to plan and process (see also Diessel 2008). If this is correct, we may hypothesize that the above-described asymmetries in the position of relative and complement clauses reflect the effect of syntactic processing on linear order. Let me emphasize, however, that while information structure and syntactic processing are different cognitive phenomena, they are not mutually exclusive. In fact, there is good evidence that both factors influence constituent order (Wasow 2002; Diessel 2005; Wiechmann and Kerz 2013).

Another factor that can affect the linear organization of constituent structure is automatization. In Chapter 5, we saw that automatization creates associative connections between linguistic elements that are frequently processed in a particular order. Other things being equal, the more often a particular string of linguistic elements is used, the stronger the sequential associations are between them.

In the default case, automatization reinforces the conceptual links between relational expressions and their fillers, but this is not generally the case. For instance, as noted in Chapter 5, while adpositions are semantically related to nominal expressions, they are sometimes associated with a preceding verb if the combination of verb and adposition is very frequent (e.g., *belong to, rely on*), suggesting that automatization can override the conceptual motivation to combine adpositions with adjacent nominal expressions.

Similar mismatches between syntactic constituents and lexical phrases have been found with other categories. Very often, the discrepancy is reflected in the prosodic groupings of lexical expressions. For instance, although articles are generally analyzed as syntactic constituents of noun phrases, they are sometimes grouped together with adpositions rather than with nouns or noun phrases (12a–b), suggesting that the sequential link between a particular adposition and an article can be stronger (as a consequence of automatization) than the conceptual link between an article and a co-occurring noun.

(12)   a. [à [le café]]   → [au café]
        b. [zu [dem Haus]]   → [zum Haus]

Another example of this type is auxiliary contraction in English (§5.3.2). Although auxiliaries are conceptually related to verbs, they often cliticize to a preceding pronoun (e.g., *I'll, he's, you're*). Since the contraction rate correlates with the joint frequency of auxiliary and pronoun, it is a plausible hypothesis that automatization has created chunks of pronouns and contracted auxiliaries (e.g., *I'll, he's, you're*) that deviate from the canonical groupings of syntactic constituents (Krug 1998; Bybee and Scheibman 1999; Barth and Kapatsinski 2017).

To summarize the previous discussion, we have seen that constituent structure is shaped by several interacting factors: (i) the conceptual properties of relational expressions, (ii) the diachronic developments of certain grammatical function words, (iii) the analogical treatment of similar expressions, (iv) the tendency to place long constituents after short ones and (v) the creation of sequential links by automatization. Taken together, these factors explain both the parallels between syntactic constituents that have been emphasized in traditional phrase structure grammar (in particular in X-bar theory; Radford 1997: 167–333) and the many idiosyncrasies that are characteristic of syntactic constituency (Bybee 2002).

9.7   Filler–Slot Relations

Having analyzed the cognitive processes that shape syntactic constituents and constituent order, let us now take a closer look at filler–slot relations. To repeat the central hypothesis from the beginning of the chapter, (hierarchical) phrase structure involves associative connections between constructional schemas and particular phrasal fillers. Consider, for instance, the structure of the noun phrase in Figure 9.13.

The noun phrase schema in this example includes two slots for nominal expressions – a genitive attribute and a head noun. In traditional phrase structure grammar, a genitive NP (like the one in Figure 9.13) is defined over formal syntactic categories, but in the current approach, it is associated with

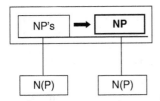

Figure 9.13 Filler–slot relations of genitive NP

particular lexical and phrasal fillers that affect the way a genitive construction is used and processed. If we look at the use of English genitive constructions in corpora, we find that head and modifier occur with very different fillers. As it turns out, the (genitive) modifier is often a pronoun or proper name referring to a human being, whereas the head is usually a common noun or noun phrase referring to an inanimate entity (e.g., *John's coat*).

In order to better understand the filler–slot relations in Figure 9.13, let us compare the *s*-genitive to the so-called *of*-genitive (e.g., *a friend of mine*), which can be seen as an alternative construction (e.g., Rosenbach 2002, 2005; Szmrecsanyi and Hinrichs 2008; Wolk et al. 2013). The two constructions (i.e., the *s*-genitive and the *of*-genitive) are marked by different function morphemes and occur with different word orders. Crucially, while both constructions have special uses, there is an area of overlap where speakers can choose between them (see 13a–b).

(13)   a. [England's capital] is London.
        b. [The capital of England] is London.

Concentrating on the area of overlap, a number of studies have shown that speakers' choice between the two constructions is predictable from several semantic and pragmatic factors. Of particular importance are (i) the animacy of the two referents, (ii) their length and (iii) their topicality (e.g. Rosenbach 2002; Szmrecsanyi and Hinrichs 2008; Wolk et al. 2013). Needless to say that some of these features correlate with each other. Animate referents, for instance, are more often topics than inanimate referents, and topics tend to be shorter than nontopics. However, while animacy, length and topicality are closely related, a number of studies have shown that they influence the genitive alternation as independent factors (Szmrecsanyi and Hinrichs 2008; Wolk et al. 2013). This is not only evident from the statistical analysis of corpus data, but also from experimental studies that were specifically designed to examine the effects of animacy, length and topicality on the genitive alternation under controlled conditions (Rosenbach 2002, 2005).

Interestingly, some of the factors that influence the genitive alternation have also been encountered in research on other alternating pairs of constructions. The dative alternation, for instance, also correlates with animacy, length and topicality. As Bresnan and colleagues have shown in a series of corpus and behavioral studies, there is a conspicuous asymmetry between recipient and theme in ditransitive constructions (Bresnan et al. 2007; Bresnan and Hay 2008; Bresnan and Ford 2010; see also Wasow 2002; Wolk et al. 2013). In the double-object construction, the recipient is usually short, highly accessible, or topical, and animate. Very often, it is a pronoun or proper name, whereas the theme is usually an inanimate noun that is longer and less topical than the dative (pro)noun (Figure 9.14).

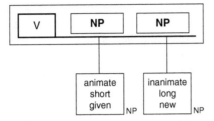

Figure 9.14 Filler–slot relations of the double-object construction

In the *to*-dative construction, however, recipient and theme do not only occur in reverse order, they also differ in terms of length, topicality and animacy from their double-object counterparts. As it turns out, the recipient of the *to*-dative construction is usually a full NP (rather than a pronoun) that tends to be longer and less topical than the preceding theme and that is less often animate than the recipient of the double-object construction.

Using multivariate statistical methods, Bresnan et al. (2007) showed that all of these factors influence speakers' choice between the double-object and *to*-dative constructions, suggesting that the dative alternation is subject to the same semantic and pragmatic constraints as the genitive alternation (see Wolk et al. 2013 for an explicit comparison of the two types of constructions).

Taken together with the results of similar studies on other alternating pairs of constructions (Mair 1990; Hawkins 1994; Arnold et al. 2000; Wasow 2002; Gries 2003; Diessel 2005, 2008; Gast and Wiechmann 2012; Wiechmann and Kerz 2013), this research provides strong evidence for the hypothesis that the filler–slot relations of the genitive and dative alternations are influenced by the same semantic and pragmatic factors, i.e., animacy, length and topicality.

Note that all of these factors are primarily descriptive. In order to understand their influence on language use, they have to be linked to general psychological processes, but these links are not yet fully understood. As pointed out above, there is an ongoing debate about the effect of length on constituent order (§9.6) and there is also a debate about the role of animacy in grammar and language change in linguistic typology (Gildea and Zúñiga 2016).

More research is needed to better understand the psychological processes behind the effects of animacy, length and topicality. However, irrespective of the fact that we do not yet fully understand these processes, it must be emphasized that filler–slot relations are not only determined by semantic and/or pragmatic factors. As we have seen in Chapters 7 and 8, while filler–slot relations are semantically and/or pragmatically motivated, they also reflect language users' experience with particular co-occurrence patterns. In other words, speakers "know" from their experience with genitive and ditransitive constructions that the alternating pairs of constructions are associated with different fillers and this knowledge affects the (future) use of these constructions in addition to semantic and pragmatic factors.

One piece of evidence for this hypothesis comes from the fact that filler–slot relations are often idiosyncratic or lexically particular. For instance, in Chapter 7 we saw that argument-structure constructions may be associated with individual verbs that do not really match the meaning of the construction (e.g., the use of *envy* and *ask* in the double-object construction), and in Chapter 8 we saw that word class schemas are sometimes associated with lexical expressions that are at odds with the conceptual specifications of a particular word class schema (e.g., the use of *head* as a verb and of *walk* as a noun).

Similar idiosyncrasies occur with filler–slot relations in the domain of phrase structure. For instance, although the verb *want* is semantically similar to *wish* (and other desiderative verbs), *want* does not occur with finite complement clauses, like *wish*, but takes instead infinitive constructions (14a–c). Note that in many other languages the semantic equivalent of English *want* can occur with finite complement clauses, just like *wish* (cf. German *Ich will/wünsche, dass du kommst* 'I want/wish that you come'), indicating that the (restrictive) use of *want* with infinitives is a particular trait of English grammar that cannot be explained by general semantic or pragmatic factors.

(14)   a. I wish that he would come.
        b. *I want that he comes.
        c. I want him to come.

Idiosyncratic constraints on constituent structure have also been noted in research on (English) varieties. For instance, one oft-noted feature of the double object construction that varies across English dialects concerns the use of pronouns and noun phrases. In standard English, the double-object construction does not usually occur with a lexical recipient and a pronominal theme, but in some northern varieties of British English, notably in the dialect of Lancashire, this pattern is well attested (cf. *Show your father them*). It occurs in linguistic corpora and is accepted as correct by speakers of this variety (Siewierska and Hollmann 2007). Moreover, it is not uncommon in the Lancashire dialect to place the recipient after the theme in the double-object construction, especially when the theme is a pronoun and the recipient a noun (e.g., *She gave it the man*), but also when both arguments are expressed by pronouns (e.g., *Give it me*) (Gast 2007). However, thus far, this pattern has only been found with three verbs, namely, with *give, send* and *show* (Siewierska and Hollmann 2007), suggesting that the order theme-recipient is lexically particular and unpredictable from general semantic and pragmatic criteria.

Similar idiosyncrasies have been noticed in studies of other constructions and other varieties, in both synchronic and diachronic corpora (Rosenbach

2002; Bresnan and Hay 2008; Bresnan and Ford 2010; Wolk et al. 2013). Thus, while the filler–slot relations of syntactic phrase structure are motivated by general semantic and pragmatic factors, they are also influenced by speakers' and listeners' experience with particular lexemes and constructions.

9.8   Conclusion

In conclusion, this chapter has outlined a usage-based analysis of phrase structure. The discussion can be summarized in three main points.

First, syntactic phrases are shaped by several interacting factors including conceptualization, grammaticalization, analogy and categorization, the short-before-long preference and automatization. Since all of these factors concern domain-general processes of language use, there are parallels in the organization of phrases across languages and constructions. For instance, the common distinction between NPs, VPs and APs is motivated by the conceptual processes that underlie the major parts of speech (Chapter 8), and the distinction between compound phrases and grammatical phrases is created by general processes of grammaticalization (§9.4).

Second, word order correlations emerge from the cognitive processes that shape syntactic constituents. Two basic types of word order correlations have been distinguished: correlations between compound phrases and grammatical phrases, which are usually the product of grammaticalization, and correlations between two or more compound phrases, which are primarily the result of analogy and categorization. Both types of correlations are also influenced by other factors that interact with analogy and grammaticalization (e.g., language contact, genetic inheritance, information structure, animacy).

And finally, the cognitive organization of phrase structure involves associative connections between particular syntactic schemas and phrasal fillers. Building on the analysis of filler–slot relations in Chapters 7 and 8, the present chapter has argued that the connections between lexical phrases and phrase structure schemas are determined by two general factors: semantic and pragmatic aspects of language use and speakers' experience with particular phrase structure patterns.

Part IV

Constructional Relations

10   Construction Families

10.1   Introduction

In the three previous chapters, the focus of analysis has been on filler–slot relations. Combining evidence from various subfields of linguistics and cognitive psychology, it was argued that argument structure, word classes and phrase structure are best analyzed in the framework of a dynamic network model in which constructional schemas are associated with particular lexical or phrasal fillers. In the remainder of this book, we will be concerned with constructional relations (§2.5.2).

Like lexemes, constructions are linguistic signs that are interconnected in various ways. In Chapter 4 we saw that speakers' knowledge of grammar involves a taxonomic network of hierarchically related constructions. The current chapter argues that, in addition to taxonomic relations, the grammar network involves horizontal, or lateral, relations between semantically or formally similar constructions at the same level of abstraction.

10.2   Horizontal Relations

In the classic version of generative grammar, syntactic structures with similar forms and meanings were connected by transformations. Passive sentences, for instance, were derived from (underlying) active sentences by a set of syntactic operations such as movement, deletion and auxiliary insertion, which together constitute the passive transformation (Chomsky 1965: 103–106). Parallel analyses were proposed for other semantically and/or formally related structures such as the two constructions of the dative alternation or finite and nonfinite subordinate clauses.

Like generative grammar, many other grammatical theories assume that syntactic structures are related by derivational processes, but construction grammar has abandoned the concept of syntactic derivation. According to Goldberg (2006: 25), every surface pattern "is best analyzed on its own terms, without relying on explicit or implicit reference to a possible alternative phrase." As a consequence, construction grammarians have paid relatively little attention to semantic and formal similarities between constructions and have focused on the taxonomic organization of grammar.

Several recent studies have argued, however, that the grammar network does not only involve taxonomic relations between constructions at different levels of abstraction, but also horizontal relations between similar or contrastive constructions, even when these constructions are not (immediately) subsumed under a schema in the taxonomic network (e.g., Cappelle 2006; Van de Velde 2014; Perek 2015).

Evidence for this hypothesis comes from research on language acquisition and language change. For instance, Abbot-Smith and Behrens (2006) argued that the acquisition of stative passives in German is crucially influenced by children's prior knowledge of semantically and formally similar constructions. Specifically, they showed that copular clauses have a marked impact on the acquisition of German passive sentences. Although copular clauses and stative passives are not taxonomically related, they are very similar in German: Both constructions include the verb *sein* 'be', occur with the order NP-*be*-ADJ/PTC and designate resultant states (i.e., *Die Tür ist offen/geöffnet* 'The door is open/ opened'). Analyzing extensive corpus data from a 2-year-old child, Abbot-Smith and Behrens showed that copular clauses facilitate the acquisition of German stative passives. Although event passives are more frequent in the ambient language than stative passives, the latter cause fewer problems in L1 acquisition because stative passives are supported by children's knowledge of copular-clause constructions, which they learn long before they begin to produce passive sentences. Similar analyses have been proposed for other semantically (or formally) related constructions in English and other languages (e.g., Rosenbach 2007; Brandt et al. 2008; Van de Velde 2014; Perek 2015; Fonteyn and van de Pol 2016; de Smet et al. 2018).

Building on this research, the current chapter argues that every construction has a particular "ecological location" in the grammar network that is defined by its relationship to other constructions in the system (Lakoff 1987: 462–494; see also Diessel 1997). These relationships can be characterized in terms of two general concepts: similarity and contrast.

In the current chapter, we will be concerned with the effect of similarity on the use and the development of grammatical constructions, and, in Chapter 11, we turn to the encoding of contrastive constructions. Since the horizontal associations between constructions are reminiscent of the associations between lexemes in the mental lexicon, we begin with a short discussion of the mental lexicon, before we turn to the analysis of constructions.

10.3   The Mental Lexicon

There is general agreement among psychologists and (most) linguists that words and lexemes are stored and processed in an activation network (Collins and Loftus 1975; Dell 1986; Bybee 1995). In order to investigate the cognitive organization of this network, psychologists have used a wide range of experimental tasks, e.g., lexical decision tasks, naming tasks, priming tasks. Many of these tasks have been devised to investigate how lexemes are accessed, or activated, in language use. Lexical access can be seen as a competition process whereby a particular item is selected from a set of alternative expressions. One factor that has been shown to have a strong impact on lexical access is frequency of occurrence. Other things being equal, frequent items are more easily accessed, or activated, than infrequent ones (Forster and Chambers 1973, among many others).

In addition to frequency, there are several other factors that influence lexical access (and that interact with frequency in complex ways). One of these other factors is priming, a recency effect of language use that facilitates (or inhibits) the activation of semantically or formally similar items (§3.5.3). Lexical priming provides strong evidence for the network organization of the mental lexicon and is commonly explained by "activation spreading" (Collins and Loftus 1975). When a word is activated in language use, activation spreads to semantically and/or phonologically similar items, making these items more easily accessible in subsequent use (see also Anderson 1983; Dell 1986; Hudson 2007: 37–41).

Another factor that can influence lexical access is "neighborhood density," or "neighborhood size," which refers to the number of items that are phonetically similar to a particular target word.[1] The word *cat*, for instance, has a large number of phonetic neighbors (e.g., *rat, hat, mat, sat, vat, fat, pat, at*), but *cup* has only a few (e.g., *cut, up*). Some studies suggest that a dense neighborhood can slow down lexical access in comprehension (Luce and Pisoni 1998), but there is good evidence that it facilitates the activation of lexical items in production (Vitevitch 2002). All else being equal, items of a dense neighborhood are produced more quickly and more accurately than items of a sparse neighborhood (Andrews 1997; Dąbrowska 2008; Gahl et al. 2012). Moreover, there is evidence that the early stages of lexical development are crucially influenced by the family size of phonetic neighbors. Disregarding high-frequency words (which are not, or only weakly influenced by phonetic neighbors), there is a clear correlation between neighborhood density and age of acquisition. Other things being equal, high-density words are learned earlier than low-density words (Storkel 2004) and are more easily recognized and memorized in learning studies (Hollich et al. 2002).

Closely related to the notion of neighborhood density is the notion of "morphological family size," which Schreuder and Baayen (1997) defined as the set of complex words that share a common lexical root. *House*, for instance,

---

[1] Usually, a "phonetic neighbor" is defined as an item that differs from the target word by one phoneme or letter (Andrews 1997).

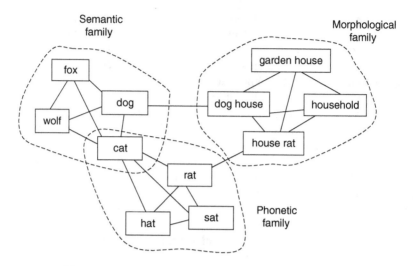

Figure 10.1 Lexical network with three lexical families

pertains to a large morphological family with more than 30 members (including compounds) (e.g., *household, garden house, housing*), whereas the family of *horizon* is very small (e.g., *horizontal*). Here again, items that reside in a large family are more easily activated and produced than items that reside in a small family (see Mulder et al. 2014 for a review). Figure 10.1 summarizes the essence of the previous discussion. It illustrates how semantically and formally similar lexemes are interconnected and grouped together into families in an association network.

In what follows, we will see that many of the phenomena that have been observed in the study of the mental lexicon can also be observed in the study of constructions in the grammar network. In particular, we will see that the use and development of constructions are crucially influenced by constructional frequency, semantic and formal similarity, and constructional family size, or neighborhood density.

10.4   Structural Priming

One piece of evidence for the hypothesis that constructions are interconnected like words and lexemes in the mental lexicon comes from research on structural priming (see Pickering and Ferreira 2008 for a review). Structural priming has been a central topic of psycholinguistic research since the pioneering study by Kathryn Bock (1986). In this study, Bock showed that speakers' choice of a construction is crucially influenced by the use of the same or a similar construction in the previous discourse. For instance, in one of her experiments, Bock showed that speakers of English are more likely to describe a ditransitive scene depicting an act of transfer with the *to*-dative construction, rather than the double-object construction, if they had used a semantically unrelated *to*-dative sentence in prior picture descriptions.

Parallel results were obtained for the active–passive alternation and various other pairs of related constructions. Crucially, while this type of priming is especially strong if it involves the same sentence type (e.g., *to*-dative primes *to*-dative), Bock and Loebell (1990) showed that structural priming also occurs between distinct grammatical constructions that share some of their properties. For instance, in one of their experiments, they found that active sentences including a locative *by*-phrase prime passive sentences with an agentive *by*-phrase (1a–b) and that sentences including a directional prepositional phrase prime the prepositional dative construction (2a–b).

(1)   a. The 747 was landing by the airport's tower.
        b. The 747 was alerted by the airport's tower.

(2)   a. The wealthy widow drove an old Mercedes to the church.
        b. The wealthy widow gave an old Mercedes to the church.

Since these priming effects occur despite the fact that prime and target have different meanings, Bock and colleagues argued that structural priming is independent of semantic factors. Later research showed, however, that structural priming also occurs with (structurally distinct but) semantically similar constructions. For instance, Hare and Goldberg (1999) showed that a *provide-with* sentence such as *The officer provided the soldier with guns* has a facilitatory effect on the activation of the double-object construction. *Provide-with* sentences share properties with both constructions of the dative alternation (3a–c): They have the same surface form as the prepositional dative construction (i.e., NP-V-NP-PP), but recipient and theme are arranged in the same order as in the double-object construction (i.e., AGENT-V-RECIPIENT-THEME). Using the same experimental task as Bock and Loebell, Hare and Goldberg showed that *provide-with* sentences prime the double-object construction although they are structurally more similar to the prepositional dative construction, indicating that semantic similarity has a priming effect on the choice of syntactic constructions (see also Bencini and Goldberg 2000; Chang et al. 2003; Goldwater et al. 2011).

(3)   a. His editor offered [Bob]$_{NP}$ [the hot story]$_{NP}$.   DOUBLE-OBJECT
        b. His editor credited [Bob]$_{NP}$ [with the hot story]$_{PP}$.   PROVIDE-WITH
        c. His editor promised [the hot story]$_{NP}$ [to Bob]$_{PP}$.   PREPOSITIONAL DATIVE

Another factor that has been shown to influence structural priming is the lexical overlap between prime and target. As Pickering and Branigan (1998) showed, while structural priming is not contingent on lexical overlap, it is greatly enhanced if prime and target include the same content words. Using a sentence repetition task, these researchers found that people are much more likely to complete a sentence fragment such as *The NP gave* . . . in the structural format of a previously used sentence if the sentence fragment includes the same verb as the prime than if it includes a different verb. Pickering and Branigan (1998) called this the "lexical boost" of structural priming, which has also been observed in corpus studies on structural priming (Gries 2005; Szmrecsanyi 2006).

Finally, recent research has argued that there is a close connection between priming and learning. Although priming is often characterized as a short-term phenomenon, there is now a large body of results indicating that structural priming has long-lasting effects on the development of linguistic knowledge (e.g., Savage et al. 2006; Bock et al. 2007; Rowland et al. 2012). For instance, Savage et al. (2006) noticed a marked impact of structural priming on children's linguistic choices after more than a week and moreover they found that the priming effect persists even longer when it is reinforced after a certain period of time. Considering the long-lasting effects of repetition, structural priming is now commonly characterized as a particular form of "implicit learning," which arguably plays an important role in grammar acquisition (Bock and Griffin 2000; Ellis 2002; Chang et al. 2006).

In general, structural priming has become a central topic of psycholinguistics and the results of this research are commonly explained in the framework of a dynamic network model (e.g., Pickering and Branigan 1998; Chang et al. 2006). There are conspicuous parallels between lexical and structural priming, supporting the hypothesis that constructions are stored and processed in an association network. Like lexical access, access to constructions involves competition between similar constructions that is influenced by the activation level of the competing constructions at a particular moment in time. The activation level is contingent on the degree of entrenchment and priming. Like lexemes, constructions are easily activated when they are deeply entrenched in memory or primed by the same or a similar element in the previous discourse, suggesting that speakers' grammatical knowledge involves associative connections between structurally and/or semantically similar grammatical patterns that influence constructional access through activation spreading.

Structural priming provides perhaps the best evidence for constructional relations, but there is also evidence from research on sentence processing, L1 acquisition and language change that constructions are interconnected by lateral associations. Concentrating on word order phenomena in English, the remainder of this chapter shows that frequency, similarity and constructional family size have a significant impact on the processing and development of constructions in the grammar network.

10.5   Sentence Processing

Like research on structural priming, much recent research on sentence comprehension has argued that the processing of structural information involves the same cognitive mechanisms as the processing of lexical information (e.g., MacDonald et al. 1994; Trueswell 1996). In the constraint-based approach (MacDonald and Seidenberg 2006), sentence comprehension is driven by language users' experience with particular structural and lexical patterns that compete for activation (see also Bates and MacWhinney 1989).

One phenomenon that has been studied intensively in the constraint-based model is the processing of relative clauses. In the older literature, it was generally found that subject relative clauses are more easily accessed and processed than object relative clauses (4–5), but recent research has shown that the particular processing difficulties of object relatives are contingent on certain semantic, pragmatic and lexical factors that were not controlled for in earlier studies. In particular, it was shown that the processing of object relatives is greatly facilitated if these constructions occur with particular types of nouns and verbs (e.g., Mak et al. 2006; Roland et al. 2012). Nevertheless, while object relatives are not generally more difficult to comprehend than subject relatives, the fact remains that in many contexts subject relatives are easier to activate and process than object relative clauses (see Gordon and Lowder 2012 for a review).

(4)   The teacher [who praised the student] . . . SUBJECT RELATIVE

(5)   The student [who the teacher praised] . . . OBJECT RELATIVE

Considering the overall results of this research, we may hypothesize that the asymmetry in the processing of subject and object relatives reflects the influence of frequency on sentence comprehension. However, when we look at linguistic corpora, we find that while subject relatives prevail in written genres (e.g., the Wall Street Journal), in conversational discourse object relatives are usually more frequent than subject relatives (Table 10.1), suggesting that the processing asymmetry between subject and object relatives cannot be due to an asymmetry in frequency between the two types of relative clauses.

But how then do we explain that object relatives tend to cause longer reading times in many comprehension studies? If we take a closer look at the use of object relatives in spontaneous language, it is immediately obvious that these structures are very different from the relative-clause stimuli that have been used

Table 10.1 *Subject and object relatives in written and spoken registers of English*

	Wall Street Journal	ICE (written)	ICE (spoken)	Switchboard (spoken)	BNC (spoken)
SUBJ-RC	5585 (78%)	393 (89%)	212 (43%)	760 (46%)	25,024 (35%)
OBJ-RC	1589 (22%)	46 (11%)	279 (57%)	870 (54%)	46,474 (65%)
	7174	439	491	1630	71,474

Source: Roland et al. (2007: 355) and Wiechmann (2015: 104)

in comprehension experiments. There are two important points to note here: First, while the relative clauses of most psycholinguistic studies are formed with two lexical NPs (e.g., *The senator who the reporter bothered* ...), the object relatives of spontaneous language typically include a pronominal subject (e.g., *The senator I bothered* ...) (Reali and Christiansen 2007; Fox and Thompson 2007); and second, while the relative clauses of most psycholinguistic studies modify an animate head noun (e.g., *The teacher who the student asked* ...), the object relatives of spontaneous language typically modify an inanimate NP (e.g., *The book I read* ...) (Roland et al. 2007: 359; Wiechmann 2015).

Given these tendencies, it does not come as a surprise that object relatives are difficult to comprehend if they occur with animate heads and lexical subjects as in many psycholinguistic studies. As Mak et al. (2006) have demonstrated, when object relatives modify an inanimate head and include a pronominal subject, they do NOT cause greater comprehension problems than subject relatives, suggesting that the processing of object relatives is crucially influenced by language users' experience with this construction (see also Traxler et al. 2005; Roland et al. 2012).

More surprising is the fact that language users' experience with subject relatives does not have the same influence on relative-clause processing. For instance, although the vast majority of subject relatives in spontaneous speech are attached to an animate head (Roland et al. 2007: 359), there is no indication that listeners find subject relatives difficult to comprehend if they modify an inanimate noun (e.g., *the storm that destroyed the bridge, the vase that broke into pieces*). In fact, Mak et al. (2006) found that when both NPs of a transitive relative clause are inanimate, speakers (of Dutch) have fewer difficulties with subject relatives than with object relatives although subject relatives are mostly used with animate heads. It seems that the processing of subject relatives is less strongly influenced by particular semantic and pragmatic factors than the processing of object relatives.

There are various suggestions in the literature to explain the processing differences between subject and object relatives (see Gordon and Lowder 2012 for a review). A full review of these suggestions is beyond the scope of this section, but there is one proposal that is of particular importance to the current approach.

According to Wells et al. (2009), the processing difference between subject and object relatives is caused, at least in part, by the relationship between relative clauses and main clauses. Specifically, these researchers claim that subject relatives are always easy to comprehend because they have many "sentence neighbors" that share with them the same order of semantic arguments. As can be seen in (6) to (8), the two NPs of subject relatives are arranged in the same linear order as the NPs of transitive clauses, ditransitive clauses and various other types of (declarative) main clauses.

(6)   [The author]$_{AG}$ who wrote [this book]$_{TH}$ . . .   NP$_{agent}$ V (NP) . . .

(7)   [The boy]$_{AG}$ opened [the window]$_{PA}$.

(8)   [The student]$_{AG}$ sent [his teacher]$_{REC}$ [a mail]$_{TH}$.

Unlike subject relatives, object relatives deviate from the dominant word order pattern of English. Since object relatives place the patient (or semantic object) before the relative-clause subject and relative-clause verb, they essentially occur with the order O-S-V, which is very unusual in English (and most other languages). Considering this difference, Wells et al. (2009: 252) hypothesized that object relatives are difficult to process because they "have essentially no sentence 'neighbors' in terms of word order and thematic role assignment." Note, however, that English has topicalization constructions and (object) WH-questions in which the patient or theme precedes the subject and verb as in object relative clauses (9–11).

(9)   [The article]$_{TH}$ [I]$_{AG}$ read . . .   NP$_{theme}$ NP$_{agent}$ V . . .

(10)   [This argument]$_{TH}$, [I]$_{AG}$ don't understand.

(11)   [Which book]$_{TH}$ did [you]$_{AG}$ read?

In other words, contrary to what Wells et al. claim, object relatives have sentence neighbors, but of course the S-V-(O) family of declarative main clauses is much larger and more deeply entrenched than the O-S-V family, which comprises only a few special sentence types. Figure 10.2 presents a network model in which subject and object relatives are grouped together with their sentence neighbors into construction families similar to the families of related lexical items in the mental lexicon (see Figure 10.1).

Since subject relatives are supported by the large S-V-O family of declarative main clauses, Wells et al. hypothesized that the processing of subject relatives is less strongly influenced by language users' experience with relative

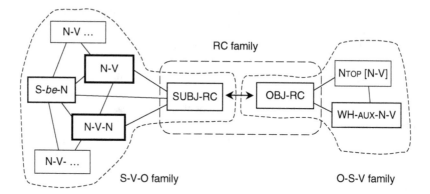

Figure 10.2 Relationship between subject and object relative clauses and their construction neighbors (in English)

clauses than the processing of object relatives. Since the latter do not receive much support from sentence neighbors, the processing of object relatives is almost exclusively contingent on language users' experience with object relatives themselves.

In order to test this hypothesis, the researchers conducted a training study in which they compared the results of two self-paced reading tasks before and after a training regime in which adult speakers of English were exposed to a large number of relative clauses. Figure 10.3 shows the (unadjusted) reading times in the critical regions of subject and object relatives in the two self-paced reading tasks before and after training.

There are three important points to note. First, subject relatives were read faster than object relatives both before and after training. Second, reading times were significantly longer for both types of relative clauses in the pretest than in the posttest, indicating that participants' additional experience with relative clauses during the experiment facilitated the processing of both subject and object relatives. And third, and most importantly, the additional experience that was provided during the training sessions had a stronger effect on the processing of object relatives than on the processing of subject relatives. In the pretest, subject relatives were read 66 ms faster (in the critical region) than object relatives, but in the posttest, the difference was reduced to only 15 ms (Figure 10.3).

Crucially, a control group that was exposed to complement and conjoined clauses, rather than to relatives, produced reading time responses with the same difference between subject and object relatives before and after training, supporting the hypothesis that the manipulation of experience in the target group had a stronger impact on object relatives than on subject relatives. Since

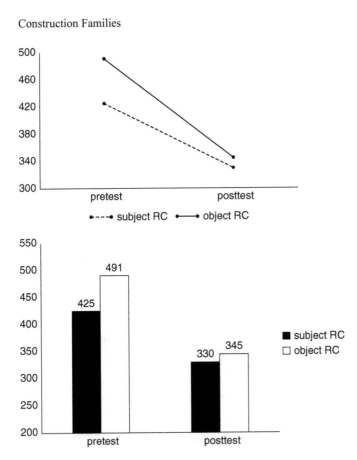

Figure 10.3 Unadjusted reading times of subject and object RCs before and after participants were exposed to a battery of subject and object relatives in four training sessions (based on data from Wells et al. 2009: 269)

subject relatives are associated with the dominant family of S-V-O constructions, they are easily activated in all contexts, whereas the activation and processing of object relatives are almost exclusively determined by language users' experience with object relatives themselves. This explains why the processing of object relative clauses is strongly influenced by speakers' experience with the particular semantic and pragmatic properties of object relatives (i.e., the animacy of the head noun and the NP type of the subject).

10.6   Language Acquisition

Additional support for the network analysis of relative clauses comes from research on L1 acquisition. Most psycholinguistic studies focus on the contrast between subject and object relatives, but Diessel and Tomasello (2005) conducted an acquisition study in which they investigated a much wider range of relative clauses in English and German. As can be seen in (12) to (16), the head of a relative clause can function not only as subject or direct object inside of a relative clause but also as indirect object, adverbial or genitive attribute. With the exception of genitive relative clauses, all English relatives are formed by the so-called gap strategy whereby the relativized role is indicated by a missing nominal inside of the relative clause (Comrie 1989: 147–153).

(12)   The man [who __ met the woman] ...   Subject RC

(13)   The woman [who the man met __] ...   Direct object RC

(14)   The boy [who the girl gave the ball to __] ...   Indirect object RC

(15)   The girl [who the boy played with __] ...   Adverbial RC

(16)   The man [whose cat caught a mouse] ...   Genitive RC

Like English, German employs a wide range of relative clauses, but in contrast to English, German uses the "relative pronoun strategy" to express the relativized role. As can be seen in (17) to (21), each of the relative clauses in these examples includes a case-marked relative pronoun that indicates the syntactic role of the head in the relative clause.

(17)   Der Mann, [*der* mich gesehen hat], ...   Subject RC

(18)   Der Mann, [*den* ich gesehen habe], ...   Direct object RC

(19)   Der Mann, [*dem* ich das Buch gegeben habe], ...   Indirect object RC

(20)   Der Mann, [*zu dem* ich gegangen bin], ...   Adverbial RC

(21)   Der Mann, [*dessen* Hund mich gebissen hat], ...   Genitive RC

What Diessel and Tomasello wanted to find out is (i) how children respond to the various types of nonsubject relatives, and (ii) how the different relativization strategies of English and German affect the acquisition process. In order to address these questions, they administered a sentence repetition task in which 4- to 5-year-old English- and German-speaking children had to repeat the various types of relative clauses shown above. The test items consisted of a copular main clause and a relative clause that was controlled for various semantic and pragmatic features. Figure 10.4 shows the percentage of children's correct responses to the various types of relative clauses.[2]

As can be seen, subject relatives (S, A) caused fewer errors than object and adverbial relatives (P, IO, ADV), which in turn caused fewer errors than

---

[2] Since previous studies had found that transitivity affects the acquisition of subject relatives, Diessel and Tomasello distinguished between transitive and intransitive subject relatives, but this will not concern us here.

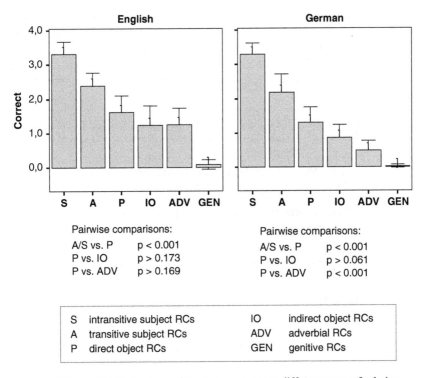

Figure 10.4 Percentage of correct responses to different types of relative clauses in an experiment with four- to five-year-old English- and German-speaking children (Diessel and Tomasello 2005: 888, 892)

genitive relatives (GEN). The results were similar across the two languages, but there was one important difference between them. With the exception of genitive relatives, the English-speaking children basically produced the same number of errors with all nonsubject relatives. As it turns out, the numerical differences between direct and indirect object relatives and adverbial relatives were not statistically significant in the English study (see the pairwise comparisons in Figure 10.4). By contrast, the German-speaking children produced significantly fewer errors with direct object relatives than with indirect object relatives and adverbial relatives. In particular, the adverbial relatives caused many more errors in the German study than in the English study (Figure 10.4).

In order to better understand children's difficulties with the various types of relative clauses, Diessel and Tomasello examined their errors and found one very common type of mistake. In both languages, there was a tendency for children to convert a given object or adverbial relative into a subject relative

(22–23). Note that while this tendency occurred in both languages, it involved a different type of change in English and German. The English-speaking children converted object and adverbial relatives into subject relatives by changing the order of subject and verb, whereas the German-speaking children converted them by changing the case roles of the relative pronoun and other nominals in the relative clause.

(22)   TEST ITEM: This is the girl [who the boy teased at school this morning].
         CHILD: This is the girl [that teased . . . the boy . . . at school this morning].

(23)   TEST ITEM: Da ist der Mann, [den das Mädchen im Stall gesehen hat].
         CHILD: Da ist der Mann, [der das Mädchen im Stall gesehen hat].

Crucially, while conversion errors of this type were very frequent, children were not consistent in their behavior. Many children produced both correct and incorrect responses with the same type of relative clause, and sometimes they noted their mistake and corrected conversion errors before a sentence was completed (24–25).

(24)   This is the girl [who bor/ Peter borrowed a football from].

(25)   Da ist der Junge, [der/ dem Paul . . . die Mütze weggenommen hat].

Taken together, these findings suggest that the vast majority of children were able to produce nonsubject relatives (with the exception of genitive relatives), but conversion errors occurred because subject relatives were more easily accessible than nonsubject relatives.

One factor that is known to affect the accessibility of linguistic knowledge is frequency of occurrence (§10.3), suggesting that subject relatives may have caused fewer errors in these experiments than nonsubject relatives because they are especially frequent; but this hypothesis is only partially supported by data from child-directed speech. As Diessel (2004: 146) noted, while subject relatives are frequent in the ambient language, object relatives are even more frequent: 57.9 percent of all relative clauses are object relatives (in Diessel's data of child-directed speech), but only 34.3 percent are subject relatives. Apart from subject and object relatives, children encounter a few adverbial relatives (7.9 percent), but indirect object relatives and genitive relatives are essentially absent from child-directed speech (see also Diessel 2009).

Considering the frequency of the various types of relative clauses in the ambient language, it is a plausible hypothesis that frequency had some influence on children's performance in this study, but given that object relatives are even more frequent than subject relatives, this cannot be the whole story. Building on an earlier proposal by Bever (1970), Diessel and Tomasello argued that children's ease with using subject relatives is due to the similarity between subject relatives and main clauses. The analysis they propose is similar to that of Wells and colleagues (§10.5). Since subject relatives share the same order of thematic roles with main clauses, their activation is reinforced by the family of declarative main clauses that children learn long before they learn relative clauses.

However, Diessel and Tomasello go beyond the study by Wells and colleagues as they suggest that similarity does not only explain the difference between subject and direct object relatives but also several other aspects of their study. In particular, they claim that constructional similarity accounts for the fact that the English-speaking children produced the same amount of errors in response to direct and indirect object and adverbial relatives (Figure 10.4). Although indirect object and adverbial relatives are much less frequent than direct object relatives, they did not cause more errors because indirect object and adverbial relatives are so similar to direct object relatives in English that they constitute a subfamily of relative-clause constructions that reinforce each other (26).

(26) NP [V ...]REL   SUBJ-relative
      NP [NP V ...]REL   DO-relative
      NP [NP V ...]REL   IO-relative
      NP [NP V ...]REL   ADV-relative
      NP [[GEN N] V ...]REL   GEN-relative

Note that German is different in this regard. There are no particular similarities between direct and indirect object relatives and adverbial relatives in German that would characterize them as a construction (sub)family distinct from other types of relative clauses. Since indirect object relatives and adverbial relatives are not supported by direct object relatives in German, they caused significantly greater difficulties in the German study. In particular, German adverbial relatives were mostly incorrect. Note that they caused more errors (in the German study) than indirect object relatives.

Here again, similarity provides a plausible explanation for children's responses. Since adverbial relatives are introduced by a preposition that precedes the relative pronoun in German, they are structurally more distinct from all other types of German relative clauses than indirect object relatives, which are similar to direct object relatives, suggesting that the German-speaking children had more difficulties with adverbial relatives than with indirect object relatives because the latter were supported by their relationship to direct object relatives.

Finally, genitive relatives were almost always incorrect in both languages. One reason for this is that genitive relatives are extremely rare in the ambient language (Diessel 2004: 146), but given that indirect object relatives are also very rare in the ambient language, frequency alone is not sufficient to explain children's difficulties with genitive relatives in this study. In addition, it is the greater structural (and semantic) distance between genitive relatives and all

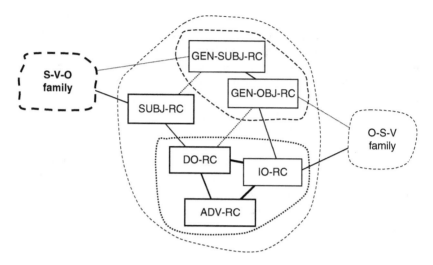

Figure 10.5 Family of English relative clauses and their relationship to other construction families

other types of relative clauses (in both languages) that explains why children had particular difficulties with these constructions.

To summarize, similarity had a great impact on children's responses in this experiment. It explains (i) why subject relatives caused fewer errors than nonsubject relatives, (ii) why in the English study direct and indirect object relatives and adverbial relatives caused the same amount of errors, (iii) why indirect object relatives were not always incorrect (despite the fact that they are essentially absent from the ambient language), and (iv) why genitive relatives and German adverbial relatives caused so many problems compared to other types of relative clauses.

Considering these results, Diessel and Tomasello argued that relative clauses constitute a network, or family, of semantically and formally similar constructions (Figure 10.5) that children acquire in a piecemeal, bottom-up way whereby new relative clauses are learned based on constructions they already know. The development begins with subject relatives in copular constructions that are only a little different from simple main clauses (see also Diessel and Tomasello 2000), and it ends with genitive relatives that are structurally and semantically distinct from all other types of relative clauses and that are therefore only loosely integrated into the construction family.[3]

---

[3] Inspired by this research, Fitz et al. (2011) conducted a connectionist study in which they showed that the ability of a neural network to learn subject and nonsubject relatives is crucially influenced by the network's prior processing of SVO constructions.

10.7   Language Change

Concluding this chapter, we will consider the role of construction families in the diachronic development of English word order. Specifically, we will be concerned with the rise of subject–auxiliary inversion in Early Modern English. The section draws on data and analyses from several studies (Ellegård 1953; Hawkins 1986; Kroch 1989; Ogura 1993; Bybee 2010: Chapter 7) but presents them from a novel perspective.

10.7.1   Subject–Auxiliary Inversion in English

Subject–auxiliary inversion, short SAI, is found in a wide range of constructions including yes/no questions (27), nonsubject WH-questions (28), sentences with an initial negative phrase or the conjunctive adverb *so* (29–30), counterfactual conditions (31), exclamative and optative sentences (32–33) and several other minor sentence types (Green 1985).

(27)   Will she be there?

(28)   Where do you live?

(29)   Never would she say that.

(30)   So do I.

(31)   Had she been there, . . .

(32)   Boy do I hate this!

(33)   May the best one win!

Note that while subject–auxiliary inversion is often treated as a uniform phenomenon, it involves two distinct construction families: (i) the AUX-S-V family, in which the auxiliary precedes all other constituents of the sentence, and (ii) the X-AUX-S-V family, in which the auxiliary follows a clause-initial lexeme or phrase (34).

(34)

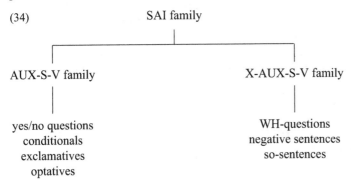

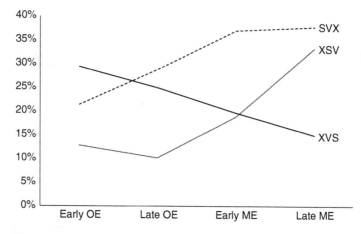

Figure 10.6 Proportions of the three most frequent word orders of declarative sentences in Old and Middle English (based on data from Bech 2001: 73)

In what follows, we will see that the two SAI families are diachronically related to two general word order patterns in Old and Middle English: The AUX-S-V family is related to a family of V1 constructions that served as nonassertive speech acts (Diessel 1997), and the X-AUX-S-V family is related to the V2 word order pattern that was characteristic of the entire Germanic language family (and is still found in Present-Day German). Importantly, the development of both SAI families was influenced by the increasing dominance of the S-V-(O) family of declarative sentences.

In Old and Middle English, word order was much more diverse and variable than it is today. Analyzing a large corpus of declarative sentences from this period, Bech (2001) identified more than a dozen ordering patterns based on the order of subject, verb and some other constituent X (subsuming both complements and adjuncts). However, while word order was more diverse in Old and Middle English than it is today, it was not random. There were clear statistical tendencies. The three most frequent word order patterns, Bech found in her data were S-V-X, X-S-V and X-V-S. At the beginning of the examined time period, X-V-S was the most frequent pattern, but, as can be seen in Figure 10.6, the two SV patterns (i.e., S-V-X and X-S-V) increased in frequency and X-V-S dropped down to 15 percent.

10.7.2   The Diachronic Sources of X-AUX-S-V and AUX-S-V

In Modern English, X-V-S has almost entirely disappeared, but it survived, at least in part, in X-AUX-S-V constructions. If we look at the X-V-S pattern in Old and Middle English, we find that this order was especially frequent with adverbs, notably with the negative adverbs *ne* and *naþer* and with conjunctive adverbs such as *þa* and *þonne* (35–36).

(35)   **Ne**   com   se   here.
       not   come   the   army
       'The army did not come.' (Mitchell and Robinson [1964] 2001: 64)

(36)   **þa**   siglde   he   þonan   suðryhte   be lande.
       then   sailed   he   from.there   southwards   along coast
       'Then he sailed southwards from there along the coast.' (Bech 2001: 3)

Since subject–auxiliary inversion (in Modern English) can be triggered by a negative phrase or a conjunctive adverb, notably by *so*, we may hypothesize that NEG-AUX-S-V and *So*-AUX-S-V are relics of an earlier stage that have survived because they have been frequent. To put it another way, since negative inversion and *so*-inversion are deeply entrenched in memory, they did not change to SVO under the influence of declarative main clauses (Hawkins 1986: 168, 209–210). Note, however, that negative inversion and *so*-inversion are more constrained in the modern language than they were in Old and Middle English. There are two important differences: first, the verb slot after the initial element is now generally filled by an auxiliary or modal (i.e., main verbs are excluded), and second, there is now always a second verb, that is, the main verb, after the subject, if we disregard copular clauses (cf. *Where is he?*) and verb ellipsis (cf. *Neither do I*). We will come back to this below.

Like negative inversion and *so*-inversion, nonsubject WH-questions are related to the X-V-S pattern of Old and Middle English. As can be seen in (37) and (38), in Old English, nonsubject WH-questions had the same word order as in Modern English except that the position after the question word is now restricted to auxiliaries and modals, whereas in Old English the question word could also be followed by a simple main verb, as in example (38).

(37)   Hwæt   *sceal*   ic   *winnan?*   cwæð   he.
       What   shall   I   gain?   said   he
       'What shall I gain? said he.' (Junius, Genesis 278)

(38)   Hwæt   *sægest*   þu,   yrþlincg?
       what   say   you,   earthling
       'What do you say, ploughman?' (Æ Coll., 22.23)

The second type of subject–auxiliary inversion, that is, AUX-S-V, is diachronically related to a family of V1 constructions that were introduced by the finite verb. Like X-V-S, V1 constitutes a particular word order schema of Germanic that is still found in some of the modern Germanic languages. In Modern German, for instance, yes/no questions, exclamatives, optatives, hortatives and conditionals can be expressed by V1 sentences in which the finite verb precedes all other constituents (39–43).

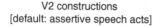

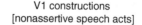

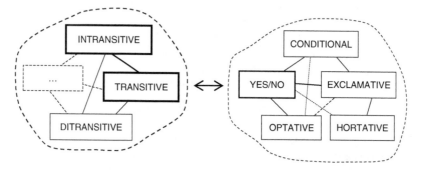

Figure 10.7 V2 and V1 constructions in German (based on Diessel 1997: 66)

(39)	Kommst du zu meiner Party?	'Will you come to my party?'
(40)	Ist das fantastisch!	'That is fantastic!'
(41)	Käme er bloß!	'I wish he would come!'
(42)	Gehen wir!	'Let's go!'
(43)	Kommst du, (so) geht er.	'If you come, he will leave.'

In Diessel (1997) I argued that the various German V1 sentences contrast with the default use of V2 constructions in Present-Day German. While V2 sentences are semantically versatile, they typically function as assertive speech acts and convey factual information. By contrast, all of the V1 sentences in (39) to (43) are nonassertive speech acts and do not convey factual information. In other words, the German V1 sentences constitute a family of particular speech act constructions that complement the default use of the V2 constructions in terms of their pragmatic functions (Diessel 1997: 52–66) (Figure 10.7).

A parallel analysis applies to the V1 constructions of Old English. Like Modern German, Old English had a family of V1 constructions that served as nonassertive and nonfactual speech acts. As can be seen in (44) to (46), Old English had yes/no questions, imperative/hortative sentences and conditional clauses that included the finite verb in clause-initial position.

(44)   Gehyrst   þu, sælida?
         hear   you sailor
         'Do you hear, sailor?' (Mitchell and Robinson [1964] 2001: 64)

(45)   Læremon   siððan   furður   on   Lædengeðiode ...
        teach man   after.that further in   Latin
        'Let those be afterwards taught more in the Latin language ...' (King Alfred's
        Preface)

(46)   Hæfde ic ælteowe þenas,   nære   ic þus eaðelice oferswiðed.
        had I faithful servants not.be.SBJV.PST I so easily   conquered
        'Had I faithful servants, I should not be thus overcome.' (Ælfric's Lives of
        Saints)

All of these constructions have survived in Modern English, but in contrast to
Old English, Modern English restricts the use of V1 constructions to auxiliaries. In fact, with the exception of yes-no questions, all V1 constructions of
Modern English can only appear with a subset of auxiliaries and modals. V1
conditionals, for instance, can only occur with three auxiliaries, namely, with
had, should and *were* (e.g., *Should this happen, ...*), and V1 optatives are
exclusively used with *may* (e.g., *May the best one win*).

To summarize the previous discussion, we have seen that the SAI constructions of Modern English are related to two general word order patterns, or word
order families, of Old English: (i) the X-AUX-S-V family is related to the V2
pattern of Germanic, and (ii) the AUX-S-V family is related to a family of V1
constructions that served as nonassertive speech acts.

10.7.3   The Rise of V_{AUX}-S-V

As pointed out above, the main difference between the SAI constructions of
Modern English and the V2 and V1 constructions of Old English is that the former
are more constrained: They generally involve a periphrastic verb form consisting of
an auxiliary before the subject and a main verb after it. The same pattern occurred
in Old English, but in contrast to the SAI constructions of Modern English, the Old
English V2 and V1 constructions were not only used with periphrastic verb forms,
they also appeared with simple verbs (as in 37 and 38 above).

An important prerequisite for the rise of subject–auxiliary inversion is the
increasing tendency to combine main verbs with auxiliaries in the development
from Old to Middle English (Bybee 2010: Chapter 7). While periphrastic verb
forms were not uncommon in Old English, some of them are diachronic
innovations (e.g., the progressive verb forms). Moreover, and this is crucial,
while Modern English has preserved two simple verb forms (in basic declarative sentences), namely simple present tense (e.g., *go*) and simple past tense
(e.g., *went*), these simple forms are now generally combined with the dummy
auxiliary *do* in SAI constructions (e.g., *do/does/did subj go*). As Ellegård
(1953) showed in a large-scale study, the new pattern emerged at the end of
Middle English and soon increased in frequency. As can be seen in Figure 10.8,

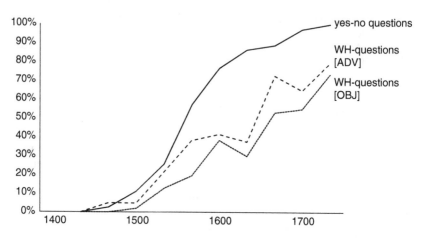

Figure 10.8 Proportions of periphrastic *do* in yes/no questions and adverbial/object WH-questions between 1450 and 1750 (based on data from Ellegård 1953: 204–205)

at the beginning of Early Modern English, *do* was rarely used in questions, but at the end of the seventeenth century, the vast majority of yes/no questions and WH-questions occurred with the dummy auxiliary *do* if they did not include an ordinary auxiliary or modal verb.

Crucially, while the diachronic origins of periphrastic *do* are uncertain (Bybee 2010: 129–130), there is good evidence that the rise of this construction is related to the increasing dominance of S-V-(O) in declarative sentences (Kroch et al. 1982). As Hawkins (1986) and others have pointed out, subject–auxiliary inversion creates a word order pattern in which the main verb follows the subject as in simple main clauses. In other words, while SAI constructions deviate from other sentence types by the position of the auxiliary, they include the same ordering of subject, (main) verb and object as main clauses. On this account, subject–auxiliary inversion can be seen as a syntactic blend, or amalgam, that has preserved the original (X)-V-S pattern in the initial part of the construction and has acquired the obligatory use of S-V-(O) under the influence of declarative main clauses in the second part of the construction (Figure 10.9).

The interaction between the two ordering patterns (i.e., (X)-V-S and S-V-O) is evident in the diachronic data of WH-questions. As Ogura (1993) showed, the rise of subject–auxiliary inversion proceeded in an item-specific fashion that was crucially influenced by the frequency of individual verbs in object questions. Drawing on data from Ellegård (1953), Ogura divided the verbs in his corpus into two groups: (i) a small group of four verbs that were frequently used in object questions (i.e., *say, mean, do, think*), and (ii) a much larger group

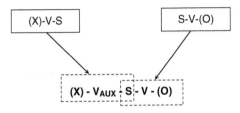

Figure 10.9 Diachronic sources of SAI constructions

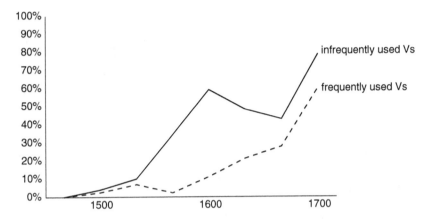

Figure 10.10 Proportions of periphrastic *do* in object WH-questions between 1450 and 1700: WH-questions with frequently used verbs versus WH-questions with infrequently used verbs (based on data from Ogura 1993: 75)

of all other verbs that was infrequent in object questions. As can be seen in Figure 10.10, the four verbs that frequently appeared in object questions retained the old word order pattern longer than verbs that were not frequently used in object questions. Since the former were more deeply entrenched in the original V2 pattern, they were not so easily accommodated to the new peri-phrastic *do* construction than questions with infrequent verbs (Ellegård 1953; Ogura 1993).

Interestingly, while the AUX-S-V pattern is conventional with all verbs in Modern English, the SAI constructions are still under pressure from the S-V-(O) family. As Rowland (2007) and others have shown, SAI constructions can cause tremendous problems in L1 acquisition. Analyzing a large sample of both yes/no questions and WH-questions from the CHILDES database, Rowland found that children have no difficulties with subject–auxiliary inversion if the combination of auxiliary and subject is frequent. Frequent "frames" such as *Can I __?* or *Why don't you __?* are almost always correct in early child language, but questions with infrequent word combinations cause many word order errors. In particular, Rowland found that children often repeat the auxiliary after the subject (47) or use them right before the main verb (48). Both types of mistakes suggest that the acquisition of subject–auxiliary inversion is subject to analogical pressure from S-V-(O) constructions (see also Rowland and Pine 2000).

(47)   What *can* he *can* do?

(48)   Where he *does* go?

In sum, subject–auxiliary inversion is diachronically related to two general word order patterns of Old English, V2 and V1, that have been modified under the influence of the S-V-(O) family of declarative sentences. The latter has become increasingly more prominent in the history of English and has replaced most other word order patterns. The diachronic connections of SAI to V2 and V1 are still noticeable in the distinction between AUX-S-V and X-AUX-S-V, though these constructions have become more similar to each other and to the family of SVO constructions in the development from Old to Modern English.

10.8   Conclusion

To conclude, in the construction-based literature, grammar is commonly characterized as a taxonomic network, but in accordance with several recent studies, the current chapter has argued that the grammar network does not only include taxonomic relations between constructions at different levels of abstraction, it also includes horizontal, or lateral, relations between semantically and/or formally similar constructions.

The horizontal relations considered in this chapter are reminiscent of lexical associations between items in the mental lexicon. There are conspicuous parallels between the network structure of the mental lexicon and the cognitive organization of grammar. Considering research from various quarters of the language sciences, the chapter has argued that constructions are stored and processed in an activation network similar to lexemes in the mental lexicon. Specifically, it has been shown that the availability, or accessibility, of constructions is influenced by the same cognitive factors as lexical access, that is, by frequency, priming, similarity and neighborhood density or family size.

11 Encoding Asymmetries of Grammatical Categories

11.1 Introduction

Having analyzed families of similar constructions in Chapter 10, we now consider pairs, or groups, of (semantically) contrastive constructions such as active and passive sentences or singular and plural nouns. Since constructions of this type express an opposition, they are commonly analyzed as "paradigmatic alternatives" of grammatical categories, such as the categories of voice and nominal number.

Crucially, paradigmatic alternatives of this type are often asymmetrical. The active–passive alternation, for instance, consists of an unequal pair of constructions. Active sentences are more frequent than passive sentences (Xiao et al. 2006), they occur in a wider range of pragmatic contexts (Weiner and Labov 1983) and are associated with a larger number of verb types (Gries and Stefanowitsch 2004). Moreover, and this is of particular importance, there is a cross-linguistic tendency to mark passive constructions more explicitly than active constructions. In English, for instance, passive sentences include two extra morphemes: the auxiliary *be* and the adposition *by* (if the agent is not omitted) (1a–b).

(1)   a. The boy kicked the ball.
        b. The ball **was** kicked **by** the boy.

Parallel asymmetries between active and passive voice have been found in many other languages and with other paradigmatically related constructions (as we will see shortly). Some typologists refer to these asymmetries by the notion of "structural markedness" (e.g., Croft 2003: 87–95; Bybee 2011).[1] Markedness is an important concept of linguistic typology that has been interpreted from a usage-based perspective. Since the asymmetries in the encoding of grammatical categories correlate with frequency, it is widely assumed that structural markedness is shaped by frequency of language use (e.g., Greenberg 1966; Bybee 1985, 2010; Haspelmath 2008a, 2008b). More

---

[1] Since the notion of markedness has also been used in many other contexts, Haspelmath (2006) argued against the use of this term in linguistic typology.

specifically, it has been claimed that the encoding asymmetries in the expression of many grammatical categories are the product of an economical strategy to mark only the less frequent member of an alternating pair of constructions and to leave the more frequent category member formally unmarked (e.g., Croft 2003: 87–117; Hawkins 2004: 63–69; Haspelmath 2008a, 2008b).

Building on this research, the current chapter argues that the encoding asymmetries of grammatical categories arise from an intricate interplay between speaker-oriented and hearer-oriented processes of language use (§3.6). In Chapter 5 we saw that language use involves an anticipatory component. Speakers plan an utterance before production starts and listeners anticipate, or "predict," upcoming elements in the unfolding speech stream. Since language users' linguistic expectations are influenced by their experience with language, listeners usually anticipate the occurrence of the more frequent member of an alternating pair of constructions. As a consequence of this, there is a tendency to signal the occurrence of the less frequent, or less expected category member by an extra morpheme. On this account, the encoding asymmetries of grammatical categories originate from a hearer-oriented (or other-oriented) strategy to indicate constructions that deviate from listeners' linguistic expectations (Haspelmath 2008a, 2008b, 2014).

Note, however, that while the asymmetries in the encoding of grammatical categories are related to listeners' needs in comprehension, they are also influenced by speaker-oriented (or self-oriented) processes of memory and activation spreading. As we will see, once a new marker has been established as a grammatical signal of an unexpected category or construction, it becomes routinized through frequency or repetition and is then often extended to similar lexemes and constructions by analogy or priming.

The chapter begins with a short overview of grammatical categories that exhibit encoding asymmetries from a cross-linguistic perspective but then concentrates on the analysis of case marking (in the encoding of grammatical relations).

11.2   Cross-Linguistic Asymmetries in the Encoding of Grammatical Categories

One of the most frequently noted asymmetries in the encoding of grammatical categories concerns the encoding of nominal number. As pointed out in Chapter 8, there is a cross-linguistic tendency to indicate the contrast between singular and plural nouns by an extra marker on the plural (cf. *car* vs. *car-s*). Singular nouns are often "zero-marked" (Bybee 2011: 144), or "zero-coded" (Haspelmath 2006: 30), but if they take a number affix, plural nouns are also "marked" by an extra morpheme (Croft 2003: 88–89).

Table 11.1 *Proportions of singular and plural nouns in five languages*

Language	Singular	Plural (& dual)	Total
Sanskrit	70.3%	29.7%	93,277
Latin	85.2%	14.8%	8342
Russian	77.7%	22.3%	8194
French	74.3%	25.7%	1000
English	68.4%	31.6%	24,615,657

Source: Greenberg (1966: 32) and COCA

The structural asymmetry between singular and plural nouns correlates with an asymmetry in frequency. This was already noted by Greenberg (1966), who provided frequency counts of singular and plural nouns in Sanskrit, Latin, Russian and French. As can be seen in Table 11.1, in all four languages, Greenberg found a larger proportion of singular nouns than plural nouns (Greenberg 1966: 32). Similar proportions of singular and plural nouns have been found in large electronic corpora of several languages (Haspelmath and Karjus 2017). The Contemporary Corpus of American English (COCA), for instance, includes 16.9 million singular (count) nouns and only 7.8 million plural nouns (Table 11.1).

Other grammatical categories that have been shown to exhibit cross-linguistic asymmetries between zero and overt coding are illustrated below with examples from English (2–5), Turkish (6–7) and Abun (8) (Haspelmath 2008a, 2008b, 2014; Haspelmath et al. 2014).

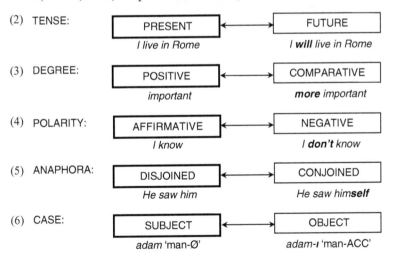

(2) TENSE: PRESENT ⟷ FUTURE
                 I live in Rome   *I **will** live in Rome*

(3) DEGREE: POSITIVE ⟷ COMPARATIVE
                 important   ***more** important*

(4) POLARITY: AFFIRMATIVE ⟷ NEGATIVE
                 I know   *I **don't** know*

(5) ANAPHORA: DISJOINED ⟷ CONJOINED
                 He saw him   *He saw him**self***

(6) CASE: SUBJECT ⟷ OBJECT
                 adam 'man-Ø'   *adam-ı* 'man-ACC'

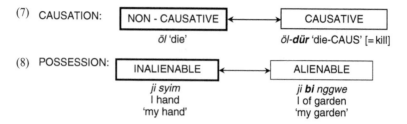

(7) CAUSATION:

| NON - CAUSATIVE | ⟷ | CAUSATIVE |

öl 'die'   *öl-dür* 'die-CAUS' [= kill]

(8) POSSESSION:

| INALIENABLE | ⟷ | ALIENABLE |

ji syim   *ji bi nggwe*
I hand   I of garden
'my hand'   'my garden'

While linguistic typologists have just begun to examine the frequencies of the various grammatical categories with corpus linguistic methods, the data at hand show a clear tendency: For all of the categories above (and several others), there is evidence from a substantial number of languages that the zero-marked construction is significantly more frequent than the paradigmatically related construction with overt coding (Greenberg 1966; Bybee 1985; Croft 1991; Haspelmath 2008a, 2008b; Haspelmath et al. 2014; Haspelmath and Karjus 2017).

Note that some of the categories in (2) to (8) can be combined to complex paradigms that can be seen as networks of semantically contrastive constructions. The structure of these networks is predictable from the relative frequency of individual category members. For instance, as can be seen in Figure 11.1, in Turkish, nouns are inflected for two features, case and number, that are asymmetrically marked. The most frequent construction of the paradigm, that is, nominative-singular, is zero-coded. Singular nouns in accusative case and plural nouns in nominative case occur with one suffix each. And plural nouns in accusative case occur with two suffixes, creating a hierarchy of morphological coding (SG.NOM < SG.ACC/PL.NOM < PL.ACC) that reflects the relative frequency

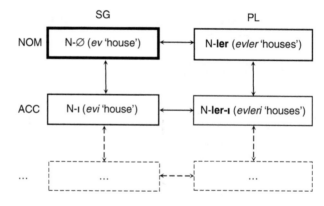

Figure 11.1 Constructional relations between case-marked NPs in Turkish

of the four nominals in linguistic corpora (see Haspelmath 2014 for some corpus evidence).

The correlation between frequency and coding is also manifest in a phenomenon known as "local markedness" or "markedness reversal." The phenomenon was first described by Tiersma (1982) and has been investigated in more detail in a recent study by Haspelmath and Karjus (2017). The best evidence for the correlation between frequency and local markedness comes again from the analysis of nominal number.

Above, we have seen that there is a cross-linguistic tendency to mark plural nouns by a particular number affix or free morpheme, whereas singular nouns are often zero-coded. In the case of local markedness, however, we find the reverse pattern with certain semantic types of nouns. Maltese, for instance, has a class of nouns, including the words for 'shoe', 'apple', 'fly' and 'goose', that take a singular suffix when they refer to a single entity but are zero-coded with plural reference (see 9–12 from Haspelmath and Karjus 2017: 1221).

(9)	a. zarbun-**a** shoe-SG	'shoe'	b. zarbun-Ø shoe-PL	'shoes'
(10)	a. tuffieħ-**a** apple-SG	'apple'	b. tuffieħ-Ø apple-PL	'apples'
(11)	a. dubbien-**a** fly-SG	'fly'	b. dubbien-Ø fly-PL	'flies'
(12)	a. wizz-**a** goose-SG	'goose'	b. wizz-Ø goose-PL	'geese'

Markedness reversals of this type occur in Arabic (e.g., Maltese), Celtic (e.g., Welsh), Cushitic (e.g., Arbore) and a few other languages of northeast Africa (e.g., Turkana) (Haspelmath and Karjus 2017). The phenomenon is generally restricted to certain semantic types of nouns denoting entities that typically occur in groups or pairs. Haspelmath and Karjus provide evidence that these nouns are usually more frequent in the plural than in the singular. Analyzing corpus data from several European languages, they found that nouns denoting small animals (e.g., fly, bee), fruits and vegetables (e.g., bean, potato), body parts (e.g., ear, leg), people (e.g., child, American) and paired items (e.g., shoe, ski) are considerably more frequent in the plural than in the singular, whereas a control group of randomly selected nouns showed the reverse pattern, that is, they were more frequent in the singular than in the plural. Since the test items were selected from semantic classes of nouns that have overtly marked singulars and zero-marked plurals in languages like Maltese, Welsh, Arbore and Turkana, Haspelmath and Karjus conclude that frequency is not only the driving force behind the dominant pattern of overtly coded plurals and zero-coded singulars, but also behind the occurrence of local markedness patterns with overtly coded singulars and zero-coded plurals.

11.3   Frequency, Economy and Social Cognition

There is compelling evidence that the encoding asymmetries in paradigmatically related constructions correlate with frequency. As pointed out above, this is often explained by some notion of economy (Croft 2003: 87–117; Hawkins 2004: 63–69, among many others). The general idea is simple: Given a semantically contrastive pair of constructions such as singular and plural nouns or active and passive sentences, speech production is most economical if only the less frequent member of the semantic pair is overtly expressed by a particular morpheme. Clearly, if the marker occurred on the more frequent category member or, worse, if both members of a semantic pair appeared with a particular morpheme, the speaker would need more energy to produce the two constructions.

However, while this view of economy is frequently invoked in the functional and typological literature, it must be emphasized that the encoding asymmetries in grammatical categories are NOT only motivated by speaker-oriented processes of efficient speech production, but also by hearer-oriented processes of communication and social cognition. As Haspelmath (2014) and others have pointed out, the ultimate motivation for the development of encoding asymmetries in grammatical categories is the predictability of a particular expression or construction. More precisely, it is speakers' assessment of what listeners are likely to predict in a particular context that gives rise to the development of encoding asymmetries in paradigmatically related constructions. Since frequency is one of the main determinants of listeners' linguistic predictions (§5.6), there is a cross-linguistic tendency to mark or signal the less frequent category member.

Consider for instance the category of polarity or negation. The vast majority of sentences (and phrases) are affirmative. There is a striking asymmetry in frequency between affirmative and negative constructions that affects language users' linguistic expectations or predictions. With no further information given, listeners assume that the propositional content of a declarative sentence fits some state of affairs in the world (Searle 1969). If a speaker intends to deny the usual fit between language and world, s/he must use an explicit marker to signal the unexpected (negative) content of the construction. This explains why negation is almost always overtly expressed by a negative marker, whereas affirmative statements are only rarely expressed by an affirmative morpheme (Greenberg 1966).

The same analysis applies to other grammatical categories such as tense, case and possession. It is the central claim of the current chapter that the cross-linguistic tendency to differentiate the constructions of an alternating pair by zero and overt coding is ultimately motivated by a hearer-oriented strategy to signal the occurrence of the unexpected (that is, the less frequent) category member (Haspelmath 2008a, 2008b, 2014).

Note that the whole idea of zero coding is based on the assumption that constructions are organized in paradigms or networks. In the morphological literature, it is often assumed that zero coding involves a "zero morph," that is, a morpheme that has meaning, but no form. However, while one might think of zero coding in terms of zero morphs, it is important to recognize that the meaning of a zero morph is based on a particular constellation of paradigmatically related constructions. It is only because language users conceive of singular and plural nouns and affirmative and negative sentences as pairs of semantically contrastive constructions that we can speak of zero coding. In other words, the meaning of a zero morph is derived from a network of related constructions and is not based on linguistic reference or denotation.

In the remainder of this chapter, we will elaborate these hypotheses based on data and analyses of one particular category, that is, the category of case in the domain of grammatical relations (also known as syntactic functions).

11.4   Grammatical Relations

Traditionally, the term grammatical relations refers to a set of categories such as subject and object that specify the function or role of an argument in a clause. The functions are expressed by three main strategies: case marking, cross-reference marking (also known as verb-argument agreement) and word order. Following Keenan (1976), typologists refer to these strategies as the "encoding properties" of grammatical relations. In addition to encoding properties, grammatical relations have "behavioral properties" such as control and anaphor binding (Croft 2001: 147–152).

11.4.1   Grammatical Relations are Language- and Construction-Particular

In the traditional approach, grammatical relations are primitive categories that are defined prior to the analysis of any particular structure, but recent research in typology has argued that grammatical relations are emergent categories that are language- and construction-particular (Dryer 1997; Croft 2001; Cristofaro 2009). The main reason for this claim is that the few primitive categories of traditional grammar are not sufficient to characterize the enormous amount of inter- and intralinguistic variation in the encoding (and development) of grammatical relations. Let us briefly consider the notion of subject to explain this point.

In English, the most salient reason for positing a (general) category of subject is word order. In basic declarative sentences, the subject is commonly defined as the nominal that precedes the (finite) verb, but, as we have seen in Chapter 10, in the case of subject–auxiliary inversion, the subject comes only after the finite verb (cf. *At no time did I say that*). Moreover, if the sentence includes a locative phrase or direct quote, the subject may even follow the main verb (13–14), though this is not obligatory.

(13)   Down the hill rolled the car.

(14)   "We are going to lose," said John.

Syntactically, the subject is the controller of reduced coordinate sentences and purpose clauses (15–16), but nonfinite complement clauses are usually controlled by the direct object (in NVNV-constructions) (17), unless the main verb is *promise*, which occurs with subject control (18).

(15)   John$_i$ moved to London and __$_i$ gave up his apartment in Rome.

(16)   She$_i$ drove to Berlin to __$_i$ attend the conference.

(17)   She persuaded Mary$_i$ __$_i$ to help her.

(18)   He$_i$ promised John __$_i$ to help him.

Similar item- and construction-specific idiosyncrasies have been observed in other languages in which grammatical relations are expressed by case- and cross-reference marking. In Icelandic, for instance, the subject usually occurs in nominative case, but there are also constructions in which dative NPs have subject properties (Barðdal 2006).

If we look at grammatical relations from a cross-linguistic perspective, there is even more variation. In English, the term subject applies to the single argument of an intransitive clause and the most agent-like argument of a transitive clause, but in languages with ergative morphology, it is the patient of a transitive clause that patterns with the single argument of an intransitive clause (Dixon 1994). Moreover, in languages with split intransitivity, agent-like arguments of intransitive clauses are encoded in the same way as the subject of a transitive clause, whereas patient-like arguments of intransitive clauses are encoded in the same way as the direct object of a transitive clause (Mithun 1991).

What is more, in many languages, case- and cross-reference marking are restricted to particular constructions. Some constructions occur with nominative-accusative alignment, others occur with ergative-absolutive alignment, or split intransitivity, and yet other constructions occur with a mixed alignment pattern, as the following examples of in/transitive constructions in Nepali, in which case marking shows ergative alignment while cross-reference marking occurs with accusative alignment.

(19)   a. ma   ga-**ē̃**
            1SG.NOM go-1SG.PST
            'I went.' (Bickel 2011: 400)
      b. mai-**le** timro ghar   dekh-**ē̃**
            1SG-ERG your house.NOM see-1SG.PST
            'I saw your house.' (Bickel 2011: 400)

Finally, the behavioral properties of grammatical relations do not always coincide with the encoding properties. In fact, in most languages with ergative morphology, complex sentences are conjoined in the same way as in languages with accusative morphology. There are languages in which certain types of subordinate clauses and coordinate sentences are controlled by absolutive NPs (e.g., Dyirbal), but "syntactic ergativity" is a rare phenomenon that is always restricted to particular constructions (Kazenin 1994).

In general, there is a great deal of inter- and intralinguistic variation in the encoding of grammatical relations. Traditionally, researchers have abstracted away from this variation and have defined grammatical relations as primitive concepts with very general (or abstract) properties, but in more recent research, (most) typologists have abandoned this view in favor of a bottom-up approach in which grammatical relations are analyzed as emergent categories of particular languages and argument-structure constructions. While the traditional notions of subject and object are still often used to describe grammatical relations, they are no longer seen as primitive concepts. Rather, it has become a standard assumption of linguistic typology that grammatical relations are construction- and language-particular (Dryer 1997; Croft 2001; Cristofaro 2009; Bickel 2011).

Note, however, that while grammatical relations are not uniform across languages and constructions, there are conspicuous parallels in the encoding of argument roles that reflect the influence of general cognitive processes on the encoding of grammatical relations. In order to characterize these parallels, linguistic typologists have developed an alternative approach in which grammatical relations are analyzed in a way that is easily compatible with the current network approach.

11.4.2   The Network Approach

Arguments bear specific relations to the predicates of argument-structure constructions (§6.4.1 and §9.3). These relations are commonly analyzed in terms of two general concepts: (i) a hierarchy of semantic roles and (ii) several (related) hierarchies of referential properties.

11.4.2.1 A hierarchy of semantic roles.   Every verb (or predicate) specifies particular semantic roles. The verb *run*, for instance, specifies a 'runner', and the verb *hit* specifies a 'hitter' and a 'hittee'. Across languages, semantic roles correlate with the encoding of grammatical relations. In order to characterize these correlations, linguistic typologists have developed a (descriptive) framework in which the arguments of simple (in)transitive clauses are defined in terms of two general concepts: (i) numerical valency and (ii) some basic force dynamic contrasts (Dixon 1994; Croft 2003).

Numerical valency refers to the number of arguments that are included in argument-structure constructions, which usually varies between one and three: intransitive clauses include a single argument, transitive clauses include two arguments and ditransitive clauses include three arguments. In what follows, we focus on the encoding of arguments in basic (in)transitive clauses; that is, ditransitive clauses will not be considered in this chapter.

The notion of force dynamics refers to a conceptual theory of causation, introduced by Talmy (1988), which Croft (1991) applied to the analysis of grammatical relations. In this approach, the participants of an event are defined by their role relative to the exertion of force in a "causal chain." The verb *break*, for instance, designates an event that constitutes a causal chain with various participant roles: an antagonist that initiates the force, an object that is affected by the exertion of force and several other entities that may or may not be involved in a breaking event, e.g., an instrument, an obstacle, a counterforce and a goal. Crucially, the various participant roles constitute a scale or hierarchy that is defined by the order of the various roles in a causal chain or causal sequence (20; see Croft 2001: 63–55):[2]

(20)   SEMANTIC ROLE HIERARCHY: initiator of force ⟶ endpoint of force

Individual verbs designate particular segments of a causal chain, which can involve a wide range of participant roles, but irrespective of the meaning of a particular verb, there is always an asymmetry between the two roles of a causal or transitive event such that one of them precedes the other in the causal sequence (or on the semantic role hierarchy).

If we combine the two verb-based properties of arguments (i.e., numerical valency and force dynamics), we can distinguish three "macro roles," which linguistic typologists represent by the labels of S, A and P: (i) S is the single argument of an intransitive clause, which may or may not be the initiator of force, (ii) A is the most agent-like argument role of a transitive clause, which is usually the initiator of force, and (iii) P is the most patient-like argument of a

---

[2] The idea that participant roles constitute a hierarchy has a long tradition in linguistics (Fillmore 1968), but while earlier research on this topic has treated participant roles as primitive concepts, Croft derives the various roles from a general theory of event structure or causation, that is, from Talmy's model of force dynamics (see Levin and Hovav 2005: 78–130 for related accounts by other scholars).

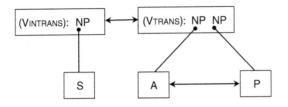

Figure 11.2 Argument roles of (in)transitive clauses

transitive clause, which is usually affected by the exertion of force (Croft 2001: 134–137).

Figure 11.2 summarizes the previous discussion in form of a network with two semantically contrastive constructions: first there is the contrast between transitive and intransitive clauses, and second there is the contrast between the two nominals of a transitive clause (i.e., A vs. P).

11.4.2.2 Referential scales   The second factor that correlates with the encoding of grammatical relations is reference. The referential properties of arguments comprise a wide range of concepts including animacy, humanness, person, definiteness, topicality, specificity and contrastiveness. In the older typological literature, most of these concepts were included in one comprehensive hierarchy (Silverstein 1976), but in more recent research, they are usually described in terms of several (related) scales (Croft 2003: 128–132).

There are various proposals in the typological literature to define referential scales (Haude and Witzlack-Makarevich 2016), but for the purpose of the current discussion let us assume that the referential properties of arguments involve (only) three basic hierarchies or scales: (i) the animacy hierarchy, which is defined by inherent semantic properties of the referent (human animate > nonhuman animate > inanimate), (ii) the definiteness hierarchy, which is defined by the familiarity of a referent in a particular context (specific definite > specific indefinite > nonspecific indefinite), and (iii) the topicality hierarchy, which is defined by the continuity of the current discourse topic across two or more sentences (21–23).

(21)   ANIMACY HIERARCHY: human   ⟶   inanimate

(22)   DEFINITENESS HIERARCHY: definite   ⟶   indefinite

(23)   TOPICALITY HIERARCHY: topic continuity ⟶ topic shift

The analysis of the various hierarchies and their interactions has been subject to much debate in typology and cognitive linguistics (e.g., Cristofaro 2013; Haude and Witzlack-Makarevich 2016). A review of this debate is beyond the scope of this chapter, but there is general consensus among researchers that the various concepts of the above-mentioned hierarchies are interconnected. There is, for instance, a well-known connection between agentivity (or force dynamics), animacy and topicality. Since people often talk about social affairs, topics are usually animate agents, and since people often talk about the same topic in several consecutive sentences, topics are usually given or definite. Figure 11.3 presents a semantic network model that shows how the various hierarchies are related.[3]

Crucially, while the associative connections in Figure 11.3 are motivated by general principles of communication and cognition, they also constitute an

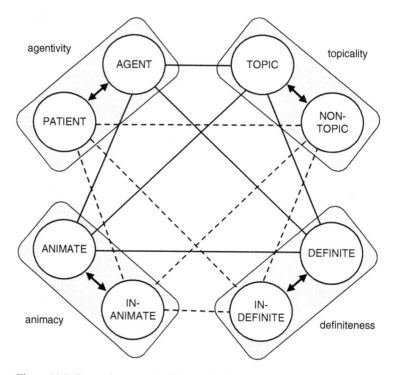

Figure 11.3 Semantic network of thematic roles and referential hierarchies

---

[3] In addition to the hierarchies in Figure 11.3, linguistic typologists have proposed several other hierarchies for the analysis of grammatical relations (e.g., the person hierarchy: first/second > third). There is good evidence that the encoding of grammatical relations correlates with a wide range of semantic and pragmatic properties, but the hierarchies in Figure 11.3 are sufficient to illustrate the network approach.

important aspect of speakers' linguistic knowledge. That is, speakers "know" from their experience with language that the categories of the various scales are interconnected, and this knowledge plays an important role in the cognitive organization of grammar, as the semantic categories of the network in Figure 11.3 are associated with S, A and P. There is a large amount of research indicating that grammatical relations correlate with animacy, topicality, agentivity and definiteness (e.g., Comrie 1989; Givón 1990; Croft 2001, 2003). In particular, A and P are associated with different values of the four scales (in Figure 11.3) as shown in Figure 11.4.

As many scholars of grammar have noted, A and P are not only linked to different force dynamic concepts (as discussed above), they also differ with regard to animacy, topicality and definiteness. Across languages, the A argument is commonly an animate (human) referent that serves as the agent or initiator of a causal chain and that is usually familiar to the speech participants from the context so that A typically designates a (definite) topic. By contrast,

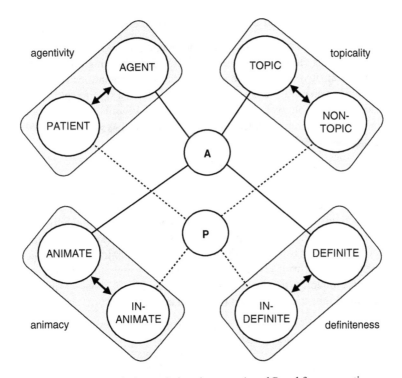

Figure 11.4 Prototypical associations between A and P and four semantic hierarchies

the P argument denotes the patient of a causal chain, which often involves an inanimate referent that may or may not be known to the speech participants from the context but usually does not serve as (primary) topic. The semantic and pragmatic properties of A and P vary with lexical and contextual factors (which can differ to some extent across languages and constructions), but the links in Figure 11.4 indicate the prototypical associations between A and P and the various semantic hierarchies that occur across both languages and constructions.

Note that the S argument is less strongly associated with these hierarchies. It is well known that intransitive verbs occur with both agentive and nonagentive arguments and that the S role is somewhere in between A and P in terms of animacy, definiteness and topicality. As DuBois (1987) showed in a classic study, while the subject of a transitive clause is mostly expressed by a pronoun denoting an animate being as topic, the subject of an intransitive clause is often a lexical NP which may or may not be an animate being that is usually less topical and less definite than A (see also Haig and Schnell 2016).

11.5   Optional and Differential Object Marking

Having characterized the semantic and pragmatic properties of S, A and P, let us now take a closer look at case marking. Concentrating on the arguments of simple transitive clauses, we will see that the associations of A and P with particular semantic and pragmatic properties have a significant impact on case marking morphology. In order to illustrate this, we will consider a phenomenon known as "differential object marking" (Bossong 1985).

11.5.1   Differential Object Marking

Thus far, we have looked at case marking from a broad perspective in which S, A and P were treated as uniform categories. However, if we take a closer look at the encoding of these roles, we find that they are NOT semantically uniform and NOT always consistently expressed by a specific morpheme. In particular, the encoding of P is often restricted to certain semantic types of objects. The phenomenon is well known from Spanish, in which animate and specific Ps are accompanied by the accusative preposition *a*, whereas inanimate and nonspecific Ps are zero-coded or unmarked (24a–b).

(24)   a. Vi   **a**   la   mujer.
            see.PST.1.SG   ACC   the   woman
            'I saw the woman.' (von Heusinger and Kaiser 2005: 34)
         b. Vi   la   mesa.
            see.PST.1.SG the table
            'I saw the table.' (von Heusinger and Kaiser 2005: 35)

Similar restrictions occur in many other languages. In Turkish, for instance, P arguments are only marked by a case suffix if they designate a specific referent (25a). All other types of direct objects lack overt case marking (25b).

(25)　　a. (Ben)　bir　kitab-ı　　oku-du-m.
　　　　　　(I)　　a　　book-ACC　read-PST-1SG
　　　　　　'I read a certain book.' (von Heusinger and Kornfilt 2005: 5)
　　　　b. (Ben)　bir　kitap　oku-du-m.
　　　　　　(I)　　a　　book　read-PST-1SG
　　　　　　'I read a book.' (von Heusinger and Kornfilt 2005: 5)

Linguistic typologists refer to case marking systems in which only a subset of P arguments occurs with an overt case marker as differential object marking, or short DOM (Bossong 1985). DOM systems are very frequent. In fact, it seems that only a minority of all case marking languages apply object case markers to all Ps. More frequently we find that object case marking alternates with zero coding as in Spanish and Turkish (Sinnemäki 2014).[4]

　　Crucially, while DOM systems are not completely uniform, there is a clear cross-linguistic tendency to restrict the use of object case markers to atypical Ps, that is, Ps denoting animate and human beings, Ps that are high in animacy and/or definiteness and Ps that outrank the subject as sentence topic, whereas inanimate, indefinite and nontopical Ps are commonly unmarked in these languages (e.g., Bossong 1985; Comrie 1989: 129–136; Aissen 2003; von Heusinger and Kaiser 2005; von Heusinger and Kornfilt 2005; Malchukov 2008; Iemmolo 2010, 2011; Schmidtke-Bode and Levshina 2018).[5]

　　The correlations between overt P marking and the various semantic and pragmatic properties that are associated with typical objects are language-particular. In some languages, overt P marking is predictable from animacy; in other languages, it correlates primarily with definiteness and specificity; and in yet other languages, it is linked to grammatical features such as the NP type of the object (which in turn correlates with definiteness and topicality). DOM systems are cross-linguistically versatile, but there is a general tendency to indicate atypical Ps that are semantically and/or pragmatically similar to the subject by an extra morpheme, whereas typical Ps are often zero-coded (e.g., Bossong 1985; Comrie 1989: 129–136; Aissen 2003).

---

[4]　Some typologists use the notion of DOM in a broad sense for all case marking systems in which P is not marked in a uniform way. This does not only include languages like Spanish and Turkish, in which overt case marking alternates with zero-coding, but also languages like Lithuanian, in which P occurs with two different case markers, that is, accusative and genitive (Witzlack-Makarevich and Seržant 2018: 18). Nevertheless, here we focus on DOM systems in which some P arguments are not overtly indicated by a case morpheme.

[5]　Bickel et al. (2015) claim that these tendencies are only found in languages of certain geographical areas, but Schmidtke-Bode and Levshina (2018) show (based on a reanalysis of Bickel et al.'s data) that, while there are areal effects, the above tendencies are universal.

Considering this finding, differential object marking is commonly characterized as an efficient strategy to mark only those objects that need to be distinguished from the subject (e.g., Aissen 2003; von Heusinger and Kaiser 2005; Haspelmath 2014; Kurumada and Jaeger 2015). As Aissen (2003: 438) put it:

Functionally, the overt marking of atypical objects facilitates comprehension where it is most needed, but not elsewhere. DOM systems are thus relatively economical.

What is implicit in this claim is that differential object marking is tailored to hearers' needs in comprehension. If P is likely to deviate from listeners' linguistic expectations, it may cause comprehension problems and therefore it is expressed by a particular morpheme, but if P is likely to be consistent with listeners' linguistic expectations, there is no need to provide an extra cue for comprehension.

The argument seems plausible, but there is good evidence that the alternation between case marking and zero coding is not always directly determined by a listener's needs in a particular situation. As Aissen (2003: 437) and others have pointed out, while DOM may be seen as an efficient strategy to guide listeners' comprehension of argument roles, it is clear that in many languages with differential object marking, P arguments are also often case-marked when a zero-coded P cannot possibly cause comprehension problems (see also Malchukov 2008: 213; Witzlack-Makarevich and Seržant 2018: 38–39).

Like many other grammatical phenomena (e.g., argument structure and word classes; see Chapters 7, 8 and 9), differential object marking is both semantically motivated and entrenched in memory. Speakers "know" from their experience with transitive clauses (in a particular language) that only certain types of objects occur with an overt case marker. Speakers of Spanish, for instance, know that a definite animate nominal such as *la mujer* 'the woman' is preceded by the accusative marker *a* if it functions as direct object, whereas an indefinite inanimate nominal such as *una mesa* 'a table' does not occur with *a* in object function. As a consequence, P marking is often triggered automatically by particular semantic, pragmatic or grammatical features of the object rather than by speakers' assessment of hearers' needs (or common ground).

11.5.2   *Optional Object Marking*

While DOM systems are (usually) governed by automated processes of speech production, there is good reason to assume that the alternation between case marking and zero coding has its roots in a hearer-oriented strategy to facilitate comprehension. One piece of evidence for this hypothesis comes from languages with "optional case marking," in which the occurrence of an overt case marker is not strictly tied to particular properties of the object. In Japanese, for instance, almost every noun (and pronoun) can occur with or without an overt case marker so that speakers can really choose between case marking and zero coding in many contexts (26).

(26)   Taro=(ga)   Hanako=(o)   mi-ta.
         Taro-(SUBJ) Hanako-(OBJ) see-PST
         'Taro saw Hanako.' (Kurumada and Jaeger 2015: 155)

Grammatical relations are expressed by two structural cues in Japanese: word order and (optional) case marking. Basic word order is SOV, but since subject and object can also occur in reverse order (i.e., OSV), word order alone is not sufficient to formally distinguish between A and P. Moreover, since arguments are often omitted, many transitive clauses include only a single argument that is potentially ambiguous between A and P if it is not accompanied by a case clitic (Fry 2003). In formal written registers, A and P are almost always accompanied by a case marker in Japanese, but in casual conversation, both arguments are often zero.

Crucially, while the use of case clitics is not predetermined by particular properties of the object in Japanese, it correlates with the same semantic and pragmatic properties as the occurrence of overt case markers in DOM systems. Consider, for instance, the numbers in Table 11.2, which summarize the results of a small corpus study of the use of object case markers in conversational Japanese (Minashima 2001).

As can be seen, pronouns and proper names, which are high in definiteness and animacy, are usually marked by an object clitic in conversational Japanese. In particular, personal pronouns are almost always accompanied by an overt case marker if they function as object, whereas common nouns denoting indefinite and inanimate entities are often unmarked in object function (see also Fry 2003). Similar proportions of case marking and zero coding have been found with direct objects in conversational Korean (Lee 2006).

Table 11.2 *Proportions of case-marked NPs in a corpus of spontaneous Japanese*

NP Type	P-case	P-zero	Total
Personal pronouns	99.1%	0.9%	116
Proper names	95.3%	4.7%	105
Definite animate nouns	90.5%	9.5%	179
Definite inanimate nouns	81.9%	18.1%	1228
Indefinite animate nouns	68.9%	31.1%	61
Indefinite inanimate nouns	49.4%	50.6%	354

In order to determine the cognitive motivations behind the optional use of case markers in Korean and Japanese, a number of recent studies have examined the alternation between overt P marking and zero coding under controlled experimental conditions (Lee 2010, 2011; Lee and Kim 2012; Fedzechkina et al. 2013; Kurumada and Jaeger 2015). In one of these studies, Kurumada and Jaeger (2015) conducted a series of recall production experiments in which speakers of Japanese had to reproduce a set of transitive sentences consisting of a subject, a direct object, a locational adverb and a transitive verb. The test sentences always occurred in the order of S-O-ADV-V, but included different semantic types of nouns that appeared with or without a case clitic.

In the first experiment, the subject was always animate and overtly marked for case by the clitic =ga, but the object varied with regard to both animacy and case marking (27a–b). The two variables (i.e., animacy and case marking) were crossed according to a 2-by-2 factorial design that allowed the researchers to examine the potential influence of animacy on object case marking. The great majority of participants' responses matched the recall stimuli, but in about 30 percent of all responses, participants produced an object case marker although the object of the recall item was not overtly marked. Crucially, this type of "recall error" correlated with the animacy of the direct object. As expected, participants were significantly more likely to add an object case marker to an animate P than to an inanimate one, supporting the hypothesis that animacy has a significant impact on object case marking in Japanese.

(27) [animate-animate]
a. Sensei=ga   seito=(o)   ekimae=de mi-ta-yo.
   teacher=SUBJ   student=(OBJ) station=LOC see-PST-SFP
   'The teacher saw a student near the train station.'
   (Kurumada and Jaeger 2015: 156)
   [animate-animate]
b. Sensei=ga   shobosha=(o)   ekimae=de   mi-ta-yo.
   teacher=SUBJ fire.engine=(OBJ) station=LOC see-PST-SFP
   'The teacher saw a fire-engine near the train station.'
   (Kurumada and Jaeger 2015: 156)

In a second experiment, the researchers manipulated the plausibility of the recall stimuli by combining particular nouns and verbs. For instance, given the nouns *keisatsu* 'police officer' and *hannin* 'criminal' and the verbs *taiho* 'arrest' and *osou* 'attack', it is likely that *taiho* selects *keisatsu* as subject and *hannin* as object, whereas *osou* is likely to occur with *hannin* as subject and *keisatsu* as object. As in experiment 1, the subject was always marked for case, but the P argument occurred with or without an overt case marker (28–29).

(28)   a. Police officer=SUBJ criminal=(OBJ) ADVERB arrest.   [plausible]
        b. Police officer=SUBJ criminal=(OBJ) ADVERB attack.   [implausible]

(29)   a. Criminal=SUBJ police officer=(OBJ) ADVERB arrest.   [implausible]
        b. Criminal=SUBJ police officer=(OBJ) ADVERB attack.   [plausible]

In accordance with the experimental hypothesis, Kurumada and Jaeger found a highly significant correlation between case marking and plausibility. Specifically, they observed that participants were more likely to use object case markers in semantically implausible sentences than in sentences that are consistent with language users' semantic expectations.

Note that the results of this experiment cannot be explained by a simple strategy to disambiguate A and P. Since the A argument was always marked for case, the test sentences were structurally unambiguous without an object case marker. In the literature, it is often assumed that case marking serves to disambiguate the argument roles of a sentence, but this view of ambiguity avoidance is difficult to reconcile with the results of the current study.

In Chapter 6, it was argued that comprehension is a dynamic process that is determined by competing factors. Since this process is often disturbed by noise in the environment or perceptual system (Kurumada and Jaeger 2015: 153), sentence comprehension is probabilistic. Listeners do not just recognize the meaning of a sentence, but interpret the various cues they encounter in an utterance against the background of their linguistic knowledge and expectations. If we think of comprehension in this way, we may characterize participants' performance in this study as a hearer-oriented strategy to reinforce the interpretation of P when there is reason to believe that P violates listeners' linguistic expectations. In other words, while object case marking can help to differentiate between A and P, it is not a simple disambiguation strategy but serves to manipulate listeners' mental states, notably their linguistic predictions, when this is needed.

Further support for this conclusion comes from a learning experiment by Fedzechkina et al. (2013). In this study, speakers of English were taught an artificial language resembling Japanese in word order and case marking. After training was completed, the researchers tested participants' knowledge of the new language in a production task in which learners overused the object case marker (compared to its use in the input language) under two conditions: First, learners were more likely to use case markers with animate than with inanimate Ps; and second, they were more likely to use the object case marker when constituent order was OSV rather than SOV. Both animate objects and objects that precede the subject are atypical Ps that deviate from language users' normal expectations regarding grammatical relations in simple transitive clauses. Thus, it seems that the participants of this study modified the input language so as to facilitate sentence comprehension.

In general, there is good evidence for the hypothesis that speakers of languages with an optional case marking system adjust the use of overt P marking to a hearer's needs in a particular context. If the object is atypical and thus likely to deviate from a listener's expectations, there is a tendency to indicate the status of P by an overt case marker, but if the object is typical and thus likely to accord with a listener's expectations (or predictions), there is a tendency to leave P unmarked (for similar results from parallel studies with speakers of Korean, see Lee 2010, 2011; Lee and Kim 2012).

Languages with optional case marking are similar to languages with differential object marking. In both types of languages, P marking correlates with animacy, definiteness and topicality, suggesting that optional and differential case marking are motivated by the same factors (Kurumada and Jaeger 2015).

There is, however, an important difference between the two types of case marking systems. In systems with optional P marking, speakers have a true choice between case marking and zero coding (in many contexts) and this choice is influenced by their assessment of listeners' needs in a particular situation. In systems with differential object marking, however, speakers do not really have a choice between P marking and zero coding, as the occurrence of an overt case marker is (usually) triggered automatically by particular semantic, pragmatic or grammatical features of the object. In other words, DOM systems are governed by linguistic conventions rather than by speakers' assessment of listeners' needs in a particular context.

That does not mean that DOM systems are not also motivated by hearer-oriented processes of language production. In §11.6, we will see that DOM systems are commonly derived from information-structure constructions that are immediately concerned with listeners' linguistic expectations, but these constructions develop into categorical case marking systems in which the alternation between P marking and zero coding is primarily determined by the type of object rather than by hearers' needs in a particular context.

11.6   The Diachronic Evolution of Object Case Marking

In Chapter 8 it was noted that case markers are commonly derived from adpositions, which in turn are often based on relational nouns or serial verbs. Once a language has acquired a case marking system, individual markers are often extended to novel uses (Heine et al. 1991; Lehmann [1995] 2015). The diachronic developments of case markers are diverse, but there are recurrent paths that are important for understanding the organization of these systems from a synchronic point of view.

In the case of DOM, the alternation between overt P marking and zero coding can often be traced back to an earlier alternation between different information-structure constructions. As Iemmolo (2011) showed, in a number of languages with differential object marking, the P marker first appeared with direct objects that were fronted or left-dislocated to indicate a topic shift (see also Iemmolo 2010; Dalrymple and Nikoleava 2011). In Spanish, for instance, the accusative preposition *a* was originally used to mark animate, topical P arguments that occurred at the beginning of a new sentence. Consider, for instance, the following examples from Old Spanish (twelfth century).

(30)   En   braços   tenedes   *mis*   *fijas*   tan blancas commo
        in   arms   hold.PRS.2PL   POSS1.PL   daughters   so   white   as
        el   sol.
        the sun
        'In your arms you hold my daughters as white as the sun.' (Iemmolo 2011: 265)

(31)   *A   la   sus   fijas*   en braços las   prendia.
        DOM the POSS3.PL daughters in arms   3.PL.F.OBJ take.IMPF.3SG
        'His daughters he took in his arms.' (Iemmolo 2011: 265)

As can be seen, when the P argument occurred after the verb, Old Spanish did not require the use of an overt case marker even when P was animate and definite, as *mis fijas* 'my daughters' in (30), but when P was fronted, it was generally accompanied by *a* and usually resumed by a pronoun, as in example (31). While *a*-marking also occurred with certain postverbal objects in Old Spanish (von Heusinger and Kaiser 2005: 43), it was especially prominent with left-dislocated Ps that were fronted to organize a topic shift (Iemmolo 2010, 2011). In other words, there was a highly conspicuous contrast between topical and nontopical Ps in Old Spanish that was formally expressed by word order and the presence or absence of *a* (see also Bossong 1985, 1991).

Interestingly, Iemmolo (2011) showed that a similar contrast occurs in several modern varieties of other Romance languages in which DOM is much less developed than in Modern Spanish. In Northern Italian, for instance, DOM is very limited. P arguments that follow the verb are never marked for case in (Northern) Italian, but in sentences in which a first or second person pronoun is left-dislocated, P marking is obligatory as in example (32), which would not be acceptable without the marker *a* (in Northern Italian).

(32)   **A**   te,   non   ti   sopporto   più!
        ACC   you   NEG   CLIT.2SG   tolerate.PRS.1SG   longer
        'I cannot stand you any longer.' (Iemmolo 2010: 249)

Similar contrasts between fronted and postverbal direct objects occur in other modern varieties of Romance languages (Languedoc French, Brussels French, Catalan, Balearic Catalan, Sicilian). Every variety has particular constraints on P marking (Iemmolo 2011: Chapter 8), but what all of them have in common is that the occurrence of *a* is restricted to direct objects that are high in topicality.

According to Iemmolo, fronted objects of this type are used to direct listeners' attention onto a new topic. Since these constructions are similar to the early constructions of *a*-marked Ps in Old Spanish, it seems reasonable to assume that topic marking has paved the way for differential object marking in Romance languages (see also von Heusinger and Kaiser 2005). Additional support for this view comes from the fact that the accusative marker *a* developed from the Latin postposition *ad* 'toward', which already in Classical Latin was often used to introduce an *as-for* topic (33).

(33)   **Ad**   Dolabell-am,   ut   scrib-is,   ita   puto
       TOP   Dolabella-ACC.SG.F   as   write.PRS-2SG   so   believe.PRS.1SG
       faci-end-um.
       do-GER-ACC.SG.N
       'As for D., as you write, I think that we should act in this way.' (Iemmolo 2010: 259)

A similar connection between DOM and topicality has been found in the history of several other languages in which P marking alternates with zero coding. The (differential) object markers of Persian (*-râ*) and Hindi (*-ko*), for example, developed from directional postpositions that were also used as topic markers, similar to Latin *ad* (Bossong 1985: 90; Iemmolo 2010: 266).

Generalizing across these findings, we may conclude that the marked variants of DOM systems are commonly derived from constructions that were originally used to organize a topic shift (von Heusinger and Kaiser 2005; Iemmolo 2010, 2011; Dalrymple and Nikoleava 2011). If this is correct, it is very plausible, as Iemmolo and others have claimed, that incipient DOM systems are motivated by the need to focus listeners' attention onto a new topic, which is basically a hearer-oriented strategy to mark an atypical P argument that deviates from listeners' linguistic expectations, similar to the strategy that underlies the alternation between overt P marking and zero coding in languages with optional case marking like Korean and Japanese.

Note, however, that while incipient DOM systems are motivated by cognitive processes that are geared toward listeners' needs, the subsequent development of these systems is also influenced by speaker-oriented processes, notably by analogy (or priming). As Iemmolo (2011) and others have shown, once a morpheme is routinely used to mark the occurrence of a topical P, it is often extended to other, nontopical uses of direct objects (see also von Heusinger and Kaiser 2005; von Heusinger and Kornfilt 2005).

Interestingly, the development proceeds along the referential scales that characterize A and P (Figure 11.4). In Spanish, for instance, the *a*-marker first appeared with personal pronouns and proper names (which are at the top of the topicality scale) and then spread to lexical objects that were animate, definite and specific. In the modern language, inanimate direct objects are never marked by *a* in European Spanish, but in some American varieties of Present-Day Spanish, *a*-marking is also occasionally found with specific inanimate and nonspecific animate Ps (von Heusinger and Kaiser 2005), suggesting that the development of the Spanish DOM system has not yet come to an end. In the extreme case, a differential object marker may spread to all direct objects regardless of their semantic and pragmatic properties.

However, given that most languages (with case-marked objects) restrict the marker of P to atypical objects (Sinnemäki 2014), we may hypothesize that the development of differential object marking usually comes to a halt when the object case marker has spread to all direct objects that deviate in one way or another from listeners' linguistic expectations. If this is correct, case spreading is not only driven by speaker-oriented processes of analogy (or priming), but also by hearer-oriented processes of social cognition and common ground that motivate the extension of direct object marking up to a point where P is fully consistent with listeners' linguistic expectations.

11.7   Case Marking and Semantic Maps

More research is needed to determine the interaction between speaker- and hearer-oriented processes in the extension of case markers, but irrespective of the question as to whether case spreading is motivated by speaker- and/or hearer-oriented processes, we find that these processes give rise to diachronic trajectories that are strikingly similar from a cross-linguistic perspective. As many scholars of grammaticalization have noted, adpositions and case markers tend to evolve along recurrent paths, known as "grammaticalization channels," that are similar across languages (Heine et al. 1991; Lehmann [1995] 2015; Hopper and Traugott 2003). In the case of differential object marking, the following trajectory is very frequent:

(34)   ALLATIVE (directional) > DATIVE (recipient) > ACCUSATIVE (patient)

As Bossong (1985) and others have shown, in many languages with DOM, the accusative marker has evolved from a marker of dative case, which in turn is often based on an allative (or directional) adposition. Spanish *a* provides a case in point, but this development also occurred in several other languages including Persian, Hindi and Semitic (Bossong 1991; Iemmolo 2010, 2011).

Interestingly, while adpositions and case markers tend to evolve along certain paths, they also often feed into other grammaticalization channels. The Latin adposition *ad,* for instance, did not only develop into a dative case marker and then further into a marker of P (in Spanish), it also evolved into various other grammatical morphemes in Romance languages. For instance, the French preposition *à* (which is cognate with Spanish *a*) did not only develop into an allative adposition and dative case marker, but also into a marker of time

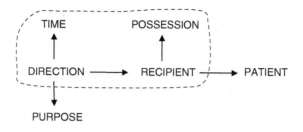

Figure 11.5 Semantic map of French *à*

(cf. *Nous arrivons à 5 h.* 'We arrive at 5:00.') and predicative possession (cf. *Ce chien est à moi.* 'This dog is mine.'), though it did not develop into a DOM marker like Spanish *a* (Haspelmath 2003: 214–220). The various uses of French *à* constitute a polysemy network to which typologists refer as a "semantic map." Figure 11.5 shows how the various senses of French *à* developed in language history and how these senses can be combined into a semantic map.

Semantic maps play an important role in typological research on grammar and grammatical development (Kemmer 1993; Haspelmath 1997, 2003; van der Auwera and Plungian 1998; Croft 2001, 2003; van Trijp 2010; Georgakopoulos and Polis 2018). They are commonly used to compare the meanings of multifunctional grammatical expressions (and constructions) across languages. Since grammaticalization is driven by domain-general processes, grammatical morphemes tend to evolve along similar paths in different languages. Compare, for instance, the map of French *à* (Figure 11.5) to that of English *to* (Figure 11.6).[6]

As can be seen, there is overlap between French *à* and English *to*. Both markers are based on an allative adposition that has been extended to recipients and certain expressions of time. However, unlike French *à*, English *to* is also used with purpose infinitives (cf. *He came to help him*), which is not possible in French (cf. **J'ai quitté la fête tôt à arriver à la maison en bon temps.* 'I left the party early to get home in time.'), but unlike French *à*, English *to* does not appear with predicative possessors (Haspelmath 2003: 215).

Some scholars have argued that the polysemy networks of grammatical markers are based on "universal conceptual spaces" that "constrain" the use and the development of grammatical markers in individual languages (Croft 2003: 92–104; see also Gärdenfors 2014). In particular, these scholars claim that the meanings of polysemous grammatical markers are restricted to those

---

[6] Note that these maps are simplified for illustrative purposes. For a more detailed analysis of semantic maps including dative/recipient markers, see Haspelmath (2003) and Narrog (2010).

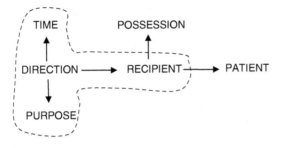

Figure 11.6 Semantic map of English *to*

senses that constitute a connected region in conceptual space. So for instance, assuming that the network that underlies Spanish *a* and English *to* (in Figures 11.5 and 11.6) constitutes a (universal) conceptual space, there should be no language in which an allative marker is also used with predicative possessors if it does not also occur with recipients because direction and possession do not constitute a connected region without the recipient node in the underlying conceptual space.

The distinction between (language-specific) semantic maps and (universal) conceptual spaces provides a useful tool for language comparison (see Haspelmath 2003 for a review), but let me emphasize that conceptual spaces are typological generalizations over language-specific polysemy networks rather than cognitive representations of semantic concepts in speakers' minds. It would be a complete misunderstanding, in my view, to assume that conceptual spaces (as defined by typologists) are hard-wired structures of the brain. They are not. Rather, conceptual spaces are "comparative concepts" (Haspelmath 2010) that typologists use in order to state typological general-izations over multifunctional grammatical markers such as Spanish *a* and English *to*. It is, thus, a bit misleading to claim that conceptual spaces "con-strain" the meanings of grammatical markers. Since conceptual spaces are descriptive generalizations, they do not have any psychological effect on language use and development. If there are any psychological constraints that restrict the meanings of grammatical morphemes, they involve the cognitive processes that motivate the use and the development of grammatical markers (and constructions).

11.8   Conclusion

In summation, in the current and previous chapters, we have been concerned with constructional relations. Every construction has a particular location in the grammar network that is defined by its relationship to other constructions in the system. Constructional relations can be characterized in terms of two general concepts: similarity and contrast. In Chapter 10, we saw that semantically and/ or formally similar constructions are organized in construction families that influence the use and the development of constructional neighbors in the network. And in the current chapter, we have seen that semantically contrastive constructions are organized in paradigms of particular categories such as voice, case and number in which infrequent and unexpected category members are often indicated by an extra morpheme.

Combining evidence from linguistic typology with evidence from psycho-linguistics, it has been argued that the asymmetries in the encoding of grammatical categories are crucially influenced by frequency of language use. Specifically, we have seen that differential object marking originates from a hearer-oriented strategy to indicate the occurrence of an atypical argument that can cause comprehension problems as it deviates from language users' linguistic expectations or predictions. Once an (object) marker is in place, however, it is often extended to more typical (object) arguments that do not really need an extra marker for comprehension. Generalizing across this research, we may say that differential object marking (and other encoding asymmetries) are the result of an intricate interplay between other-oriented processes of social cognition and self-oriented processes of memory, analogy and activation spreading.

12 Conclusion

12.1 Grammar as a Network

This book has provided a comprehensive overview of usage-based research in linguistics and psychology and has tried to integrate the many aspects of usage-based research into a more unified approach. Concluding the discussion, let us briefly recapitulate the main points.

For more than a century, linguistic scholars have analyzed grammar as a self-contained, deductive system consisting of a limited set of primitive categories and categorical rules that can generate an infinite number of sentences, but there is now an alternative approach, known as the usage-based model, in which grammar is seen as a dynamic system in which grammatical categories and rules, or schemas, are derived from language use.

Elaborating the usage-based approach, this book has presented a nested network model of grammar in which all aspects of linguistic structure, including basic categories such as word, noun and case, are defined in terms of nodes and links, or associative relations, shaped by language use. The model crucially relies on the assumption that linguistic structure consists of constructions. Since constructions are linguistic signs or symbols, similar to lexemes, it is widely assumed that constructions are associated with each other like lexical expressions in the mental lexicon. However, while the network view of grammar is frequently invoked in usage-based studies, it has not yet been developed into an explicit theory or model.

Building on research in construction grammar, usage-based morphology and lexical semantics, the current monograph has proposed a network model of grammar in which all linguistic concepts, including basic grammatical categories (e.g., word classes, grammatical relations, syntactic constituents), are defined in terms of associations between different aspects of linguistic knowledge. In this model, linguistic signs are analyzed at two different levels. In accordance with much previous research, constructions and lexemes have been analyzed as nodes of a symbolic network, but, crucially, while nodes are usually seen as basic elements of network models, in the current approach, each node is also analyzed as some kind of network.

On this account, linguistic signs are dynamic entities that involve three general associations: (i) symbolic relations, which combine a certain form or structure with a particular function or meaning, (ii) sequential relations, which connect linguistic elements that appear in linear order and (iii) taxonomic relations, which specify connections between linguistic patterns at different levels of abstraction (Chapters 4, 5 and 6).

Together the three relations define the basic units of speech, e.g., morphemes, words, phrases, collocations and constructions. Every unit constitutes a dynamic network, but these networks also serve as nodes of a higher-level network that involves three other types of associations: (i) lexical relations, which connect lexemes with similar or contrastive forms and meanings, (ii) constructional relations, which specify associative connections between similar and contrastive constructions, and (iii) filler–slot relations, which connect particular lexemes (or phrases) with certain slots of constructional schemas (Chapters 7–11).

Taken together, the six relations provide a framework for the analysis of all grammatical concepts as emergent and dynamic entities. Nouns and verbs, for instance, are defined by filler–slot relations that connect individual lexemes with particular word class schemas (Chapter 8), and inflectional categories such as case and number are based on constructional relations between semantically contrastive constructions that typically involve an encoding asymmetry between the default construction and its competitors (Chapter 11).

12.2   Cognitive Processes and Language Use

The network model of grammar provides a unified framework for the analysis of linguistic states and language development. If we think of grammar as a dynamic system, we have to analyze grammatical categories and constructions in light of their developments. There is general agreement among usage-based researchers that the development of linguistic structure is driven by domain-general processes of language use, but the nature and interaction of these processes are not yet fully understood. Drawing on general research in cognitive psychology, this book has considered language use and language development in light of a wide range of domain-general processes, which have been divided into three basic types: (i) processes of social cognition, (ii) processes of conceptualization and (iii) memory-related processes (Chapter 3).

The processes of social cognition concern the interaction between speaker and hearer. In order to communicate, interlocutors must take the other person's current mental state into account and must coordinate their shared attention and common ground. Social cognition is of central significance to the rise of symbolic associations (Chapter 6) and the encoding asymmetries of grammatical categories such as case and number (Chapter 11).

The processes of conceptualization concern the structuring of meaning (or semantic content). In order to evoke a particular meaning, speakers manipulate listeners' current mental states, which involves general conceptual processes such as deixis, metaphor and the figure–ground distinction. Conceptualization is involved in the creation of both lexical and constructional meanings (Chapters 6–10), but while previous research has emphasized the parallels between lexemes and constructions, the current study has argued that lexemes and constructions evoke meaning in very different ways. Lexemes provide access to an open-ended network of encyclopedic knowledge that listeners use to construct a semantic interpretation in a particular (linguistic and social) context, whereas constructions serve to guide listeners' interpretation of lexical expressions.

Finally, the processes of memory concern the storage, retrieval and processing of information. In order to produce (or comprehend) an utterance, language users must access linguistic concepts in long-term memory, which is influenced by a wide range of cognitive processes including priming, analogy and automatization. All of these processes have been studied intensively in cognitive psychology but have long been neglected in grammatical research. However, as we have seen (throughout the entire book), memory-related processes play a key role in the usage-based study of grammar. They have a significant impact on language users' choice of linguistic means, which in turn determines their development in language acquisition and language change.

The various cognitive processes can reinforce each other, but can also be in competition. Of particular importance is the competition between other-oriented processes of social cognition and self-oriented processes of memory and information processing. As we have seen, language use involves a continuous decision-making process that is motivated by speakers' and listeners' assessment of the other person's mental state in a particular context. Nevertheless, while the communicative partners must take the other person's knowledge and perspective into account, they often proceed in a routine fashion that is primarily determined by memory-related processes such as priming and automatization.

One general advantage of the network model is that it can easily explain the role of memory-related processes in both language use and grammar. As we have seen, many grammatical categories are motivated by semantic and pragmatic factors (which are ultimately based on cognitive processes of conceptualization and social cognition), but in addition to these factors, it is language users' experience with particular lexical and grammatical patterns that determines their choice of linguistic means and the organization of linguistic structure. One piece of evidence for this hypothesis comes from the many idiosyncrasies of grammar that cannot be explained by general rules but are readily explained by association learning. If a language user repeatedly encounters a particular co-occurrence pattern, his/her experience becomes entrenched in the associative connections of the grammar network and these connections affect his/her choice of linguistic means and the development of linguistic structure as an independent factor (Chapters 6, 7, 8 and 11).

In conclusion, the dynamic network model of grammar presents a radical alternative to traditional research on grammar. It combines the study of linguistic structure with the study of language use and language development and provides a unified framework for the analysis of lexical, structural and semantic phenomena. It is inspired by computational research with dynamic network models in cognitive science and situates the linguistic theory of grammar in a general theory of cognition.

References

Abbot-Smith, Kirsten and Heike Behrens. 2006. How known constructions influence the acquisition of other constructions: The German passive and future constructions. *Cognitive Science* 30: 995–1026.

Abbot-Smith, Kirsten and Michael Tomasello. 2006. Exemplar-learning and schematization in a usage-based account of syntactic acquisition. *The Linguistic Review* 23: 275–290.

Aissen, Judith. 2003. Differential object marking: Iconicity vs. economy. *Natural Language and Linguistic Theory* 21: 435–483.

Akthar, Nameera and Michael Tomasello. 1996. Two-year-olds learn words for absent objects and actions. *British Journal of Developmental Psychology* 14: 79–93.

Albright, Adam and Bruce Hayes. 2003. Rules vs. analogy in English past tenses: A computational/experimental study. *Cognition* 90: 119–161.

Alegre, Maria and Peter Gordon. 1999. Frequency effects and the representational status of regular inflections. *Journal of Memory and Language* 40: 41–61.

Altmann, Gerry T. M. and Yuki Kamide. 1999. Incremental interpretation at verbs: Restricting the domain of subsequent reference. *Cognition* 73: 247–264.

Altmann, Gerry T. M. and Jelena Mirković. 2009. Incrementality and prediction in human sentence processing. *Cognitive Science* 33: 583–609.

Ambridge, Ben, Julian M. Pine, Caroline F. Rowland and Chris R. Young. 2008. The effect of verb semantic class and verb frequency (entrenchment) on children's and adults' graded judgments of argument-structure overgeneralization errors. *Cognition* 106: 87–129.

Ambridge, Ben, Julian M. Pine, Caroline F. Rowland and Franklin Chang. 2012. The roles of verb semantics, entrenchment, and morphophonology in the retreat from dative argument-structure overgeneralization errors. *Language* 88: 45–81.

Andersen, Paul Kent. 1979. Word order typology and prepositions in Old Indic. In Bela Brogyani (ed.), *Festschrift for Oswald Szemerényi on the Occasion of His 65th Birthday*, 23–34. Amsterdam: John Benjamins.

Anderson, John R. 1983. Retrieval of information from long-term memory. *Science* 220: 25–30.

2005. *Cognitive Psychology and Its Implications*. New York: Worth Publisher. [Sixth edition]

Andrade, Manuel José. 1933. Quileute. In Franz Boas (ed.), *Handbook of American Indian Languages*, 149–292. New York: Augustin.

Andrews, Sally. 1997. The effect of orthographic similarity on lexical retrieval: Resolving neighborhood conflicts. *Psychonomic Bulletin and Review* 4: 439–461.

Arbib, Michael A. 2012. *How the Brain Got Language: The Mirror System Hypothesis*. Oxford: Oxford University Press.

Ariel, Mira. 1990. *Accessing Noun-Phrase Antecedents*. London: Routledge.

Arnold, Jennifer E. 2008. Reference production: Production-internal and addressee-oriented processes. *Language and Cognitive Processes* 23: 495–527.

Arnold, Jennifer E., Thomas Wasow, Anthony Losongco and Ryan Ginstrom. 2000. Heaviness vs. newness: The effects of structural complexity and discourse status on constituent ordering. *Language* 76: 28–55.

Arnon, Inbal and Uriel Cohen Priva. 2013. More than words: The effect of multi-word frequency and constituency on phonetic duration. *Language and Speech* 56: 349–371.

Arnon, Inbal and Neal Snider. 2010. More than words: Frequency effects for multi-word phrases. *Journal of Memory and Language* 62: 67–82.

Arunachalam, Sudha. 2017. Preschoolers' acquisition of novel verbs in the double-object dative. *Cognitive Science* 41: 831–854.

Aslin, Richard N. and Elissa L. Newport. 2012. Statistical learning: From acquiring specific items to forming general rules. *Current Directions in Psychological Science* 21: 170–177.

Auer, Peter. 2005. Projection in interaction and projection in grammar. *Text* 25: 7–36.

Austin, John. 1962. *How to Do Things with Words*. Cambridge, MA: Harvard University Press.

Aylett, Matthew and Alice Turk. 2004. The smooth signal redundancy hypothesis: A functional explanation for relationships between redundancy, prosodic prominence, and duration in spontaneous speech. *Language and Speech* 47: 31–56.

Baddeley, Alan D. 1986. *Working Memory*. Oxford: Clarendon Press.

Bannard, Colin and Danielle Matthews. 2008. Stored word sequences in language learning. The effect of familiarity on children's repetition of four-word combinations. *Psychological Science* 19: 241–248.

Barcelona, Antonio. 2015. Metonymy. In Ewa Dąbrowska and Dagmar Divjak (eds.), *Handbook of Cognitive Linguistics*, 143–167. Berlin: Mouton de Gruyter.

Bard, Ellen Gurman, Anne H. Anderson, Catherine Sotillo, Matthew Aylett, Gwyneth Doherty-Sneddon and Alison Newlands. 2000. Controlling the intelligibility of referring expressions in dialogue. *Journal of Memory and Language* 42: 1–22.

Barðdal, Johanna. 2006. Construction-specific properties of syntactic subjects in Icelandic and German. *Cognitive Linguistics* 17: 39–106.

2008. *Productivity: Evidence from Case and Argument Structure in Icelandic*. Amsterdam: John Benjamins.

Baronchelli, Andrea, Ramon Ferrer-i-Cancho, Romualdo Paster-Satorras, Nick Chater and Morten H. Christiansen. 2013. Networks in cognitive science. *Trends in Cognitive Science* 17: 348–360.

Barsalou, Lawrence W. 1999. Perceptual symbol systems. *Behavioral and Brain Sciences* 22: 577–660.

Barth, Danielle and Vsevolod Kapatsinski. 2017. A multimodel inference approach to categorical variant choice: Construction, priming and frequency effects on the choice between full and contracted forms of am, are and is. *Corpus Linguistics and Linguistic Theory* 13: 1–58.

Bates, Elizabeth and Brian MacWhinney. 1989. Functionalism and the competition model. In Brian MacWhinney and Elizabeth Bates (eds.), *The Crosslinguistic Study of Sentence Processing*, 3–73. Cambridge: Cambridge University Press.

Bech, Kristin. 2001. Word order patterns in Old and Middle English: A syntactic and pragmatic study. PhD dissertation. University of Bergen.

Beckner, Clay, Richard Blythe, Joan Bybee, Morton H. Christiansen, William Croft, Nick C. Ellis, John Holland, Jinyun Ke, Diane Larsen-Freeman and Tom Schoenemann. 2009. Language is a complex adaptive system: Position paper. *Language Learning* 59: 1–26.

Behaghel, Otto. 1932. *Deutsche Syntax. Eine geschichtliche Darstellung. Vol. 4. Wortstellung, Periodenbau*. Heidelberg: Winter.

Behrens, Heike. 2005. Wortartenerwerb durch Induktion. In Clemens Knobloch and Burkhard Schaeder (eds.), *Wortarten und Grammatikalisierung: Perspektiven in System und Erwerb*, 177–198. Berlin: Walter de Gruyter.

2009. Usage-based and emergentist approaches to language acquisition. *Linguistics* 47: 383–411.

2017. The role of analogy in language processing and acquisition. In Marianne Hundt, Sandra Mollin and Simone E. Pfenniger (eds.), *The Changing English Language*, 215–239. Cambridge: Cambridge University Press.

Behrens, Heike and Stefan Pfänder (eds.). 2016. *Experience Counts: Frequency Effects in Language*. Berlin: Mouton de Gruyter.

Bell, Alan, Daniel Jurafsky, Eric Fosler-Lussier, Cynthia Girand, Michelle Gregory and Daniel Gildea. 2003. Effects of disfluencies, predictability, and utterance position on word form variation in English conversation. *Journal of the Acoustic Society of America* 113: 1001–1024.

Bell, Alan, Jason Brenier, Michelle Gregory, Cynthia Girand and Daniel Jurafsky. 2009. Predictability effects on durations of content and function words in conversational English. *Journal of Memory and Language* 60: 92–111.

Bencini, Guilia M. L. and Adele E. Goldberg. 2000. The contribution of argument structure constructions to sentence meaning. *Journal of Memory and Language* 43: 640–651.

Bergen, Benjamin K. 2012. *Louder than Words: The New Science of How the Mind Makes Meaning*. New York: Basic Books.

Bergs, Alexander and Gabriele Diewald (eds.). 2008. *Constructions and Language Change*. Berlin: Mouton de Gruyter.

Bever, Thomas G. 1970. The cognitive basis for linguistic structure. In John R. Hayes (ed.), *Cognition and Development of Language*, 279–352. New York: Wiley.

Bickel, Balthasar. 2011. Grammatical relations typology. In Jae Jung Song (ed.), *The Oxford Handbook of Linguistic Typology*, 399–444. Oxford: Oxford University Press.

Bickel, Balthasar, Alena Witzlack-Makarevich and Taras Zakharko. 2015. Typological evidence against universal effects of referential scales on case alignment. In Ina Bornkessel-Schlesewsky, Andrej L. Malchukov and Marc Richards (eds.), *Scales and Hierarchies: A Cross-Disciplinary Perspective*, 7–43. Berlin: Mouton de Gruyter.

Boas, Hans C. 2003. *A Constructional Approach to Resultatives*. Stanford, CA: CSLI Publications.

2008. Determining the structure of lexical entries and grammatical constructions in Construction Grammar. *Annual Review of Cognitive Linguistics* 6: 113–144.

2010. The syntax-lexicon continuum in Construction Grammar: A case study of English communication verbs. *Belgian Journal of Linguistics* 24: 54–82.

Bock, Kathryn. 1986. Syntactic persistence in language production. *Cognitive Psychology* 18: 355–387.

Bock, Kathryn and Zenzi Griffin. 2000. The persistence of structural priming: Transient activation or implicit learning? *Journal of Experimental Psychology: General* 129: 177–192.

Bock, Kathryn and Helga Loebell. 1990. Framing sentences. *Cognition* 35: 1–39.

Bock, J. Kathryn, Gary S. Dell, Franklin Chang and Kristine H. Onishi. 2007. Persistent structural priming from language comprehension to language production. *Cognition* 104: 437–458.

Bod, Rens. 2009. From exemplar to grammar: A probabilistic analogy-based model of language learning. *Cognitive Science* 33: 752–793.

Bolinger, Dwight. 1967. Adjectives in English: Attribution and predication. *Lingua* 18: 1–34.

Bossong, Georg. 1985. *Differentielle Objektmarkierung in den neuiranischen Sprachen*. Tübingen: Narr.

1991. Differential object marking in Romance and beyond. In Dieter Wanner und Douglas A. Kibbee (eds.), *New Analyses in Romance Linguistics. Selected Papers from the XVIII Linguistics Symposium on Romance Languages*, 143–170. Amsterdam: John Benjamins.

Bowdle, Brian F. and Dedre Gentner. 2005. The career of metaphor. *Psychological Review* 112: 193–216.

Bower, Gordon H. 2000. A brief history of memory research. In Endel Tulving and Fergus I. M. Craik (eds.), *The Oxford Handbook of Memory*, 3–32. Oxford: Oxford University Press.

Bowerman, Melisa. 1988. The "no negative evidence" problem: How children avoid constructing an overgeneral grammar. In John A. Hawkins (ed.), *Explaining Language Universals*, 73–101. Oxford: Basil Blackwell.

Boye, Kasper and Peter Harder. 2012. A usage-based theory of grammatical status and grammaticalization. *Language* 88: 1–44.

Braine, Martin D. S. 1976. Children's first word combinations. *Monographs of the Society for Research in Child Development* 41.

Brandt, Silke, Holger Diessel and Michael Tomasello. 2008. The acquisition of German relative clauses: A case study. *Journal of Child Language* 35: 325–348.

Breban, Tine and Kristin Davidse. 2003. Adjectives of comparison: The grammaticalization of their attribute uses into postdeterminer and classifier uses. *Folia Linguistica* 37: 269–318.

Breban, Tine, Kristin Davidse and Lobke Ghesquière. 2011. A typology of anaphoric and cataphoric relations expressed by English complex determiners. *Journal of Pragmatics* 43: 2689–2703.

Bresnan, Joan and Marilyn Ford. 2010. Predicting syntax: Processing dative constructions in American and Australian varieties of English. *Language* 86: 186–213.

Bresnan, Joan and Jennifer Hay. 2008. Gradient grammar: An effect of animacy on the syntax of give in New Zealand and American English. *Lingua* 118: 245–259.

Bresnan, Joan and Jessica Spencer. 2013. Frequency and variation in English subject-verb contraction. Manuscript. Stanford University.

Bresnan, Joan, Anna Cueni, Tatiana Nikitina and Harald R. Baayen. 2007. Predicting the dative alternation. In Gerlof Boume, Irene Kraemer and Joost Zwarts (eds.), *Cognitive Foundations of Interpretation*, 69–94. Amsterdam: Royal Netherlands Academy of Science.

Brooks, Patricia and Michael Tomasello. 1999. Young children learn to produce passives with nonce verbs. *Developmental Psychology* 35: 29–44.

Brooks, Patricia, Michael Tomasello, Kelly Dodson and Lawrence B. Lewis. 1999. Young children's overgeneralizations with fixed transitivity verbs. *Child Development* 70: 1325–1337.

Broschart, Jürgen. 1997. Why Tongan does it differently: Categorial distinctions in a language without nouns and verbs. *Linguistic Typology* 1: 123–165.

Brown, Dunstan and Andrew Hippisley. 2012. *Network Morphology. A Default-Based Theory of Word Structure*. Cambridge: Cambridge University Press.

Buchanan, Mark. 2002. *Nexus. Small Worlds and the Groundbreaking Science of Networks*. New York: W. W. Norton.

Bühler, Karl. 1934. *Sprachtheorie. Die Darstellungsfunktion der Sprache*. Jena: Fischer.

Bybee, Joan. 1985. *Morphology: A Study on the Relation between Meaning and Form*. Amsterdam: John Benjamins.

   1988. Morphological and lexical organization. In Michael Hammond and Michael Noonan (eds.), *Theoretical Morphology*, 191–141. San Diego, CA: Academic Press.

   1995. Regular morphology and the lexicon. *Language and Cognitive Processes* 10: 425–455.

   2001. *Phonology and Language Use*. Cambridge: Cambridge University Press.

   2002. Sequentiality as the basis of constituent structure. In Talmy Givón and Bertram F. Malle (eds.), *The Evolution of Language out of Pre-Language*, 109–132. Amsterdam: John Benjamins.

   2006. From usage to grammar: The mind's response to repetition. *Language* 82: 711–733.

   2007. *Frequency of Use and the Organization of Language*. Cambridge: Cambridge University Press.

   2010. *Language, Cognition, and Usage*. Cambridge: Cambridge University Press.

   2011. Markedness: Iconicity, economy, and frequency. In Jae Jung Song (ed.), *The Oxford Handbook of Linguistic Typology*, 131–147. Oxford: Oxford University Press.

Bybee, Joan and Paul Hopper (eds.). 2001. *Frequency and the Emergence of Linguistic Structure*. Amsterdam: John Benjamins.

Bybee, Joan and Carol Lynn Moder. 1983. Morphological classes as natural categories. *Language* 59: 251–270.

Bybee, Joan and Joanne Scheibman. 1999. The effect of usage on degrees of constituency: The reduction of *don't* in English. *Linguistics* 37: 575–596.

Bybee, Joan and Dan I. Slobin. 1982. Rules and schemas in the development of the English past tense. *Language* 58: 265–289.

Bybee, Joan and Sandra A. Thompson. 2000. Three frequency effects in syntax. *Berkeley Linguistics Society* 23: 65–85.

Bybee, Joan, William Perkins and Revere Pagliuca. 1990. On the asymmetries in the affixation of grammatical material. In William Croft, Susanne Kemmer and Keith Denning (eds.), *Studies in Typology and Diachrony: Papers Presented to Joseph H. Greenberg on his 75th Birthday*, 1–42. Amsterdam: John Benjamins.

Bybee, Joan, William Perkins and Revere Pagliuca. 1994. *The Evolution of Grammar. Tense, Aspect and Modality in the Languages of the World*. Chicago: Chicago University Press.

Cappelle, Bert. 2006. Particle placement and the case for "allostructions." *Constructions* 1: 1–28.

Carey, Susan and Elsa Bartlett. 1978. Acquiring a single new word. *Proceedings of the Stanford Child Language Conference* 15: 17–29.

Carpenter, Malinda, Katherine Nagell and Michael Tomasello. 1998. Social cognition, joint attention, and communicative competence from 9 to 15 months of age. *Monographs of the Society for Research in Child Development* 63.

Chafe, Wallace. 1994. *Discourse, Consciousness, and Time: The Flow and Displacement of Conscious Experience in Speaking and Writing*. Chicago: University of Chicago Press.

Chang, Franklin, Kathryn Bock and Adele E. Goldberg. 2003. Can thematic roles leave traces of their places? *Cognition* 90: 29–49.

Chang, Franklin, Gary S. Dell and Kathryn Bock. 2006. Becoming syntactic. *Psychological Review* 113: 234–272.

Chomsky, Noam. 1965. *Aspects of a Theory of Syntax*. Cambridge, MA: MIT Press.

  1972. *Studies on Semantics in Generative Grammar*. The Hague: Mouton Publishers.

  1980. *Rules and Representations*. New York: Columbia University Press.

  1981. *Lectures on Government and Binding*. Dordrecht: Foris Publications.

  1986. *Knowledge of Language: Its Nature, Origin and Use*. Westport, CT: Praeger.

Christiansen, Morten H. 2000. Using artificial language learning to study language evolution: Exploring the emergence of word order universals. In Laleh Ghadakpour and Jean-Louis Dessalles (eds.), *The Evolution of Language: Third International Conference*, 45–48. Paris: Ecole Nationale Supérieure des Télécommunications.

Christiansen, Morten H. and Nick Chater. 2008. Language as shaped by the brain. *Behavioral and Brain Sciences* 31: 489–509.

  2016. The now-or-never bottleneck: A fundamental constraint on language. *Behavioral and Brain Sciences* 62: 1–72.

Christiansen, Morten H. and Maryellen C. MacDonald. 2009. A usage-based approach to recursion in sentence processing. *Language Learning* 59: 126–161.

Chung, Sandra. 2012. Are lexical categories universal? The view from Chamorro. *Theoretical Linguistics* 2012: 1–56.

Cienki, Alan. 2007. Frames, idealized cognitive models, and domains. In Dirk Geeraerts and Hubert Cuyckens (eds.), *The Oxford Handbook of Cognitive Linguistics*, 170–187. Oxford: Oxford University Press.

Clark, Eve V. 2003. *First Language Acquisition*. Cambridge: Cambridge University Press.

Clark, Eve V. and Herbert H. Clark. 1979. When nouns surface as verbs. *Language* 55: 767–811.

Clark, Herbert H. 1996. *Using Language*. Cambridge: Cambridge University Press.

Clark, Herbert H. and Susan E. Brennan. 1991. Grounding in communication. In Lauren B. Resnick, John M. Levine and Stephanie D. Teasley (eds.), *Perspectives on Socially Shared Cognition*, 127–149. Washington, DC: American Psychology Association.

Clark, Herbert H. and Catherine R. Marshall. 1981. Definite reference and mutual knowledge. In Aravind K. Joshe, Bruce H. Webber and Ivan A. Sag (eds.), *Elements of Discourse Understanding*, 10–63. New York: Cambridge University Press.

Clay, Zanna and Klaus Zuberbühler. 2011. Bonobos extract meaning from call sequences. *PLoS ONE* 6(4). https://doi.org/10.1371/journal.pone.0018786

Colleman, Timothy and Bernard de Clerck. 2011. Constructional semantics on the move: On semantic specialization in the English double-object construction. *Cognitive Linguistics* 22: 183–209.

Collins, Alan M. and Elizabeth F. Loftus. 1975. A spreading-activation theory of semantic processing. *Psychological Review* 82: 407–428.

Collins, Jeremy. 2012. The evolution of the Greenbergian word order correlations. In *Proceedings of the 9th International Conference (EVOLANG9)*, 72–79. Singapore: World Scientific.

Comrie, Bernard. 1976. *Aspect: An Introduction to the Study of Verbal Aspect and Related Problems*. Cambridge: Cambridge University Press.

1989. *Language Universals and Linguistic Typology*. Chicago: Chicago University Press. [Second edition]

1998. Attributive clauses in Asian languages: Towards an areal typology. In Winfried Boeder, Christopher Schroeder, Karl Heinz Wagner and Wolfgang Wildgen (eds.), *Sprache, Raum und Zeit. In Memorium Johannes Bechert. Band 2: Beiträge zur empirischen Sprachwissenschaft*, 51–60. Tübingen: Narr.

Conwell, Erin and Katherine Demuth. 2007. Early syntactic productivity: Evidence from dative shift. *Cognition* 103: 163–179.

Coventry, Kenny R. and Simon C. Garrod. 2004. *Saying, Seeing and Acting: The Psychological Semantics of Spatial Prepositions*. Hove, UK: Psychology Press.

Cowan, Nelson. 2005. *Working Memory Capacity*. New York: Psychology Press.

Cristofaro, Sonia. 2003. *Subordination*. Oxford: Oxford University Press.

2009. Grammatical categories and relations: Universality vs. language-specificity and construction-specificity. *Language and Linguistics Compass* 3: 441–479.

2013. The referential hierarchy: Reviewing the evidence in diachronic perspective. In Dik Bakker and Martin Haspelmath (eds.), *Languages across the Boundaries*, 69–94. Berlin: Mouton de Gruyter.

Crockford, Catherine, Roman M. Wittig, Roger Mundry and Klaus Zuberbühler. 2012. Wild chimpanzees inform ignorant group members of danger. *Current Biology* 22: 142–146.

Croft, William. 1991. *Syntactic Categories and Grammatical Relations: The Cognitive Organization of Information*. Chicago: Chicago University Press.

    2000. *Explaining Language Change: An Evolutionary Approach*. London: Longman.

    2001. *Radical Construction Grammar*. Oxford: Oxford University Press.

    2003. *Typology and Universals*. Cambridge: Cambridge University Press. [Second edition]

Croft, William and Alan Cruse. 2004. *Cognitive Linguistics*. Cambridge: Cambridge University Press.

Culbertson, Jennifer. 2010. Convergent evidence for categorical change in French: From subject clitic to agreement marker. *Language* 86: 85–132.

Culbertson, Jennifer and Elissa L. Newport. 2015. Harmonic biases in child learners: In support of language universals. *Cognition* 139: 71–82.

Culbertson, Jennifer, Paul Smolensky and Géraldine Legendre. 2012. Learning biases predict a word order universal. *Cognition* 122: 306–329.

Culicover, Peter W. 1999. *Syntactic Nuts: Hard Cases, Syntactic Theory, and Language Acquisition*. Oxford: Oxford University Press.

Dąbrowska, Ewa. 1997. The LAD goes to school: A cautionary tale for nativists. *Linguistics* 35: 735–766.

    2000. From formula to schema: The acquisition of English questions. *Cognitive Linguistics* 11: 83–102.

    2008. The effects of frequency and neighbourhood density on adult speakers' productivity with Polish case inflections: An empirical test of usage-based approaches to morphology. *Journal of Memory and Language* 58: 931–951.

    2012. Different speakers, different grammars: Individual differences in native language attainment. *Linguistic Approaches to Bilingualism* 2: 219–253

    2018. Experience, aptitude and individual differences in native language ultimate attainment. *Cognition* 178: 222–235.

Dąbrowska, Ewa and Elena V. M. Lieven. 2005. Towards a lexically specific grammar of children's question constructions. *Cognitive Linguistics* 16: 437–474.

Dalrymple, Mary and Irina Nikoleava 2011. *Objects and Information Structure*. Cambridge: Cambridge University Press.

Deacon, Terrance W. 1997. *The Symbolic Species: The Co-Evolution of Language and the Brain*. New York: W. W. Norton.

Dell, Gary S. 1986. A spreading-activation theory of retrieval in sentence production. *Psychological Review* 93: 283–321.

Deppermann, Arnulf. 2006. Von der Kognition zur verbalen Interaktion: Bedeutungskonstitution im Kontext aus Sicht der Kognitionswissenschaften und der Gesprächsforschung. In Arnulf Deppermann and Thomas Spranz-Fogasy (eds.), *Wie Bedeutung im Gespräch entsteht*, 11–33. Tübingen: Stauffenburg. [Second edition]

De Smet, Hendrik, Frauke D'hoedt, Lauren Fonteyn and Kristel Van Goethem. 2018. The changing functions of competing forms: Attraction and differentiation. *Cognitive Linguistics* 29: 197–234.

Deutscher, Guy. 2000. *Syntactic Change in Akkadian: The Evolution of Sentential Complementation*. Oxford: Oxford University Press.

Diessel, Holger. 1997. Verb-first constructions in German. In Marjolijn Verspoor, Lee Kee Dong and Eve Sweetser (eds.), *Lexical and Syntactical Constructions and the Construction of Meaning*, 51–68. Amsterdam: John Benjamins.

1999. *Demonstratives: Form, Function, and Grammaticalization*. Amsterdam: John Benjamins.

2004. *The Acquisition of Complex Sentences*. Cambridge: Cambridge University Press.

2005. Competing motivations for the ordering of main and adverbial clauses. *Linguistics* 43: 449–470.

2006. Demonstratives, joint attention, and the emergence of grammar. *Cognitive Linguistics* 17: 463–489.

2007. Frequency effects in language acquisition, language use, and diachronic change. *New Ideas in Psychology* 25: 108–127.

2009. On the role of frequency and similarity in the acquisition of subject and non-subject relative clauses. In Talmy Givón and Masayoshi Shibatani (eds.), *Syntactic Complexity*, 251–276. Amsterdam: John Benjamins.

2011a. Review article of "Language, Usage and Cognition" by Joan Bybee. *Language* 87: 830–844.

2011b. Grammaticalization and language acquisition. In Bernd Heine and Heiko Norrog (eds.), *Handbook of Grammaticalization*, 130–141. Oxford: Oxford University Press.

2012a. Buehler's two-field theory of pointing and naming and the deictic origins of grammatical morphemes. In Tine Breban, Lieselotte Brems, Kristin Davidse and Tanja Mortelmans (eds.), *New Perspectives on Grammaticalization: Theoretical Understanding and Empirical Description*, 35–48. Amsterdam: John Benjamins.

2012b. Language change and language acquisition. In Alexander Bergs and Laural Brinton (eds.), *Historical Linguistics of English: An International Handbook*, Vol. 2, 1599–1613. Berlin: Mouton de Gruyter.

2013. Construction grammar and first language acquisition. In Thomas Hoffmann and Graeme Trousdale (eds.), *The Oxford Handbook of Construction Grammar*, 347–364. Oxford: Oxford University Press.

2014. Demonstratives, frames of reference, and semantic universals of space. *Language and Linguistics Compass* 8: 116–132.

2015. Usage-based construction grammar. In Ewa Dąbrowska and Dagmar Divjak (eds.), *Handbook of Cognitive Linguistics*, 295–321. Berlin: Mouton de Gruyter.

2016. Frequency and lexical specificity: A critical review. In Heike Behrens and Stefan Pfänder (eds.), *Experience Counts: Frequency Effects in Language*, 209–237. Berlin: Mouton de Gruyter.

2017. Usage-based linguistics. In Mark Aronoff (ed.), *Oxford Research Encyclopedia of Linguistics*. New York: Oxford University Press. https://doi.org/10.1093/acre fore/9780199384655.013.363

2019. Preposed adverbial clauses: Functional adaptation and diachronic inheritance. In Karsten Schmidtke-Bode, Natalia Levshina, Susanne Maria Michaelis and Ilja A. Seržant (eds.), *Explanation in Linguistic Typology: Diachronic Sources,*

Functional Motivations and the Nature of the Evidence, 191–126. Leipzig: Language Science Press.

Diessel, Holger and Martin Hilpert. 2016. Frequency effects in grammar. In Mark Aronoff (ed.), *Oxford Research Encyclopedia of Linguistics*. New York: Oxford University Press. https://doi.org/10.1093/acrefore/9780199384655.013.120

Diessel, Holger and Michael Tomasello. 2000. The development of relative clauses in spontaneous child speech. *Cognitive Linguistics* 11: 131–151.

2005. A new look at the acquisition of relative clauses. *Language* 81: 1–25.

Dik, Simon. 1997. *The Theory of Functional Grammar*. Berlin: Mouton de Gruyter.

Dixon, Robert M. W. 1977. Where have all the adjectives gone. *Studies in Language* 1: 19–80.

1994. *Ergativity*. Cambridge: Cambridge University Press.

2004. Adjective classes in typological perspective. In Robert M. W. Dixon and Alexandra Y. Aikhenvald (eds.), *Adjective Classes: A Cross-Linguistic Typology*, 1–49. Oxford: Oxford University Press.

Dixon, Robert M. W. and Alexandra Y. Aikhenvald. 2002. Word: A typological framework. In Robert M. W. Dixon and Alexandra Y. Aikhenvald (eds.), *Word: A Cross-Linguistic Typology*, 1–41. Cambridge: Cambridge University Press.

Dryer, Matthew S. 1988. Object-article order and adjective-noun order: Dispelling a myth. *Lingua* 74: 185–217.

1991. SVO languages and the OV: VO typology. *Journal of Linguistics* 27: 443–482.

1992. The Greenbergian word order correlations. *Language* 68: 81–138.

1997. Are grammatical relations universal? In Joan Bybee, John Haiman and Sandra A. Thompson (eds.), *Essays on Language Function and Language Type. Dedicated to Talmy Givón*, 115–143. Amsterdam: John Benjamins

2003. Word order in Sino-Tibetan languages: From a typological and geographical perspective. In Graham Thurgood and Randy J. LaPolla (eds.), *The Sino-Tibetan Languages*, 43–55. London: Routledge.

2005. Prefixing vs. suffixing in inflectional morphology. In Martin Haspelmath, Matthew Dryer, David Gil and Bernard Comrie (eds.), *World Atlas of Language Structures*, 110–113. Oxford: Oxford University Press.

2009. The branching direction theory of word order correlations revisited. In Sergio Scalise, Elisabetta Magni and Antonietta Bisetto (eds.), *Universals of Language Today*, 185–207. Berlin: Springer.

2013. Relationship between the order of object and verb and the order of relative clause and noun. In Matthew S. Dryer and Martin Haspelmath (eds.), *The World Atlas of Language Structures Online*. Leipzig: Max Planck Institute for Evolutionary Anthropology. Available online at http://wals.info/

2019. Grammaticalization accounts of word order correlations. In Karsten Schmidtke-Bode, Natalia Levshina, Susanne Maria Michaelis and Ilja A. Seržant (eds.), *Explanation in Linguistic Typology: Diachronic Sources, Functional Motivations and the Nature of the Evidence*, 67–100. Leipzig: Language Science Press.

DuBois, John W. 1985. Competing motivations. In John Haiman (ed.), *Iconicity in Syntax*, 343–366. Berlin: Mouton de Gruyter.

1987. The discourse basis of ergativity. *Language* 63: 805–855.

Ellegård, Alvar. 1953. *The Auxiliary do: The Establishment and Regulation of Its Use in English*. Stockholm: Almqvist & Wiksell.

Ellis, Nick C. 1996. Sequencing in SLA: Phonological memory, chunking, and points of order. *Studies in Second Language Acquisition* 18: 91–126.

2002. Frequency effects in language processing: A review with implications for theories of implicit and explicit language acquisition. *Studies in Second Language Acquisition* 24: 143–188.

Ellis, Nick C., Ute Römer and Matthew Brook O'Donnel. 2016. *Usage-Based Approaches to Language Acquisition and Processing: Cognitive and Corpus Investigations of Construction Grammar*. Chichester, UK: John Wiley.

Elman, Jeffrey L. 1990. Finding structure in time. *Cognitive Science* 14: 179–211.

2009. On the meaning of words and dinosaur bones: Lexical knowledge without a lexicon. *Cognitive Science* 33: 1–36.

Elman, Jeffrey L., Elizabeth A. Bates, Mark H. Johnson, Annette Karmiloff-Smith, Domencio Parisi and Kim Plunckett. 1996. *Rethinking Innateness: A Connectionist Perspective on Development*. Cambridge, MA: Bradford Books/MIT Press.

Erman, Britt and Beatrice Warren. 2000. The idiom principle and the open choice principle. *Text* 20: 29–62.

Evans, Vyvyan and Melanie Green. 2006. *Cognitive Linguistics: An Introduction*. Edinburgh: Edinburgh University Press.

Evans, Nicholas and Toshiki Osada. 2005. Mundari: The myth of a language without word classes. *Linguistic Typology* 9: 351–390.

Fauconnier, Gilles and Mark Turner. 2002. *The Way We Think: Conceptual Blending and the Mind's Hidden Complexities*. New York: Basic Books.

Faulhaber, Susen. 2011. *Verb Valency Patterns: A Challenge for Semantic-Based Accounts*. Berlin: Mouton de Gruyter.

Fedzechkina, Maryia, T. Florian Jaeger and Elissa L. Newport. 2013. Language learners restructure their input to facilitate efficient communication. In *Proceedings of the 23th Annual Meeting of the Cognitive Science Society*, 430–435.

Fillmore, Charles J. 1968. The case for case. In Emmon Bach and Robert T. Harms (eds.), *Universals in Linguistic Theory*, 1–81. New York: Holt, Reinhart & Winston.

1970. The grammar of *hitting* and *breaking*. In Roderick Jacobs and Peter Rosenbaum (eds.), *Readings in English Transformational Grammar*, 120–133. Washington, DC: Georgetown University Press.

1975. Checklist theories of meaning. *Berkeley Linguistics Society* 1: 123–131.

1982. Frame semantics. In Dirk Geeraerts (ed), *Cognitive Linguistics. Basic Readings*, 373–400. Berlin: Mouton de Gruyter. [Reprinted from Linguistics in the Morning Calm, Linguistic Society of Korea, 111–137. Seoul: Hanshin Publishing Company.]

1985. Frames and the semantics of understanding. *Quaderni di Semantica* 6: 222–254.

Fillmore, Charles J. and Paul Kay. 1999. Construction Grammar. Manuscript. Berkeley: University of California.

Fillmore, Charles J., Paul Kay and Catherine O'Connor. 1988. Regularity and idiomaticity in grammatical constructions: The case of let alone. *Language* 64: 501–538.

Fillmore, Charles J., Christopher R. Johnson and Miriam R. L. Petruck. 2003. Background to framenet. *International Journal of Lexicography* 16: 235–250.

Fine, Alex B., T. Florian Jaeger, Thomas A. Farmer and Ting Qian. 2013. Rapid expectation adaptation during syntactic comprehension. *Plos One* 8: e77661.

Fitz, Hartmut, Franklin Chang and Morton H. Christiansen. 2011. A connectionist account of the acquisition and processing of relative clauses. In Evan Kidd (ed.), *The Acquisition of Relative Clauses: Processing, Typology and Function*, 39–60. Amsterdam: John Benjamins.

Fonteyn, Lauren and Nikki van de Pol. 2016. Divide and conquer: The formation and functional dynamics of the Modern English ing-clause network. *English Language and Linguistics* 35: 1–35.

Ford, Marilyn, Joan Bresnan and Ronald M. Kaplan. 1982. A competence-based theory of syntactic change. In Joan Bresnan (ed.), *Mental Representations and Grammatical Relations*, 727–796. Cambridge, MA: MIT Press.

Forster, Kenneth I. and Susan M. Chambers. 1973. Lexical access and naming time. *Journal of Verbal Learning and Verbal Behavior* 12: 627–635.

Fox, Barbara A. and Sandra A. Thompson. 2007. Relative clauses in English conversations. *Studies in Language* 31: 293–326.

Fowler, Carol A. and Jonathan Housum. 1987. Talkers' signaling of "new" and "old" words in speech and listeners' perception and use of the distinction. *Journal of Memory and Language* 26: 489–504.

Frank, Stefan L. and Morten H. Christiansen. 2018. Hierarchical and sequential processing of language: A response to: Ding, Melloni, Tian, and Poeppel (2017). Rule-based and word-level statistics-based processing of language: insights from neuroscience. *Language, Cognition and Neuroscience* 33: 1213–1218.

Frank, Stefan L., Rens Bod and Morten H. Christiansen. 2012. How hierarchical is language use? *Proceedings of the Royal Society B: Biological Sciences* 22: 4522–4531.

Frauenfelder, Uli H. and Robert Schreuder. 1992. Constraining psycholinguistic models of morphological processing and representation: The role of productivity. *Yearbook of Morphology* 1991: 165–183.

Frazier, Lyn. 1985. Syntactic complexity. In David R. Dowty, Lauri Karttunen and Arnold Zwicky (eds.), *Natural Language Parsing: Psychological, Computational and Theoretical Perspectives*, 129–189. Cambridge: Cambridge University Press.

Fried, Mirjam. 2015. *Construction Grammar*. In Artemis Alexiadou and Tibor Kiss (eds.), *Syntax – Theory and Analysis: An International Handbook*, 974–1003. Berlin: Walter de Gruyter.

Fried, Mirjam and Jan-Ola Östman. 2005. Construction Grammar: A thumbnail sketch. In Mirjam Fried and Jan-Ola Östman (eds.), *Construction Grammar in Cross-Language Perspective*, 11–86. Amsterdam: John Benjamins.

Fry, John. 2003. *Ellipsis and wa-Marking in Japanese Conversation*. New York: Routledge.

Gahl, Susan and Susan M. Garnsey. 2004. Knowledge of grammar, knowledge of usage: Syntactic probabilities affect pronunciation variation. *Language* 80: 748–775.

Gahl, Susan, Yao Yao and Keith Johnson. 2012. Why reduce? Phonological neighborhood density and phonetic reduction in spontaneous speech. *Journal of Memory and Language* 66: 789–806.

Gärdenfors, Peter. 2014. *The Geometry of Meaning: Semantics Based on Conceptual Spaces*. Cambridge, MA: MIT Press.

Garnsey, Susan M., Neal J. Pearlmutter, Elizabeth E. Myers and Melanie A. Lotocky. 1997. The contributions of verb bias and plausibility to the comprehension of temporarily ambiguous sentences. *Journal of Memory and Language* 7: 58–93.

Gast, Volker. 2007. I gave it him – on the motivation of the "alternative double-object construction" in varieties of British English. *Functions of Language* 14: 31–56.

Gast, Volker and Daniel Wiechmann. 2012. W(h)-Clefts im Deutschen und Englischen: eine quantitative Untersuchung auf der Grundlage des Europarl Korpus. In Lutz Gunkel and Gisela Zifonun (eds.), *Deutsch im Sprachvergleich: Grammatische Kontraste und Konvergenzen*, 333–362. Berlin: Mouton de Gruyter.

Gentner, Dedre. 1983. Structure-mapping: A theoretical framework for analogy. *Cognitive Science* 7: 155–170.

Georgakopoulos, Thanasis and Stéphane Polis. 2018. The semantic map model: State of the art and future avenues for linguistic research. *Language and Linguistic Compass* 12: e12270.

Gerken, LouAnn. 2006. Decisions, decisions: Infant language learning when multiple generalizations are possible. *Cognition* 98: 67–74.

Gil, David. 2013. Riau Indonesian: A language without nouns and verbs. In Jan Rijkhoff and Eva von Lier (eds.), *Flexible Word Classes: Typological Studies of Underspecified Parts of Speech*, 89–130. Oxford: Oxford University Press.

Gildea, Spike and Fernando Zúñiga. 2016. Referential hierarchies: A new look at some historical and typological patterns. *Linguistics* 54: 483–529.

Givón, Talmy. 1971. Historical syntax and synchronic morphology: An archaeologist's field trip. *Chicago Linguistic Society* 7: 394–415.

1975. Serial verbs and syntactic change: Niger Congo. In Charles N. Li (ed.), *Word Order and Word Order Change*, 47–112. Austin: University of Texas Press.

1979. *On Understanding Grammar*. New York: Academic Press.

(ed.). 1983. *Topic Continuity in Discourse: A Quantitative Cross-Language Study*. Amsterdam: John Benjamins.

1984. *Syntax: A Functional-Typological Introduction*. Vol. 1. Amsterdam: John Benjamins.

1990. *Syntax: A Functional-Typological Introduction*. Vol. 2. Amsterdam: John Benjamins.

Gobet, Fernand. 2017. Entrenchment, gestalt formation and chunking. In Hans-Jörg Schmid (ed.), *Entrenchment and the Psychology of Language Learning*, 245–268. Berlin: Mouton de Gruyter.

Gobet, Fernand, Peter C. R. Lane, Steve Croker, Peter C.-H. Cheng, Gary Jones, Iain Oliver and Julian M. Pine. 2001. Chunking mechanisms in human learning. *Trends in Cognitive Science* 5: 236–243.

Goldberg, Adele E. 1995. *Constructions: A Construction Grammar Approach to Argument Structure*. Chicago: University of Chicago Press.

2002. Surface generalizations: An alternative to alternations. *Cognitive Linguistics* 13: 327–356.

2006. *Constructions at Work: The Nature of Generalization in Language*. Oxford: Oxford University Press.

Goldberg, Adele E., Devin M. Cashenhiser and Nitya Sethuraman. 2004. Learning argument structure generalizations. *Cognitive Linguistics* 15: 289–316.

Goldwater, Micah B., Marc T. Tomlinson, Catharine H. Echols and Bradley C. Love. 2011. Structural priming as structure mapping: Children use analogies from previous utterances to guide sentence production. *Cognitive Science* 35: 156–170.

Gómez, Rebecca L. and LouAnn Gerken. 1999. Artificial grammar learning by 1-year-olds leads to specific and abstract knowledge. *Cognition* 70: 109–135.

2000. Infant artificial language learning and language acquisition. *Trends in Cognitive Science* 4: 178–186.

Gordon, Peter C. and Matthew W. Lowder. 2012. Complex sentence processing: A review of theoretical perspectives on the comprehension of relative clauses. *Language and Linguistics Compass* 6: 403–415.

Green, Clarence. 2017. Usage-based linguistics and the magic number four. *Cognitive Linguistics* 28: 209–237.

Green, Georgia M. 1985. The description of inversion in generalized phrase structure grammar. *Berkeley Linguistics Society* 11: 117–145.

Greenberg, Joseph H. 1966. *Language Universals, with Special Reference to Feature Hierarchies*. The Hague: Mouton.

1978. How does a language acquire gender markers. In Joseph H. Greenberg, Charles A. Ferguson and Edith A. Moravcsik (eds.), *Universals of Human Language*, Vol. 3, 47–82. Stanford, CA: Stanford University Press.

Gries, Stefan T. 2003. *Multifactorial Analysis in Corpus Linguistics: A Study of Particle Placement*. London: Continuum.

2005. Syntactic priming: A corpus-based approach. *Journal of Psycholinguistic Research* 34: 365–399.

Gries, Stefan T. and Anatol Stefanowitsch. 2004. Extending collexeme analysis. *International Journal of Corpus Linguistics* 9: 97–129.

Gries, Stefan T., Beate Hampe and Doris Schönefeld. 2005. Converging evidence: Bringing together experimental and corpus data on the association of verbs and constructions. *Cognitive Linguistics* 16: 635–676.

Gropen, Jess, Steven Pinker, Michael Hollande, Richard Goldberg and Ronald Wilson. 1989. The learnability and acquisition of the dative alternation in English. *Language* 65: 203–257.

Güldemann, Tom. 2008. *Quotative Indexes in African Languages: A Synchronic and Diachronic Survey*. Berlin: Mouton de Gruyter.

Hagège, Claude. 2010. *Adpositions: Function-Marking in Human Languages*. Oxford: Oxford University Press.

Haig, Geoffrey. 1998. *Relative Constructions in Turkish*. Wiesbaden: Harrassowitz.

Haig, Geoffrey and Stefan Schnell. 2016. The discourse basis of ergativity revisited. *Language* 92: 591–618.

Haiman, John. 1985. *Iconicity in Syntax*. Cambridge: Cambridge University Press.

1994. Ritualization and the development of language. In William Pagliuca (ed.), *Perspectives on Grammaticalization*, 3–28. Amsterdam: John Benjamins.

Hale, John. 2001. A probabilistic earley parser as a psycholinguistic model. In *Proceedings of the Second Meeting of the North American Chapter of the Association for Computational Linguistics on Language Technologies*, 1–8. Stroudsburg, PA: Association for Computational Linguistics.

Hampe, Beate. 2011. Discovering constructions by means of collostructional analysis: The English denominative construction. *Cognitive Linguistics* 22: 211–245.

Hanna, Joy E., Michael K. Tanenhaus and John C. Trueswell. 2003. The effects of common ground and perspective on domains of referential interpretation. *Journal of Memory and Language* 49: 43–61.

Hare, Mary and Jeffrey L. Elman. 1995. Learning and morphological change. *Cognition* 56: 61–98.

Hare, Mary L. and Adele E. Goldberg. 2000. Structural priming: Purely syntactic? In *Proceedings of the 21st Annual Meeting of the Cognitive Science Society*, 208–211.

Hare, Mary L., Michael Ford and William D. Marslen-Wilson. 2001. Ambiguity and frequency in regular verb inflection. In Joan Bybee and Paul Hopper (eds.), *Frequency and the Emergence of Linguistic Structure*, 181–200. Amsterdam: John Benjamins.

Harley, Trevor A. 2001. *The Psychology of Language: From Data to Theory*. Hove: Psychology Press. [Second edition].

Harris, Alice C. and Lyle Campbell. 1995. *Historical Syntax in Cross-Linguistic Perspective*. Cambridge: Cambridge University Press.

Haspelmath, Martin. 1997. *Indefinite Pronouns*. Oxford: Oxford University Press.

2003. The geometry of grammatical meaning: Semantic maps and cross-linguistic comparison. In Michael Tomasello (ed.), *The New Psychology of Language*, Vol. 2, 211–242. Mahwah, NJ: Lawrence Erlbaum.

2006. Against markedness (and what to replace it with). *Journal of Linguistics* 41: 1–46.

2008a. Frequency vs. iconicity in explaining grammatical asymmetries. *Cognitive Linguistics* 19: 1–33.

2008b. Creating economical morphosyntactic patterns in language change. In Jeff Good (ed.), *Language Universals and Language Change*, 185–214. Oxford: Oxford University Press.

2010. Comparative concepts and descriptive categories in cross-linguistic studies. *Language* 86: 663–687.

2011. The indeterminacy of word segmentation and the nature of morphology and syntax. *Folia Linguistica* 45: 31–80.

2014. On system pressure competing with economic motivation. In Brian MacWhinney, Andrej Malchukov and Edith Moravcsik (eds.), *Competing Motivations in Grammar and Usage*, 197–208. Oxford: Oxford University Press.

Haspelmath, Martin and Andres Karjus. 2017. Explaining asymmetries in number marking: Singulatives, pluratives, and usage frequency. *Linguistics* 55: 1213–1235.

Haspelmath, Martin, Andreea Calude, Michael Spagnol, Heiko Narrog and Elif Bamyaci. 2014. Coding causal-noncausal verb alternations: A form-frequency correspondence explanation. *Journal of Linguistics* 50: 587–625.

Haude, Katherina and Alena Witzlack-Makarevich. 2016. Referential hierarchies and alignment: An overview. *Linguistics* 54: 433–441.

Hawkins, John A. 1983. *Word Order Universals*. San Diego, CA: Academic Press.

1986. *A Comparative Typology of English and German: Unifying the Contrast*. London: Croom Helm.

1994. *A Performance Theory of Order and Constituency*. Cambridge: Cambridge University Press.

2000. The relative order of prepositional phrases in English: Going beyond manner-place-time. *Language Variation and Change* 11: 231–266.

2004. *Efficiency and Complexity in Grammars*. Oxford: Oxford University Press.

Hawkins, John A. and Anne Cutler. 1988. Psycholinguistic factors in morphological asymmetry. In John A. Hawkins (ed.), *Explaining Language Universals*, 281–317. Oxford: Basil Blackwell.

Hay, Jennifer. 2001. Lexical frequency in morphology: Is everything relative? *Linguistics* 39: 1041–1070.

2003. *Causes and Consequences of Word Structure*. New York: Routledge.

Hay, Jennifer and Harald R. Baayen. 2005. Shifting paradigms: Gradient structure in morphology. *Trends in Cognitive Sciences* 9: 342–348.

Heine, Bernd. 2008. Grammaticalization of cases. In Andrej Malchukov and Andrew Spencer (eds.), *The Oxford Handbook of Case*, 458–479. Oxford: Oxford University Press.

Heine, Bernd and Tania Kuteva. 2002. *World Lexicon of Grammaticalization*. Cambridge: Cambridge University Press.

Heine, Bernd, Ulrike Claudi and Friederike Hünnemeyer. 1991. *Grammaticalization: A Conceptual Framework*. Chicago: Chicago University Press.

Hengeveld, Kees. 1992. Parts of speech. In Michael Fortescue, Peter Harder and Lars Kristoffersen (eds.), *Layered Structure and Reference in a Functional Perspective*, 29–55. Amsterdam: John Benjamins.

2013. Parts-of-speech as a basic typological determinant. In Jan Rijkhoff and Eva van Lier (eds.), *Flexible Word Classes: Typological Studies of Underspecified Parts-of-Speech*, 31–55. Oxford: Oxford University Press.

Hengeveld, Kees, Jan Rijkhoff and Anna Siewierska. 2004. Parts-of-speech systems and word order. *Journal of Linguistics* 40: 527–570.

Herbst, Thomas. 2014. The valency approach to argument structure constructions. In Thomas Herbst, Hans-Jörg Schmid and Susen Faulhaber (eds.), *Constructions – Collocations – Patterns*, 167–216. Berlin: Mouton de Gruyter.

Hill, Eugen. 2010. A case study in grammaticalized inflectional morphology: Origin and development of Germanic weak preterite. *Diachronica* 27: 411–458.

Hilpert, Martin. 2007. *Germanic Future Constructions: A Usage-Based Approach to Language Change*. Amsterdam: John Benjamins.

2013. *Constructional Change in English: Developments in Allomorphy, Word-Formation and Syntax*. Cambridge: Cambridge University Press.

2014. *Construction Grammar and Its Application to English*. Edinburgh: Edinburgh University Press.

Himmelmann, Nikolaus. 2008. Lexical categories and voice in Tagalog. In Peter Austin and Simon Musgrave (eds.), *Voice and Grammatical Relations in Austronesian Languages*, 247–293. Stanford, CA: CSLI.

2014. Asymmetries in the prosodic phrasing of function words: Another look at the suffixing preference. *Language* 90: 927–960.

Hoey, Michael. 2005. *Lexical Priming: A New Theory of Words and Language*. London: Routledge.

Hoffmann, Thomas and Graeme Trousdale (eds.). 2013. *The Oxford Handbook of Construction Grammar*. Oxford: Oxford University Press.

Hollich, George, Peter Jusczyk and Paul A. Luce. 2002. Lexical neighbourhood effects in 17-month-old word learning. *Proceedings of the 26th Annual Boston University Conference on Language Development*, 314–323. Boston: Cascadilla Press.

Holyoak, Keith J. and Paul R. Thagard. 1995. *Mental Leaps: Analogy in Creative Thought*. Cambridge, MA: MIT Press.

Hopper, Paul. 1987. Emergent grammar. *Berkeley Linguistics Society* 10: 139–157.

Hopper, Paul and Sandra A. Thompson. 1984. The discourse basis for lexical categories in universal grammar. *Language* 60: 703–752.

Hopper, Paul J. and Elizabeth Closs Traugott. 2003. *Grammaticalization*. Cambridge: Cambridge University Press. [Second edition]

Horton, William S. and Richard J. Gerrig. 2005. The impact of memory demands on audience design during language production. *Cognition* 96: 127–142.

Horton, William S. and Boaz Keysar. 1996. When do speakers take into account common ground? *Cognition* 59: 91–117.

Hudson, Richard. 2007. *Language Networks: The New Word Grammar*. Oxford: Oxford University Press.

Iemmolo, Giorgio. 2010. Topicality and differential object marking: Evidence from Romance and beyond. *Studies in Language* 34: 239–272.

2011. Towards a typological study of differential object marking and differential object indexation. PhD dissertation. University of Pavia.

Israel, Michael. 1996. The *way* constructions grow. In Adele E. Goldberg (ed.), *Conceptual Structure, Discourse and Language*, 217–230. Stanford, CA: CSLI.

Jach, Daniel. 2018. A usage-based approach to preposition placement in English as a second language. *Language Learning* 68: 271–305.

Jackendoff, Ray. 2002. *Foundations of Language: Brain, Meaning, Grammar, Evolution*. Oxford: Oxford University Press.

Jäger, Gerhard and Anette Rosenbach. 2008. Priming and unidirectional change. *Theoretical Linguistics* 34: 85–113.

Jakobsen, William H. 1979. Noun and verb in Nootkan. In B. S. Efrat (ed.), *The Victoria Conference on Northwestern Languages 1976*, 83–153. British Columbia Provincial Museum, Heritage Record No. 4, Victoria.

Jany, Carmen. 2008. Relativization versus nominalization strategies in Chimariko. *Santa Barbara Papers in Linguistics* 19: 40–50.

Johnson, Keith. 1997. Speech perception without speaker normalization: An exemplar model. In Keith Johnson and John W. Mullennix (eds.), *Talker Variability in Speech Processing*, 145–165. San Diego, CA: Academic Press.

Jonides, John, Richard L. Lewis, Derek Evan Nee, Cindy A. Lustig, Marc G. Berman and Katherine Sledge Moore. 2008. The mind and brain of short-term memory. *The Annual Review of Psychology* 59: 193–224.

Juliano, Cornell and Michael K. Tanenhaus. 1993. Contingent frequency effects in syntactic ambiguity resolution. *Proceedings of the 15th Annual Conference of the Cognitive Science Society*, 593–598.

Jurafsky, Daniel. 1996. A probabilistic model of lexical and syntactic access and disambiguation. *Cognitive Science* 20: 137–194.

Jurafsky, Daniel, Alan Bell, Michelle L. Gregory and William D. Raymond. 2001. Probabilistic relations between words: Evidence from reduction in lexical production. In Joan Bybee and Paul Hopper (eds.), *Frequency and the Emergence of Linguistic Structure*, 229–254. Amsterdam: John Benjamins.

Jusczyk, Peter W. 1997. *The Discovery of Spoken Language*. Cambridge, MA: Bradford/MIT Press.

Justeson, John S. and Laurence D. Stephens. 1990. Explanations for word order universals: A log-linear analysis. *Proceedings of the XIV International Congress of Linguistics*, 2372–2376. Berlin: Mouton de Gruyter.

Kamide, Yuki, Gerry T. M. Altmann and Sarah L. Haywood. 2003. The time-course of prediction in incremental sentence processing: Evidence from anticipatory eye movements. *Journal of Memory and Language* 49: 133–156.

Kapatsinski, Vsevolod. 2018. Learning morphological constructions. In Geert Booij (ed.), *The Construction of Words: Advances in Construction Morphology*, 547–582. Cham, Switzerland: Springer.

Kazenin, Konstantin I. 1994. Split syntactic ergativity: Toward an implicational hierarchy. *Sprachtypologie und Universalienforschung* 47: 78–98.

Keenan, Edward L. 1976. Towards a universal definition of "subject." In Charles Li (ed.), *Subject and Topic*, 303–334. New York: Academic Press.

Kemmer, Suzanne. 1993. *The Middle Voice*. Amsterdam: John Benjamins.

Kemmer, Suzanne and Michael Barlow (eds.). 2000. *Usage-Based Models of Language*. Stanford, CA: CSLI.

Keysar, Boaz, Dale J. Barr, Jennifer A. Balin and Jason S. Brauner. 2000. Taking perspective in conversation: The role of mutual knowledge in comprehension. *Psychological Science* 11: 32–38.

Kidd, Evan, Seamus Donnelly and Morten H. Christiansen. 2018. Individual differences in language acquisition and processing. *Trends in Cognitive Science* 22: 154–169.

Kirby, Simon. 1999. *Function, Selection, and Innateness: The Emergence of Language Universals*. Oxford: Oxford University Press.

2012. Language is an adaptive system: The role of cultural evolution in the origins of structure. In Maggie Tallerman and Kathleen R. Gibson (eds.), *The Oxford Handbook of Language Evolution*, 589–604. Oxford: Oxford University Press.

Koffka, Kurt. 1935. *Principles of Gestalt Psychology*. New York: Harcourt, Brace & World.

Konieczny, Lars. 2000. Locality and parsing complexity. *Journal of Psycholinguistic Research* 29: 627–645.

Koptjevskaja-Tamm, Maria. 1993. *Nominalizations*. London: Routledge.

Kornfilt, Jaklin. 1997. *Turkish*. New York: Routledge.

Kortmann, Bernd. 1996. *Adverbial Subordination: A Typology and History of Adverbial Subordination Based on European Languages*. Berlin: Mouton de Gruyter.

Krifka, Manfred. 1985. Harmony or consistency? Review of John A. Hawkins, Word Order Universals. *Theoretical Linguistics* 12: 73–94.

Kroch, Anthony S. 1989. Reflexes of the grammar in patterns of language change. *Language Variation and Change* 1: 199–244.

Kroch, Anthony, Susan Pintzuk and John Myhill. 1982. Understanding "do." *Chicago Linguistics Society* 18: 282–294.

Krug, Manfred. 1998. String frequency. A cognitive motivating factor in coalescence, language processing, and linguistic change. *Journal of English Linguistics* 26: 286–320.

2000. *Emerging English Modals. A Corpus-Based Study of Grammaticalization*. Berlin: Mouton de Gruyter.

2003. Frequency as a determinant of grammatical variation and change. In Günter Rohdenburg and Britta Mondorf (eds.), *Determinants of Grammatical Variation in English*, 7–67. Berlin: Mouton de Gruyter.

Kuperberg, Gina R. and T. Florian Jaeger. 2016. What do we mean by prediction in language comprehension? *Language, Cognition and Neuroscience* 31: 32–59.

Kuperman, Victor and Joan Bresnan. 2012. The effects of construction probability on word durations during spontaneous incremental sentence production. *Journal of Memory and Language* 66: 588–611.

Kurumada, Chigusa and T. Florian Jaeger. 2015. Communicative efficiency in language production: Optional case-marking in Japanese. *Journal of Memory and Language* 83: 152–178.

Labov, William. 1969. Contraction, deletion, and inherent variability of the English copula. *Language* 45: 715–762.

1972. *Sociolinguistic Patterns*. Philadelphia: University of Pennsylvania Press.

Lakoff, George. 1987. *Women, Fire, and Dangerous Things*. Chicago: University of Chicago Press.

Lakoff, George and Mark Johnson. 1980. *Metaphors We Live By*. Chicago: University of Chicago Press.

Langacker, Ronald W. 1987. *Foundations of Cognitive Grammar,* Vol. 1, *Theoretical Prerequisites*. Stanford, CA: Stanford University Press.

1988. A usage-based model. In Brygida Rudzka-Ostyn (ed.), *Topics in Cognitive Linguistics*, 127–161. Amsterdam: John Benjamins.

1991. *Concept, Image, and Symbol: The Cognitive Basis of Grammar*. Berlin: Mouton de Gryuter.

1997. Constituency, dependency, and conceptual grouping. *Cognitive Linguistics* 8: 1–32.

2000. A dynamic usage-based model. In Susanne Kemmer and Michael Barlow (eds.), *Usage-Based Models of Language*, 1–64. Stanford, CA: CSLI.

2008. *Cognitive Grammar: A Basic Introduction*. Oxford: Oxford University Press.

Lee, Hanjung. 2006. Parallel optimization in case systems: Evidence from ellipsis in Korean. *Journal of East Asian Linguistics* 15: 69–96.

2010. Explaining variation in Korean case ellipsis: Economy versus iconicity. *Journal of East Asian Languages* 19: 191–318.

2011. Gradients in Korean case ellipsis: An experimental investigation. *Lingua* 121: 20–34.

Lee, Hanjung and Nayoun Kim. 2012. Non-canonical word order and subject-object asymmetry in Korean case ellipsis. In Stefan Müller (ed.), *Proceedings of the 19th International Conference on Head-Driven Phrase Structure Grammar*, 427–442. Stanford, CA: CSLI.

Leech, Robert, Denis Mareschal and Richard P. Cooper. 2008. Analogy as relational priming: A developmental and computational perspective on the origin of a complex cognitive skill. *Behavior and Brain Sciences* 31: 357–378.

Lehmann, Christian. (1995) 2015. *Thoughts on Grammaticalization*. Leipzig: Language Science Press. [Third edition]

Levin, Beth and Malka Rappaport Hovav. 2005. *Argument Realization*. Cambridge: Cambridge University Press.

Levy, Roger. 2008. Expectation-based syntactic comprehension. *Cognition* 106: 1126–1177.

Li, Charles N. and Sandra A. Thompson. 1981. *Mandarin Chinese: A Functional Reference Grammar*. Berkeley: University of California Press.

Lieven, Elena V. M., Julian M. Pine and Gillian Baldwin. 1997. Lexically-based learning and early grammatical development. *Journal of Child Language* 24: 187–219.

Lieven, Elena V. M., Heike Behrens, Jennifer Spears and Michael Tomasello. 2003. Early syntactic creativity: A usage-based approach. *Journal of Child Language* 30: 333–370.

Lightfoot, David. 1999. *The Development of Language: Acquisition, Change, and Evolution*. Oxford: Blackwell.

Logan, Gordon D. 1988. Towards an instance theory of automatization. *Psychological Review* 95: 492–527.

Lorenz, David. 2013. From reduction to emancipation: Is gonna a word? In Hilde Hasselgård, Jarle Ebeling and Signe Oksefjell Ebeling (eds.), *Corpus Perspectives on Patterns of Lexis*, 133–152. Amsterdam: John Benjamins.

Lorenz, David and David Tizón-Couto. 2017. Coalescence and contraction of V-to-Vinf sequences in American English – Evidence from spoken language. *Corpus Linguistics and Linguistic Theory*. https://doi.org/10.1515/cllt-2015-0067

Luce, Paul A. and David P. Pisoni. 1998. Recognizing spoken words: The neighborhood activation model. *Ear and Hearing* 19: 1–36.

Lyons, John. 1968. *Introduction to Theoretical Linguistics*. Cambridge: Cambridge University Press.

MacDonald, Maryellen C. 2013. How language production shapes language form and comprehension. *Frontiers in Psychology* 4: 1–16.

MacDonald, Maryellen C. and Morton H. Chistiansen. 2002. Reassessing working memory: Comments on Just and Carpenter (1992) and Waters and Caplan (1996). *Psychological Review* 109: 35–54.

MacDonald, Maryellen C. and Mark S. Seidenberg. 2006. Constraint satisfaction accounts of lexical and sentence comprehension. In Matthew J. Traxlor and Morton Ann Gernsbacher (eds.), *Handbook of Psycholinguistics*, 581–611. London: Elsevier. [Second edition]

MacDonald, Maryellen C., Neal J. Pearlmutter and Mark S. Seidenberg. 1994. Lexical nature of syntactic ambiguity resolution. *Psychological Review* 101: 676–703.

MacWhinney, Brian (ed.). 1999. *The Emergence of Language*. Mahwah, NJ: Lawrence Erlbaum.

Madlener, Karin. 2016. Input optimization: Effects of type and token frequency manipulations in instructed second language acquisition. In Heike Behrens and Stefan Pfänder (eds.), *Experience Counts: Frequency Effects in Language*, 133–173. Berlin: Mouton de Gruyter.

Mahootian, Shahrzad. 1997. *Persian Descriptive Grammar*. London: Routledge.

Mair, Christian. 1990. *Infinitival Complement Clauses in English: A Study of Syntax in Discourse*. Cambridge: Cambridge University Press.

Mak, Willem M., Wietske Vonk and Herbert Schriefers. 2002. The influence of animacy on relative clause processing. *Journal of Memory and Language* 47: 50–68.

2006. Animacy in processing relative clauses. *Journal of Memory and Language* 54: 466–490.

Malchukov, Andrej L. 2008. Animacy and asymmetries in differential case marking. *Lingua* 118: 203–221.

Manning, Christopher D. and Hinrich Schütze. 1999. *Foundations of Statistical Natural Language Processing*. Cambridge, MA: MIT Press.

Marcus, Gary F. 1999. *The Algebraic Mind: Integrating Connectionism and Cognitive Science*. Cambridge, MA: MIT Press.

Marcus, Gary F., S. Vijayan, S. Bandi Rao and P. M. Vishton. 1999. Rule learning by seven-month-old infants. *Science* 283: 77–80.

Matsumoto, Yoshiko. 1997. *Noun-Modifying Constructions in Japanese: A Frame-Semantic Approach*. Amsterdam: John Benjamins.

McCauley, Stewart M. and Morton H. Christiansen. 2014. Acquiring formulaic language: A computational approach. *The Mental Lexicon* 9: 419–436.

Michaelis, Laura. 2004. Type shifting in construction grammar: An integrated approach to aspectual coercion. *Cognitive Linguistics* 15: 1–67.

Miller, George A. 1956. The magical number seven, plus or minus two: Some limits on our capacity for processing information. *Psychological Review* 63: 81–97.

Mintz, Toben H. 2003. Frequent frames as a cue for grammatical categories in child-directed speech. *Cognition* 90: 91–117.

Mintz, Toben H., Elissa L. Newport and Thomas G. Bever. 2002. The distributional structure of grammatical categories in speech to young children. *Cognitive Science* 26: 393–424.

Minashima, Hiroshi. 2001. On the deletion of accusative case markers in Japanese. *Studia Linguistica* 55: 175–190.

Mitchell, Bruce and Fred C. Robinson. (1964) 2001. *A Guide to Old English*. Oxford: Blackwell. [Sixth edition]

Mithun, Marianne. 1984. The evolution of noun incorporation. *Language* 60: 847–894.
1991. Active/agentive case marking and its motivations. *Language* 67: 510–546.

Monaghan, Padraic, Nick Chater and Morton H. Christiansen. 2005. The differential role of phonological and distributional cues in grammatical categorization. *Cognition* 96: 143–182.

Mondorf, Britta. 2010. Variation and change in English resultative constructions. *Language Variation and Change* 22: 397–421.

Mosel, Ulrike and Even Hovdhaugen. 1992. *Samoan Reference Grammar*. Oslo: Scandinavian University Press.

Mulder, Kimberley, Ton Dijkstra, Robert Schreuder and Harald R. Baayen. 2014. Effects of primary and secondary morphological family size in monolingual and bilingual word processing. *Journal of Memory and Language* 72: 59–84.

Murphy, Gregory L. 2002. *The Big Book of Concepts*. Cambridge, MA: MIT Press.

Narrog, Heiko. 2010. A diachronic dimension in maps of case functions. *Linguistic Discovery* 8: 233–254.

Narrog, Heiko and Bernd Heine (eds.). 2011. *The Oxford Handbook of Grammaticalization*. Oxford: Oxford University Press.

Newell, Allen. 1990. *Unified Theories of Cognition*. Cambridge, MA: Harvard University Press.

Newmeyer, Frederick. 2003. Grammar is grammar and usage is usage. *Language* 79: 682–707.

Nichols, Johanna. 1992. *Linguistic Diversity in Space and Time*. Chicago: University of Chicago Press.

Ninio, Anat. 1999. Pathbreaking verbs in syntactic development and the acquisition of isolated forms at the onset of speech. *First Language* 13: 291–314.

Nosofsky, Robert M. 1988. Similarity, frequency and category representation. *Journal of Experimental Psychology: Learning, Memory and Cognition* 14: 54–65.

Nunberg, Geoffrey, Ivan A. Sag and Thomas Wasow. 1994. Idioms. *Language* 70: 491–538.

Oberauer, Klaus. 2002. Access to information in working memory: Exploring the focus of attention. *Journal of Experimental Psychology: Learning, Memory, and Cognition* 28: 411–421.

Ogura, Mieko. 1993. The development of periphrastic *do* in English: A case of lexical diffusion in syntax. *Diachronica* 10: 51–85.

Ohara, Kyoko Hirose. 1992. On Japanese internally headed relative clauses. *Berkeley Linguistics Society* 8: 100–108.

Pagel, Mark and Andrew Meade. 2018. The deep history of number words. *Philosophical Transactions of the Royal Society, Series B* 373: 20160517.

Paul, Hermann. (1880) 1920. *Prinzipien der Sprachgeschichte*. Tübingen: Niemeyer. [Fifth edition]

Perek, Florent. 2015. *Argument Structure in Usage-Based Construction Grammar: Experimental and Corpus-Based Perspectives*. Amsterdam: John Benjamins.

Perek, Florent and Adele E. Goldberg. 2015. Generalizing beyond the input: The functions of the constructions matter. *Journal of Memory and Language* 24: 108–127.

Pickering, Martin J. and Holly P. Branigan. 1998. The representation of verbs: Evidence from syntactic priming in language production. *Journal of Memory and Language* 39: 633–651.

Pickering, Martin J. and Victor S. Ferreira. 2008. Structural priming: A critical review. *Psychological Bulletin* 134: 427–459.

Pickering, Martin J. and Simon Garrod. 2004. Toward a mechanistic psychology of dialogue. *Behavioral and Brain Sciences* 27: 169–226.

2017. Priming and language change. In Marianne Hundt, Sandra Mollin and Simone E. Pfenniger (eds.), *The Changing English Language*, 173–190. Cambridge: Cambridge University Press.

Pierrehumbert, Janet B. 2001. Exemplar dynamics: Word frequency, lenition and contrast. In Joan Bybee and Paul Hopper (eds.), *Frequency and the Emergence of Linguistic Structure*, 137–158. Amsterdam: John Benjamins.

Pinker, Steven. 1989. *Learnability and Cognition: The Acquisition of Argument Structure*. Cambridge, MA: MIT Press.

1991. Rules of language. *Science* 253: 530–535.

1994. *The Language Instinct: How the Mind Creates Language*. New York: Harper.

1999. *Words and Rules: The Ingredients of Language*. New York: Basic Books.

Pinker, Steven and Ray Jackendoff. 2005. The faculty of language: What's special about it? *Cognition* 95: 201–236.

Pinker, Steven and Alan Prince. 1988. On language and connectionism: Analysis of a parallel distributed processing model of language acquisition. *Cognition* 28: 73–193.

Pinker, Steven, David S. Lebeaux and Loren Ann Frost. 1987. Productivity and constraints in the acquisition of the passive. *Cognition* 26: 195–267.

Pluymaekers, Mark, Mirjam Ernestus and Harald R. Baayen. 2005. Lexical frequency and acoustic reduction in spoken Dutch. *Journal of the Acoustic Society of America* 118: 2561–2569.

Pollack, Irwin and J. M. Pickett. 1964. Intelligibility of excerpts from fluent speech: Auditory vs. structural context. *Journal of Verbal Learning and Verbal Behavior* 3: 79–84.

Quine, Willard van Orman 1960. *Word and Object*. Cambridge, MA: MIT Press.

Quirk, Randolph, Sidney Greenbaum, Geoffrey Leech and Jan Svartvik. 1985. *A Grammar of Contemporary English*. London: Longman.

Radford, Andrew. 1997. *Syntax: A Minimalist Introduction*. Cambridge: Cambridge University Press.

Reali, Florencia and Morton H. Christiansen. 2007. Processing of relative clauses is made easier by frequency of occurrence. *Journal of Memory and Language* 57: 1–23.

Redington, Martin, Nick Chater and Steven Finch. 1998. Distributional information: A powerful cue for acquiring syntactic categories. *Cognitive Science* 22: 425–469.

Robenalt, Clarice and Adele Goldberg. 2015. Judgment evidence for statistical preemption: It is relatively better to vanish than to disappear a rabbit, but a lifeguard can equally well backstroke or swim children to shore. *Cognitive Linguistics* 26: 467–503.

Roland, Douglas, Fredric Dick and Jeffrey L. Elman. 2007. Frequency of basic English grammatical structures: A corpus analysis. *Journal of Memory and Language* 57: 348–379.

Roland, Douglas, Gail Mauner, Carolyn O'Meara and Hongoak Yun. 2012. Discourse expectations and relative clause processing. *Journal of Memory and Language* 66: 479–508.

Rosenbach, Annette. 2002. *Genitive Variation in English: Conceptual Factors in Synchronic and Diachronic Studies*. Berlin: Mouton de Gruyter.

2005. Animacy versus weight as determinants of grammatical variation in English. *Language* 81: 613–644.

2007. Emerging variation: Determiner genitive and noun modifiers in English. *English Language and Linguistics* 11: 143–189.

Rowland, Caroline F. 2007. Explaining errors in children's questions: Auxiliary DO and modal auxiliaries. *Cognition* 104: 106–134.

Rowland, Caroline F. and Julian M. Pine 2000. Subject–auxiliary inversion errors and wh-question acquisition: "What children do know?" *Journal of Child Language* 27: 157–181.

Rowland, Caroline F., Franklin Chang, Ben Ambridge, Julian Pine and Elena V. M. Lieven. 2012. The development of abstract syntax: Evidence from priming and the lexical boost. *Cognition* 125: 49–63.

Rumelhart, David E. and James L. McClelland (eds.). 1986a. *Parallel Distributed Processing: Exploration in the Microstructures of Cognition*. 2 Vols. Cambridge, MA: MIT Press.

1986b. On learning the past tenses of English verbs. In David E. Rumelhart, James L. McClelland and PDP Research Group (eds.), *Parallel Distributed Processing: Explorations in the Microstructure of Cognition*, Vol. 2, 216–271. Cambridge, MA: MIT Press.

Saffran, Jenny R., Richard N. Aslin and Elissa L. Newport. 1996. Statistical learning in 8-month-old infants. *Science* 274: 1926–1928.

Sandra, Dominiek and Sally Rice. 1995. Network analyses of prepositional meaning: Mirroring whose mind – the linguist's or the language user's? *Cognitive Linguistics* 6: 89–130.

Sankoff, Gillian and Hélène Blondeau. 2007. Language change across the lifespan: /r/ in Montreal French. *Language* 83: 560–588.

Sapir, Edward. 1921. *Language: An Introduction to the Study of Speech.* New York: Harcourt Brace Jovanovich.

Saussure, Ferdinand de. (1916) 1994. *Course in General Linguistics.* La Salle, IL: Open Court.

Savage, Ceri, Elena V. M. Lieven, Anna Theakston and Michael Tomasello. 2006. Structural priming as implicit learning in language acquisition: The persistence of lexical and structural priming in 4-year-olds. *Language Learning and Language Development* 2: 27–49.

Schachter, Paul and Timothy Shopen. 2007. Parts-of-speech systems. In Timothy Shopen (ed.), *Language Typology and Syntactic Description, Vol. 1, Clause Structure,* 1–60. Cambridge: Cambridge University Press.

Schiering, René, Balthasar Bickel and Kristine A. Hildebrandt. 2011. The prosodic word is not universal, but emergent. *Journal of Linguistics* 46: 657–709.

Schmid, Hans-Jörg. 2015. A blueprint of the entrenchment-and-conventionalization model. *Yearbook of the German Cognitive Linguistics Association* 3: 3–26.

2016. A framework for understanding linguistic entrenchment and its psychological foundations in memory and automatization. In Hans-Jörg Schmid (ed.), *Entrenchment and the Psychology of Language Learning: How We Reorganize and Adapt Linguistic Knowledge,* 11–35. Berlin: Mouton de Gruyter.

Schmid, Hans-Jörg and Helmut Küchenhoff. 2013. Collostructional analysis and other ways of measuring lexicogrammatical attraction: Theoretical premises, practical problems and cognitive underpinnings. *Cognitive Linguistics* 24: 531–577.

Schmidtke-Bode, Karsten. 2009. *A Typology of Purpose Clauses.* Amsterdam: John Benjamins.

Schmidtke-Bode, Karsten and Holger Diessel. 2017. Cross-linguistic patterns in the structure, function and position of (object) complement clauses. *Linguistics* 55: 1–38.

Schmidtke-Bode, Karsten and Natalia Levshina. 2018. Reassessing scale effects on differential object marking: Methodological, conceptual and theoretical issues in quest of a universal. In Ilja A. Seržant and Alena Witzlack-Makarevich (eds.), *Diachrony of Differential Argument Marking,* 509–537. Leipzig: Language Science Press.

Schneider, Walter and Jason M. Chein 2003. Controlled and automatic processing: Behavior, theory, and biological mechanisms. *Cognitive Science* 27: 525–559.

Scholz, Barbara C. and Geoffrey K. Pullum. 2002. Searching for arguments to support linguistic nativism. *The Linguistic Review* 18: 185–223.

Schreuder, Robert and Harald R. Baayen. 1997. How complex simplex words can be. *Journal of Memory and Language* 37: 118–139.

Searle, John R. 1969. *Speech Acts.* Cambridge: Cambridge University Press.

Seidenberg, Mark S. and Maryellen C. MacDonald. 1999. A probabilistic constraints approach to language acquisition and processing. *Cognitive Science* 23: 569–588.

Seidenberg, Mark S. and David C. Plaut. 2014. Quasiregularity and its discontents: The legacy of the past tense debate. *Cognitive Science* 38: 1190–1128.

Sereno, Joan A. and Allard Jongman. 1999. Processing of English inflectional morphology. *Memory and Cognition* 25: 425–437.

Siewierska, Anna. 1993. Syntactic weight vs. information structure and word order variation in Polish. *Journal of Linguistics* 29: 233–265.

Siewierska, Anna and Dik Bakker. 1996. The distribution of subject and object agreement and word order type. *Studies in Language* 20: 115–161.

Siewierska, Anna and Willem Hollmann. 2007. Ditransitive clauses with special reference to Lancashire dialect. In Mike Hannay and Gerald D. Steen (eds.), *Structural-Functional Studies in English Grammar in Honor of Lacklan Mackenzie*, 83–102. Amsterdam: John Benjamins.

Silverstein, Michael. 1976. Hierarchy of features and ergativity. In Robert M. W. Dixon (ed.), *Grammatical Categories in Australian Languages*, 112–171. Canberra: Australian Institute of Aboriginal Studies.

Sinclair, John. 1991. *Corpus, Concordance and Collocation*. Oxford: Oxford University Press.

Sinnemäki, Kaius. 2014. A typological perspective on differential object marking. *Linguistics* 52: 281–313.

Soe, Myint. 1999. A Grammar of Burmese. PhD dissertation. University of Oregon.

Sommerer, Lotte. 2015. The influence of constructions in grammaticalization: Revisiting category emergence and the development of the definite article in English. In Joanna Barðdal, Elena Smirnova, Lotte Sommerer and Spike Gildea (eds.), *Diachronic Construction Grammar*, 107–136. Amsterdam: John Benjamins.

Song, Jae Jung. 2012. *Word Order*. Cambridge: Cambridge University Press.

Spencer, Andrew and Ana R. Luis. 2012. *Clitics: An Introduction*. Cambridge: Cambridge University Press.

Spivey-Knowlton, Michael J. and Julie Sedivy. 1995. Resolving attachment ambiguities with multiple constraints. *Cognition* 55: 227–267.

Stassen, Leon. 2005. Predicative adjectives. In Martin Haspelmath, Matthew Dryer, David Gil and Bernard Comrie (eds.), *World Atlas of Language Structures*, 478–481. Oxford: Oxford University Press.

Steels, Luc. 2000. Language as a complex adaptive system. In *Parallel Problem Solving from Nature (PPSN VI)*, 17–26. Berlin: Springer.

(ed.). 2011. *Design Patterns in Fluid Construction Grammar*. Amsterdam: John Benjamins.

2013. Fluid construction grammar. In Thomas Hoffmann and Graeme Trousdale (eds.), *The Oxford Handbook of Construction Grammar*, 153–167. Oxford: Oxford University Press.

2015. *The Talking Heads Experiment: Origins of Words and Meanings*. Berlin: Language Science Press.

Stefanowitsch, Anatol. 2008. Negative entrenchment: A usage-based approach to negative evidence. *Cognitive Linguistics* 19: 513–531.

Stefanowitsch, Anatol and Stefan Gries. 2003. Collostructions: Investigating the interaction of words and constructions. *International Journal of Corpus Linguistics* 8: 209–243.

Storkel, Holly L. 2004. Do children acquire dense neighborhoods? An investigation of similarity neighborhoods in lexical acquisition. *Applied Psycholinguistics* 25: 201–221.

Stukenbrock, Anja. 2015. *Deixis in der face-to-face-Interaktion*. Berlin: Mouton de Gruyter.

Suttle, Laura and Adele E. Goldberg. 2011. The partial productivity of constructions as induction. *Linguistics* 49: 1237–1269.

Szmrecsanyi, Benedikt. 2006. *Morphosyntactic Persistence in Spoken English: A Corpus Study*. Berlin: Mouton de Gruyter.

Szmrecsanyi, Benedikt and Lars Hinrichs. 2008. Probabilistic determinants of genitive variation in spoken and written English: A multivariate comparison across time, space, and genres. In Terttu Nevalainen, Irma Taavitsainen, Paivi Pahta and Minna Korhonen (eds.), *The Dynamics of Linguistic Variation: Corpus Evidence on English Past and Present*, 291–309. Amsterdam: John Benjamins.

Talmy, Leonard. 1988. Force dynamics in language and cognition. *Cognitive Science* 12: 49–100.

  2000. *Towards a Cognitive Semantics*, Vol. 1, *Concept Structuring Systems*. Cambridge, MA: MIT Press.

Tanenhaus, Michael K., Michael J. Spivey-Knowlton, Kathleen M. Eberhard and Julie C. Sedivy. 1995. Integration of visual and linguistic information in spoken language comprehension. *Science* 268: 1632–1634.

Taylor, John R. 2012. *The Mental Lexicon: How Language Is Represented in the Mind*. Oxford: Oxford University Press.

Thomason, Sarah Grey and Terrence Kaufman. 1988. *Language Contact, Creolization, and Genetic Linguistics*. Berkeley: University of California Press.

Tiersma, Peter Meijes. 1982. Local and general markedness. *Language* 59: 832–849.

Tomasello, Michael. 1992. *First Verbs: A Case Study of Early Grammatical Development*. Cambridge: Cambridge University Press.

  1999. *The Cultural Origins of Human Cognition*. Cambridge, MA: Harvard University Press.

  2000. Do young children have adult syntactic competence? *Cognition* 74: 209–253.

  2003. *Constructing a Language: A Usage-Based Approach*. Cambridge, MA: Harvard University Press.

Tomasello, Michael and Patricia Brooks. 1998. Young children's earliest transitive and intransitive constructions. *Cognitive Linguistics* 9: 379–395.

Trask, R. Larry. 1996. *Historical Linguistics*. Oxford: Oxford University Press.

Traugott, Elizabeth Closs. 1992. Syntax. In R. M. Hogg (ed.), *The Cambridge History of the English Language,* Vol. 1, *The Beginnings to 1066*, 168–289. Cambridge, MA: Cambridge University Press.

Traugott, Elizabeth Closs and Graeme Trousdale. 2013. *Constructionalization and Constructional Changes*. Oxford: Oxford University Press.

Traxler, Matthew J., Robin K. Morris and Rachel E. Seely. 2002. Processing subject and object relative clauses: Evidence from eye movements. *Cognition* 47: 69–90.

Traxler, Matthew J., Rihana S. Williams, Shelley A. Blozis and Robin K. Morris. 2005. Working memory, animacy, and verb class in the processing of relative clauses. *Cognition* 53: 204–224.

Tremblay, Antoine, Bruce Derwing, Gary Libben and Chris Westbury. 2011. Processing advantages of lexical bundles: Evidence from self-paced reading and sentence recall tasks. *Language Learning* 61: 569–613.

Trudgill, Peter. 1974. *The Social Differentiation of English in Norwich.* Cambridge: Cambridge University Press.

Trueswell, John C. 1996. The role of lexical frequency in syntactic ambiguity resolution. *Journal of Memory and Language* 35: 566–585.

Trueswell, John C. and Michael K. Tanenhaus. 1994. Towards a lexicalist framework for constraint-based syntactic ambiguity resolution. In Charles Cliften Jr., Lyn Frazier and Keith Rayner (eds.), *Perspectives on Sentence Processing*, 155–179. Hillsdale, NJ: Lawrence Erlbaum.

Trueswell, John C., Tamara Nicol Medina, Alon Hafri and Lila R. Gleitman. 2013. Propose but verify: Fast mapping meets cross-situational word learning. *Cognitive Psychology* 66: 126–156.

Tyler, Andrea and Vyvyan Evans. 2001. Reconsidering prepositional polysemy networks: The case of over. *Language* 77: 724–765.

2014. Degeneracy: The maintenance of constructional networks. In Ronny Boogaart, Timothy Colleman and Gijsbert Rutten (eds.), *Extending the Scope of Construction Grammar*, 141–179. Berlin: Mouton de Gruyter.

van der Auwera, Johan and Vladimir A. Plungian. 1998. Modality's semantic map. *Linguistic Typology* 2: 79–124.

Van de Velde, Freek. 2010. The emergence of the determiner in Dutch NP. *Linguistics* 48: 263–299.

Van Gelderen, Elly. 2011. The grammaticalization of agreement. In Bernd Heine and Heiko Norrog (eds.), *Handbook of Grammaticalization*, 491–501. Oxford: Oxford University Press.

Van Lier, Eva and Jan Rijkhoff. 2013. Flexible word classes in linguistic typology and grammatical theory. In Jan Rijkhoff and Eva van Lier (eds.), *Flexible Word Classes: Typological Studies of Underspecified Parts-of-Speech*, 1–30. Oxford: Oxford University Press.

van Trijp, Remi. 2010. Grammaticalization and semantic maps: Evidence from artificial language evolution. *Linguistic Discovery* 8: 310–326.

2016. *The Evolution of Case Grammar.* Leipzig: Language Science Press.

Van Valin, Robert D. and Randy J. LaPolla. 1997. *Syntax: Structure, Meaning and Function.* Cambridge: Cambridge University Press.

Verhagen, Arie. 2005. *Constructions of Intersubjectivity: Discourse, Syntax, and Cognition.* Cambridge: Cambridge University Press.

2007. Construal and perspectivization. In Dirk Geeraerts and Hubert Cuyckens (eds.), *The Oxford Handbook of Cognitive Linguistics*, 48–81. Oxford: Oxford University Press.

Vitevitch, Michael S. 2002. The influence of phonological neighbourhoods on speech production. *Journal of Experimental Psychology: Learning, Memory and Cognition* 28: 735–747.

Vlach, Haley and Catherine Sandhofer. 2012. Fast mapping across time: Memory processes support children's retention of learned words. *Frontiers in Psychology.* 3: 1–8.

von Heusinger, Klaus and Georg A. Kaiser. 2005. The evolution of differential object marking in Spanish. In Klaus von Heusinger, Georg A. Kaiser and Elisabeth Stark (eds.), *Proceedings of the Workshop "Specificity and the Evolution/Emergence of Nominal Determination in Romance,"* 33–69. Fachbereich Sprachwissenschaft (Arbeitspapier 119). Konstanz, Germany: Universität Konstanz.

von Heusinger, Klaus and Jaklin Kornfilt. 2005. The case of direct object in Turkish: Semantics, syntax and morphology. *Turkic Languages* 9: 3–44.

Warner, Anthony. 1993. *English Auxiliaries: Structure and History.* Cambridge: Cambridge University Press.

Wasow, Thomas. 2002. *Postverbal Behavior.* Stanford, CA: CSLI.

Weiner, E. Judith and William Labov. 1983. Constraints on agentless passive. *Journal of Linguistics* 19: 29–58.

Weinrich, Uriel, William Labov and Marvin I. Herzog. 1968. Empirical foundations for a theory of language change. In Winfrid P. Lehmann and Yakov Malkiel (eds.), *Directions for Historical Linguistics*, 95–115. Austin: University of Texas Press.

Wells, Justine B., Morton H. Christiansen, David S. Race, Daniel J. Acheson and Maryellen C. MacDonald. 2009. Experience and sentence processing: Statistical learning and relative clause comprehension. *Cognitive Psychology* 58: 250–271.

Wiechmann, Daniel. 2015. *Understanding Relative Clauses: A Usage-Based View on the Processing of Complex Constructions.* Berlin: Mouton de Gruyter.

Wiechmann, Daniel and Elma Kerz. 2013. The positioning of concessive adverbial clauses in English: Assessing the importance of discourse-pragmatic and processing-based constraints. *English Language and Linguistics* 17: 1–23.

Wiechmann, Daniel and Arne Lohmann. 2013. Domain minimization and beyond: Modeling prepositional phrase ordering. *Language Variation and Change* 25: 65–88.

Witzlack-Makarevich, Alena and Ilja A. Seržant. 2018. Differential argument marking: Patterns of variation. In Ilja A. Seržant and Alena Witzlack-Makarevich (eds.), *Diachrony of Differential Argument Marking*, 1–48. Berlin: Language Science Press.

Wolk, Christoph, Joan Bresnan, Anette Rosenbach and Benedikt Szmrecsanyi. 2013. Dative and genitive variability in Late Modern English: Exploring cross-constructional variation and change. *Diachronica* 30: 382–419.

Wonnacott, Elizabeth, Elissa L. Newport and Michael K. Tanenhaus. 2008. Acquiring and processing verb argument structure: Distributional learning in a miniature language. *Cognitive Psychology* 56: 165–209.

Wray, Alison. 2002. *Formulaic Language and the Lexicon.* Cambridge: Cambridge University Press.

Wulff, Stefanie. 2008. *Rethinking Idiomaticity: A Usage-Based Approach.* London: Continuum.

Xiao, Richard, Tomy McEnery and Yufang Qian. 2006. Passive constructions in English and Chinese. *Languages in Contrast* 6: 109–149.

Yamashita, Hiroko and Franklin Chang. 2001. "Long before short" preference in the production of a head-final language. *Cognition* 81: B45–B55.

Zehentner, Eva. 2018. Ditransitives in Middle English: On semantic specialization and the rise of the dative alternation. *English Language and Linguistics* 22: 149–175.

Author Index

Abbot-Smith, Kirsten 44, 200
Aikhenvald, Alexandra Y. 67
Aissen, Judith 237–38
Akthar, Nameera 92
Albright, Adam 166
Alegre, Maria 73
Altmann, Gerry T. M. 15, 82–84
Ambridge, Ben 54, 127, 132
Anderson, John 32, 34, 94, 201
Anderson, Paul Kent 182, 184
Andrade, Manuel J. 70
Andrews, Sally 201
Arbib, Michael 153
Ariel, Mira 27
Arnold, Jennifer E. 27, 36–37, 193
Arnon, Inbal 37, 66
Arunachalam, Sudha 137
Aslin, Richard 46
Auer, Peter 23
Austin, John 24
Aylett, Matthew 68

Baayen, Harald R. 11, 73, 201
Baddeley, Alan D. 30
Bakker, Dik 78
Bannard, Colin 66
Barcelona, Antonio 103
Bard, Ellen 37
Barðdal, Johanna 121, 130, 131
Baronchelli, Andrea 10
Barsalou, Lawrence W. 91, 93, 94
Barth, Danielle 68
Barth, Elizabeth 191
Bartlett, Elsa 92
Bates, Elizabeth 2, 9, 11, 36, 205
Bech, Kristin 216
Beckner, Clay 2, 3
Behaghel, Otto 63, 175, 189
Behrens, Heike 23, 32, 46, 49, 52, 200
Bell, Alan 37, 68
Bencini, Guilia M. L. 203
Bergen, Benjamin 90, 94

Bergs, Alexander 56
Bever, Thomas G. 150, 212
Bickel, Balthasar 231, 237
Blondeau, Hélène 38
Boas, Hans 119–21, 126
Bock, Kathryn 33, 202–4
Bod, Rens 34
Bolinger, Dwight 157
Bossong, Georg 236, 237, 243, 244, 245
Bowdle, Brian 103, 106
Bower, Gordon H. 93
Bowerman, Melisa 54, 132
Boye, Kasper 4
Braine, Martin D. S. 52–53
Brandt, Silke 200
Branigan, Holly P. 9, 204
Breban, Tine 61
Brennan, Susan E. 27
Bresnan, Joan 37, 68, 120, 189, 192, 193, 195
Brooks, Patricia 53, 55, 132
Broschart, Jürgen 153, 156
Brown, Dunstan 9
Buchanan, Mark 10
Bühler, Karl 24, 28
Bybee, Joan 1–3, 9, 11, 15, 19, 23, 32, 34, 37,
    38, 43, 44, 63, 64, 68–71, 72–77, 78–79,
    85–87, 130–31, 152, 165–66, 168, 172, 178,
    180, 182, 191, 200, 215, 219, 223, 224, 226

Cappelle, Bert 200
Carey, Susan 92
Carpenter, Malinda 26
Chafe, Wallace 26, 27, 31, 63, 190
Chambers, Susan M. 201
Chang, Franklin 10, 34, 203, 204
Chater, Nick 2, 23, 87
Chein, Jason M. 34
Chomsky, Noam 1, 3, 4, 19, 49, 172, 182, 199
Christiansen, Morton H. 2, 10, 17, 23, 30, 66,
    87, 188, 206
Chung, Sandra 153, 156
Cienki, Alan 96

Subject Index

Note: Bold page numbers of particular importance.